NOVEL CULTIVATIONS

Under the Sign of Nature: Explorations in Ecocriticism
Serenella Iovino, Kate Rigby, John Tallmadge, Editors

Michael P. Branch and SueEllen Campbell,
Senior Advisory Editors

NOVEL CULTIVATIONS

Plants in British Literature of the
Global Nineteenth Century

Elizabeth Hope Chang

UNIVERSITY OF VIRGINIA PRESS
Charlottesville and London

University of Virginia Press
© 2019 by Elizabeth Hope Chang
All rights reserved
Printed in the United States of America on acid-free paper

First published 2019

ISBN 978-0-8139-4247-6 (cloth)
ISBN 978-0-8139-4248-3 (paper)
ISBN 978-0-8139-4249-0 (e-book)

1 3 5 7 9 8 6 4 2

Library of Congress Cataloging-in-Publication Data is available for this title.

Cover art: Eucalyptus globulus, from *Köhler's Medizinal-Pflanzen*, vol. 3, 1887. (Digital image © Board of Trustees, RBG Kew http://creativecommons.org/licenses/by/3.0/)

CONTENTS

Acknowledgments vii

Introduction 1

1. Detecting the Global Plant Specimen 23

2. Strange City Gardens 49

3. Strange Country Gardens 84

4. Acclimatization Abroad 121

5. The Sentient Specimen Returns 158

Notes 183

Works Cited 209

Index 223

ACKNOWLEDGMENTS

Many people and institutions have made possible the writing of this book. I am grateful for research funding from the Mellon Foundation, which supported work at the Huntington Library; for funding from the University of Missouri Research Board and the University of Missouri Research Council, which supported travel to the British Library, the Royal Geographical Society Library and the archives of the Royal Horticultural Society in England, and the special collections of Hong Kong University in Hong Kong; as well as for support from the University of Missouri/University of Western Cape South African Exchange Program, which allowed me to visit the National Archives of South Africa in Cape Town and the National English Literary Museum in Grahamstown. I am especially grateful to the librarians at all of those collections, as well as the Special Collections librarians at the University of Missouri, for their assistance with research questions large and small. The idea for this book first came in an interdisciplinary Undergraduate Research Team on "The Life of the Garden" sponsored by Mizzou Advantage. I am deeply indebted to my fellow team leader Candace Galen for providing a plant biologist's view of *The Secret Garden*.

I am also very appreciative of the many audiences who listened to or read this work as it was in progress and offered generous feedback. I am particularly indebted to Lynn Voskuil and the other members of the V-Cologies working group. I also owe thanks to my colleagues and students in the Department of English at the University of Missouri for their conversations and questions. At the University of Virginia Press, Boyd Zenner, Morgan Myers, and Emily Shelton have improved my manuscript with care and efficiency. Vast advances in my writing and thinking were made possible by Mai-Lin Cheng, Asali Solomon, and Joanna Hearne.

I am most of all thankful for the patience, understanding, and love of my family, always and forever.

* * *

Portions of chapter 3 appear in the collection *Beyond Chinoiserie* edited by Jennifer Miliam and Petra Chu. Portions of chapter 5 appear in the collection *Strange Science: Investigating the Limits of Knowledge in the Victorian Age,* edited by Lara Karpenko and Shalyn Clagget. I am very grateful to Peter Lang and the University of Michigan Press for permission to republish, as well as the editors of those volumes for allowing me to be a part of their works.

NOVEL CULTIVATIONS

Introduction

The plant life that surrounded Victorian authors and readers was vitally different from the plant life that had surrounded their ancestors. By at least the eighteenth century, "much of English nature was now coming from somewhere else"; these elsewheres included the far-flung botanies of South America, Africa, and Asia, and other territories of the expanding British Empire.[1] The horticulturalist and garden writer John Loudon estimated in 1830 that at least five thousand new exotics had recently been imported into Britain, and that rate increased dramatically across Victoria's reign.[2] What's more, almost all of these exotic plants entered the country under cultivation and remained cultivated as they naturalized, like many, many other plants in the British Isles; Keith Thomas tells us that while in 1500 there were two hundred cultivated plants in England, by 1839 there were around eighteen thousand.[3] Thus it is no exaggeration to say that the plants that surrounded Victorians were often transported from foreign soil and almost always modified by human actions to form a second, cultivated nature so omnipresent as to seem at times invisible.[4] It was the effort of the Victorian novel, among other mediating texts, to allow—intermittently—the spadework of cultivation, and, by extension, the global origins of the category of "English nature," to once again be seen. It was also the work of the Victorian novel to make that revelation an investigation into the emotions, thoughts, wants, and needs of plants through the developing forms of narrative.

This book calls for a closer attention to cultivations of plant life and of novel characters and settings within the interdependent conditions of the nineteenth century's chief expansions: the growth of the British Empire, the rise of plant cultivation, the spread of global botanical exchange, and, of course, the reign of the novel. Reading novels that experiment with narrative form beyond the bounds of realism, this book shows how fictional plant life mediates the possibilities of character and selfhood in the genre novel as environmental form. To do this, I depend on a simple yet notable assumption: that plants in books are a buttonhole between fiction and reality, existing in and following the rules of both realms, and, by their presence, registering changes in both realms as well. Plants make the realist novel more real, but they also make the genre novel more fantastic—witness, for example, the vast gulf possible between two novels centered around trees, Thomas Hardy's *Under the Greenwood Tree* (1872) and Frank Aubrey's *The Devil Tree of El Dorado* (1896).[5] In particular, cultivated plants, the oft-ignored artificers of Victorian environmental writing, fill up nineteenth-century realist and romance novels alike, making fictional worlds grow human-made plants but also directing human settings to follow the needs and wants of plants into fictions of vegetable consciousnesses hitherto unknown.[6]

That both of these conditions, of realness and of fantasticality, can be true of plants simultaneously tells us something about Victorian relations to plants and Victorian environmentalism more generally. Most of all, it reminds us that cultivation of plants, like other kinds of human interventions in the nineteenth century, was a sign and symptom of modernity. The changes that nineteenth-century up-to-date cultivation imposed—bringing together plants from around the globe on railways and steamships; popularizing their forms and variations in new kinds of print media; and making plants change color, size, shape and lifespan at human command—were proof of technical skill.[7] But these changes also signaled a shift in the living world itself, demonstrating that organic objects could yield to human intervention, and could in turn direct human activities and compel their own circulations.[8] With this shift, native and natural became no longer linked terms, in growing conditions or in fictional life.[9] Or, as the writer of a popular Victorian work on botany explains, given the advent of "increasing civilization, characteristic plants [have] become a legend of the past."[10] Animals and material commodities tell this story of the nineteenth century too, but plants tell it subtly, pervasively, and in many ways that still need to be explained, particularly when using the methods of literary studies. This supplements work being done to describe connections between the evolving biological designations of species both exotic and naturalized to related cultural and historical discourses: a story Helen Curry has told of the rosy periwinkle, whose cultural naturalization has altered its natural history.[11] While historians and geographers have traced the routes of botanical introduction throughout the society and culture of the British nineteenth century, the trails of those traveling plants have been obscured once they move from garden bed to Victorian novel page.[12]

This is not for want of mutually assured human-plant affections across the varieties of the Victorian novel, from realist fiction to fiction decidedly resistant to realism. W. H. Hudson's 1887 futuristic romance *A Crystal Age* finds the forlorn protagonist, eager to endear himself to the race of superior beings he has unexpectedly awoken among, commenting on the dominant vegetation of this new world: "And now tell me about the rainbow lilies, for I am a great lover of flowers," he ventures. To this is returned the disapproving reply: "Are you? Is it strange you should have a taste common to all human beings?"[13] As for the 119th century, so for the 19th: a general taste for flowers connected readers of all kinds of fiction, not excluding readers of new experiments in fictive genre including the detective novel, the scientific romance, and spy fiction, as well as readers returning to older gothic, utopian, and adventure forms revived for an imperial age. These experimental genres' excursions through and beyond the human challenged the scope and scale of the mainstream novel's narrative march from realism to modernism. And those challenges, as the chapters that follow explain, used (among other things) the transcendent referentiality of plants—existing as they did both within and outside of the novel's narrative world—to explore questions of exoticism, foreignness, selfhood, and subjectivity amid the global exchanges of the British Empire and the revisions to the content and form of narrative setting that such exchanges wrought. The large and small alterations that authors on the outskirts of realism made to prose style and generic form changed how authors and readers recognized character, acknowledged interior thoughts and desires, and identified sentience: all adjustments that admitted plants as one of the era's many new kinds of thinking and feeling beings.

The history of the realist novel's narrative development premised itself from the outset on an indexically representative and silent setting, the better to prioritize the shifts in subjective individual human experience occurring in novel characters after the shift into modernism.[14] Yet many critical prods to this primacy of human character and plots over multispecies setting and communal world-building have been delivered since December 1910 was famously set in literary history by Virginia Woolf as "on or about" the date when something changed in human and literary character—despite, or perhaps because of, Woolf's insistence that changes in human characters are not comparable to the "sudden and definite" alterations of the organic world. "I am not saying that one went out, as one might into a garden, and there saw that a rose had flowered, or that a hen had laid an egg," is her lesser-known immediate qualification of her famous claim of change.[15] Some of the critical prods questioning this shift goad disregarded supernumeracies; welcome work in Victorian environmental studies grapples with the new recognition of the superhuman vastness of climate conditions, geologic eras, and energy sources that the Victorian novel awkwardly shoehorns into cramped human confines.[16] Other prods trouble assertions of dialogic relations: human-animal studies, and even more so human-plant studies, have worried over how those fields can operate as other or more than extended exegeses of the operations of anthropomorphism.[17] This book uses the experimental, borderline realist, and antirealist genres of detection, adventure, gothic, and scientific romance to build on these critical interventions. In taking plants as the transitory location between realism and fantasy within British fiction, I also point out the different registers of personhood within those divided realms. I recognize novel plants both as part of the thickly descriptive background to the operations of a singular subject and, intermittently but equally, as the operative singular subjects drawn out from that background: plants are at once the one and the many, and their individual characters tell us of the qualities of novel beings more generally.[18]

Following the methods that narrative uses to describe these plant extrusions means considering the effort of establishing sentience, consciousness, and affective emotional response from a vegetable direction. To do this is to put to work for literary studies the functional anthropomorphism described by Jane Bennett, who argues that a "touch" of this modified version "can catalyze a sensibility that finds a world filled not with ontologically distinct categories of beings (subjects and objects) but with variously composed materialities that form confederations." With this, we approach via the Victorian novel the network of multispecies interdependence that Anna Tsing charts in the collapse of capitalism.[19] Cultivation of Victorian plants, a physical and mental demonstration of one's love (and sometimes fear) of plants, involved both asserting and altering parameters by which selves could be registered and perceived. From either human affection or aversion for plants, a correspondent plant agency that returns the favor and claims its own connections can itself emerge. If this seems dramatic, it is no more so than the radical fictionalizations performed by Victorian amateur garden writers themselves, one of whom asserts that "for true appreciation we must . . . think of the plant as a living being—a friend whom we may love, and whose character must be intimately known."[20] When discovered in the Victorian novel, these promotions of plant from fictional object to fictional subject—and potential intimate—tell how late-century nonrealist fiction introduced generally new global possibilities of selfhood and self-narration to readers of popular fiction.

The stories and novels I consider, from mid- to late-Victorian writers including Wilkie Collins, Arthur Conan Doyle, Charlotte Brontë, Oscar Wilde, Frances Hodgson Burnett, H. Rider Haggard, Rudyard Kipling, H. G. Wells, and Algernon Blackwood, among others, share an often obsessive interest in the parts of the story that aren't (or don't seem to be) about people. The things surrounding novel characters—the commodities they purchase, craft, or inherit; the houses they live in, abandon, or invade; the plants they harvest or admire and the gardens and woods those plants grow in; all the countless pieces of the characters' personal landscapes that come to support the reader's understanding of fictional lived experience—exist in narrative and give shape to what narrative can be. Where these things come from, and how their ornament, shape, and purpose seems to indicate that origin, also matters for narrative.[21] Readers, trained in human prejudice, rely on human-aligned forms and figures in narrative as much as they do major and minor characters to direct their reading. As they do so, they constantly parse those forms according to assumptions about their geographical origin, race, culture, and degree of civilization. This may be so obvious as to hardly need stating. Yet authors and readers cannot conceive of or follow fictional conditions without a far broader plain of creation to which the same rules also apply. Like many other nonhuman elements, trees, flowers, shrubs, and grasses all make their way from around the globe into fiction as surely as any human character, and betray or obscure their origins as they do so—and all of these operations matter for narrative too, even as the lives and loves of the plants often mystify human perception. Plants in the novel are, in Timothy Morton's phrase, "strange strangers," and in their strangeness they change what they encounter.[22] Such strangeness, however, does not disallow closeness; in the intimate recognitions between plants and people, what Robert Mitchell has termed in the Romantic era "cryptogamia," a sense of the bounds of the human comes clear precisely because of the off-kilter premise of the plant encounter.[23]

The cultivation of these plants—the active, engaging, directive work of consciousness in perceiving and reinterpreting what plants could be and do—intersected and reinforced the goals of narrative. Plants, particularly because of their seeming resistance to fictional modes, ground novels in organic experience. And yet plant life, in fiction, also proposes expanded notions of sentience, mobility, ethics, reproduction, representation, and figural operations in general: in short, all the formal parameters by which we recognize novel fictions as such. For nineteenth-century readers and writers, one of the ways that novelistic narrative had the capacity to make both personal and social development visible existed because ideas about plants, singly and together, had organized its scope and scale. These ways of thinking questioned not only the perfectibility of the botanical condition but also its limits and constraints. In the turn to human conditions and to the kinds of narrative that articulated such conditions for the general reader, questions about plants became also questions about people, with the same attention to both heights and to ends. In this book, cultivation serves as the vector through which plants, as reality effects, real objects, or influential metonyms, connect individually and collectively to human activities of narrative-making, history-writing, and world-building of all kinds. "Worlds had to be in travail, that the meanest flower might blow," proposes Lord Henry, expanding on Wordsworth, in Oscar Wilde's *The Picture of Dorian Gray,* and despite the character's insidious effects on the plot of that novel, the sequence and causality he proposes is not in question for Wilde or for his readers.[24]

Within the multiple layers of deitic plant relations these encounters propose are embedded equally multiple lines of causation. While we know the ways that human perception and figurative thinking shaped the growth and cultivation of plants, we also have to account for the ways that plants have cultivated the human. Thus Lucy Snowe, in Charlotte Brontë's *Villette,* a work discussed in chapter 2, can scornfully claim that "happiness is not a potato, to be planted in mould, and tilled with manure" in response to the facile advice that she "*cultivate* happiness."[25] Lucy's vehement rejection of potato happiness as metaphor, and explicit disavowal of the multiple meanings of "cultivation," implicitly makes mental space for the reader to think more carefully about cultivation's bounds of time and space. The words cultivate and cultivation nudge the reader to consider not just *what* can be cultivated, but *when* and *for how long* it can be cultivated as well. A flower can be crossed to bloom in a new color, a daughter can learn to play the pianoforte, or a working man can come to understand the principles of mathematics, and each of these alterations are personally and socially significant, but each of these alterations are also significant in that they occur at a pace that is held to be artificial and conscious rather than natural and innate.[26] To cultivate, then, is to call attention to an intervention that reorders representative relationships, between part and whole, specimen and collective, but also reconfigures temporally causal relations, between beginning and end, seed and plant—making the overall act of being alive no longer necessarily a self-supporting and intuitively-managed affair. This, for Lucy, is a seriously untenable psychological position that she seems to assign merely to a failure of figurative language and the inability of potatoes to speak beyond their bed of excrement. By demanding the reader consider "what such advice mean[s]," however, she nevertheless interjects a starting point from which the cultivation of potato happiness—and their prompting of human cultivation—might be imagined.

Following this imagining several steps forward is Samuel Butler's *Erewhon* (1872) and the novel's embedded "Book of the Machines." This intertexual digression from the loose main plot of the novel offers a long extranarrative meditation, ostensibly produced by the Erewhonians themselves, on the possibilities of developing machine consciousness.[27] In one of many examples of what Philip Armstrong calls the "attempts" of this "Book" to "formulate a theory of networked agency *avant la lettre*," the Erewhonians detail the "low cunning" of a potato in a dark cellar:[28] "He knows perfectly well what he wants and how to get it. He sees the light coming from the cellar window and sends his shoots crawling straight thereto . . . we can imagine him saying, 'I will have a tuber here and a tuber there, and I will suck whatsoever advantage I can from all my surroundings. . . . The potato says these things by doing them, which is the best of languages. What is consciousness if this is not consciousness?"[29] Going far beyond Lucy's initial negative enchainment of potatoes and human emotion, Butler provides his readers with *only* a potato and asks them to work from that toward a comprehensive definition of consciousness that accommodates both humans and potatoes through the actions of self-cultivation. From the potato, we must put together a model of sentience that operates both hypothetically and in reverse—potato growth as "not not-consciousness." A key difference is that the insertion of the human is not, as it was for Lucy, in the implication of anthropogenic agriculture of planting and tilling, but rather in the abstracted activity of "imagining," which is itself both collective and conditional (not to mention being the historical activity of an invented Nowhere). As a result, we ourselves work harder to take Butler's meaning even though Brontë's proposition seemed to offer more overt resistance. If Brontë (here at least) remains largely anchored in metaphor, Butler's potato is both exemplar and metaleptic point of connection between fictive and real worlds. This is not exactly an operation of the pathetic fallacy or sympathetic self-identification with the object as someone like the critic John Ruskin (whose plant metaphors are discussed in chapter 3) would understand it, since, even more than Brontë, Butler depends on the negation of the potato to admit its nonhuman agency.[30] Instead, it is subjectivity reimagined through double negative, an inversion that the operations of cultivation help us see more clearly.

This lends another ontological layer to the conclusion of plant historians that "it is difficult to conceive of species that have had more culinary and social impact than potatoes in Europe."[31] Indeed there is no one in the Victorian novel who does not have something in common with a potato—to the extent that plant life is human subjectivity's overt or covert negative reference point for readers and authors alike. But, equally important, it was a point of reference whose cultivated European history we (mostly) know, thanks to archival records and the genetic investigations of modern scientists. The potato, after arriving in Europe from South America during the sixteenth century, travelled onward to other European colonial outposts around the globe in traceable ways, and the act of its cultivation came to carry significant influence not just for Europeans but for the culture they were working to spread around the globe. In New Zealand, for example, missionaries deemed that teaching the skill of cultivating potatoes to the Maori outweighed the value of direct food grants, while the consequences of potato cultivations in Ireland need no restating here.[32]

Further, within the insistence that human perception and figurative thinking shaped the growth and cultivation of the potato, we have to also account for the ways that the potato's low cunning cultivated the human. (What is agency if this is not agency?) As Algernon Blackwood's narrator in "The Man Whom the Trees Loved" (a work of horror and of plant sentience discussed in chapter 5) agrees, "in everything that grows, has life, that is, there's mystery past all finding out. The wonder that lies hidden in our own souls lies also hidden, I venture to assert, in the stupidity and silence of a mere potato."[33] At the overlap between a "mere" cultivated potato and the broadest possible understanding of ecological animism, a human form seeks to find and replicate itself in the plant (and other) life that surrounds it, but, equally, that life returns the inquiry, settling itself into the human form to give it shape and purpose.[34] Or, more simply, potatoes exist to be grown by humans, but humans exist to grow potatoes.[35]

Thus Blackwood's potato's silence is, of course, exactly the point. In these "stupid" moments, plants are becoming not a subject upon which knowledge can be discovered, but a way of making knowledge, or at least structuring the constituent forms of thinking within which knowledge can be made. In this book I will look at plants not exclusively in their moments of figural intervention, as in the just-explored examples from Brontë, Butler, and Blackwood, but in their introductions into the substance of both the fictional world and the activity of the narration itself. The moments in which a narrative pauses to regard a plant, whether potato, oak, or orchid, have often been seen as gaps or breaks from regular narrative work, but in the readings that follow I see them instead as different but equal opportunities to make meaning.[36] In particular, I see them as especially making meaning about what agency, consciousness, sentience, and selfhood could be for the British subject in the imperial age. They do this not only by operating as resonant shards of figuration diverting the progress of the plot, in the manner that Lucy Snowe has just eviscerated. They also do it simply by making space for their own description in the wide field of the novel's setting, and, specifically, making space for a description that reminds readers that the fictional world is filled with just as much non-native, artificial, cultivated second nature as the real world that surrounds them. Further, readers remember that to strive for affinity with these second natures, in imagination or in reality, is as much a self-altering proposition as it is one that alters the world outside the self. When Mole, the lover of home comforts and moral center of Kenneth Grahame's *The Wind in the Willows* (1908) recognizes his own desires—"he saw clearly that he was an animal of tilled field and hedgerow, linked to the ploughed furrow, the frequented pasture, the lane of evening lingerings, the cultivated garden-plot"—it registers as more than an aversion to the "asperities" of "Nature in the rough."[37] It also, like the parasitic domesticities of Beatrix Potter's animal tales, or, for that matter, the acculturation of Mowgli from jungle child to Forest Service employee described in chapter 4, recenters how such cultivated affinities could be made and who could make them.

In singling out what is particularly operative about plant fictions, then, I want to specifically propose that the epistemology of nineteenth-century fictional form makes stealthy but essential recourse to the cultivation of plants in a guise that is neither entirely functional nor deterministic, but is always dependent on the operations of empire. Before explaining the intersection of the nineteenth-century British Empire with the genre novels that are the focus of my study, I will briefly review the boundaries of my methodology and the range of my primary sources. In my discussion of cultivations, it will become quickly apparent that, though conceding our mutual potato ties, I am for the main part of this study avoiding agriculture, as well as discussion of some other common ways that plants might enter novels in this era: ground up as poisons or medicines, dissected in scientific study, consumed as delicacies, printed on wallpapers and carpets, and so on. This is because my interest is in the narrative possibilities of plants as both (usually) living and (relatively) singular specimens made mobile to move around the globe. Living ornamental plants circulate from territory to territory and from garden to novel for reasons both fuzzier and perhaps more interesting than nutrition or wholesale economic gain, taking part in a long-standing history that Jack Goody has termed the "culture of flowers."[38] As Richard White argues against Donald Worster's identification of agroecology as the primary driver of human/nature relations and thus the main proper study of environmental historians: "Humans do not eat all that it is possible to eat, and they do not regard all that they eat simply as food."[39] To distinguish horticulture from agriculture is to notice the ways that plants took on object-qualities without becoming objects, but rather existed in subject-like collusion with material culture's effects on lived experience.

The nineteenth century's immersion in its stuff is a vast ocean of scholarship. In this book I am telling the story of only one part: the story of how a rethinking of plant life as a domain apart from rural labor or economic sufficiency came to influence larger questions of ontology and the making of self-meaning. This has led me away from several other possible avenues of inquiry; most notably, the sentimental language of flowers traced by Beverly Seaton through "flower poetry, the language of flowers . . . moral and religious works in which flowers are the main source of examples, and flower folklore" which Victorians used to thematize love and marriage or forms of religious interpretations of nature including natural typology.[40] I also have not, for the most part, enfolded into this study the complicated histories of nineteenth-century botany and botanical writing, the development of botany as an elite masculine scientific practice that James Secord has described, or the passion for plant study, collection, and illustration still pursued by working-class and female botanists despite those elite developments investigated by Barbara Gates, Ann Shteir, and Ann Secord.[41] Nor, despite their obvious material interests in my study, have I been able to include attention to Victorian florist societies, wax flower modelers, flower designs reproduced in fabric patterns, pressed flower books, flower decoration in churches, or other areas in which botanical affiliations were given aesthetic declaration.[42]

Victorian novels incorporating the reach of the empire, loosely defined, accommodated and evolved in response to changing understandings of the global environment premised by the exotic plant importations with which I began. Jason Moore has succinctly explained that "the emergence of a pan-European world-economy, stretching from the Baltic to the Americas, was at once cause and consequence of an epochal reorganization of world ecology."[43] His work leads much current theory in charting the self-perpetuating cycle of empire: capitalist geographic expansion in search of commodity followed by environmental transformation which in turn drove further geographic expansion. By this process, sugar plantations came to the Caribbean, opium fields to India, rubber trees to Brazil, and acacia trees to Australia—concurrent actions of commodity extraction and settler colonialism. Though both massive environmental drivers of imperial growth, these actions were by no means identical, yet their overlapping logic cooperatively emphasized the justification and promotion of the organic spread of empire on the grounds of imperial, national, and personal amelioration. Expansive studies published over the past thirty years by Alfred Crosby, Richard Grove, and Richard Drayton have proposed that imperial history is environmental history is human history, and have also received some necessary corrections to the heavily synthetic humanism of those (particularly Crosby's) claims.[44] The nineteenth-century expansion of the British Empire drives (and is driven by) the botanical variety, and concurrent crisis of biotic nativeness, from which this book draws its source material, though this book does not itself perform such a rigorous history of imperial plants.[45]

Rather I work within the fuzzily general sense, among Victorian authors and readers, that plants and nature were coming from "somewhere else," which structured narrative innovation even as it lacked environmental specificity. As a result, I refer broadly to the ideal of imperial and colonial plants throughout, not always specifically tracing their particular origins but always being attentive to their specific characters.

What I am most interested in is the way plant migration was a frequently held analogue to colonial movement: plant invaders and colonizers paralleled human circulations and yielded at times comparable results. Though such exchanges had been going on for centuries, the botanical circulations of the Victorian era had world-defining consequence, and so the simple equation of migrant plants and migrant peoples is the first and most obvious connection of note. The invention of the Wardian case, as I'll discuss in chapter 1, allowed transport of new plants hardy in temperate climates from China, Southern Africa, and the western United States and Canada (as opposed to the tropicals sourced from older British colonies), while technological improvements in glass, steel, and hothouse design brought a wider range of exotics to grow in Britain at a lower cost, the rise of the periodical press and the appearance of hundreds of new magazines and books on horticulture created a new genre of nonfiction writing about plants that shaped fiction's progress, and, most important, the growth of a class of person possessed of adequate leisure, personal space, and income to be able to read and garden made all of the previous advances relevant.[46]

All these are examples of the ways that, as Eric Pawson has pointed out, environmental mobility via botanical transfer has been responsible for "re-making the landscapes of the last 200 years," supporting Tim Cresswell's formulation that mobility shapes "what it is to be modern."[47] Plants that could be imported, assimilated, hybridized, acculturated, and cultivated all became in some ways fictions of themselves, with identifiers—such as hybrid, exotic, invasive, alien, even "weed"—to match. These terms, all relational, situational, and contextual, were also always sociocultural: "Invasive species are anthropogenic phenomena," as plant historians point out.[48] So too, of course, are nations, and the linkage between traveling plants and diasporic peoples was not lost on Victorian explainers of science. Grant Allen, "the busiest man in England," genre author as well as frequent popularizer of botanical knowledge, sets out his project in *The Flowers and Their Pedigrees* (1883) to explain the presence of various flowers in Britain as "naturalised citizens of our own restricted petty insular floral commonwealth."[49] His goal in that collection of republished essays is to argue that plants' "distribution over [the earth's] surface has to be explained on historical grounds just as a future ethnologist would have to explain the occurrence of isolated French communities in Lower Canada and Mauritius, of African negroes in Jamaica and Brazil, or of Chinese coolies in San Francisco and the Australian colonies."[50] While such botanical geographies were widely charted both in elite botanical science and with regard to plants useful in economic agriculture, as Allen's human examples make clear, Allen's application of the colonial metaphor to flowering plants in the context of his popular writing increases the burden on vernacular plant-thinking to bear the weights and sound the limits of sovereignty.

Like botanist Hewett Cottrell Watson's *Cybele* (1847–59), which marked the culmination of a specialist's life's devotion to plant geography, Allen's texts insisted on a disciplinary humanistic framing revealed through their botanical and horticultural distinctions. *Cybele* catalogued plants present in the British Isles accorded to categories of "native,"; "denizen . . . at present maintaining its habitats, as if a native, without the aid of man, yet liable to some suspicion of having been originally introduced"; "colonist . . . a weed of cultivated land . . . seldom found except in places where the ground has been adapted for its production by the operations of man"; and "incognita . . . [r]eported as British, but requiring confirmation as such"—distinctions that Greg Garrard finds a disturbing "appropriation" revealing a "suppressed biogeographical *ethos*" that he links to Romantic-era metaphysics of species.[51] The analogies of human movements that Watson and Allen assign to representative plant varieties also tighten another loop of anthropocentric form around the discrete self-sufficiency of "naturalized citizens," "natives," and "colonists." Each term both conjures a representative, if suspicious, singular example and stands in for a class or category of immigrants whose limits are not entirely known.

As a result of these equations of plant migrations with forced and free human circulations, there is a second consequence for my study of fictional cultivated plants. Plants also changed how the British landscape and environment could be perceived and conceptualized as either native or natural—two conditions no longer mutually productive. The result was at once an appearance of global sameness and at the same time a consciousness of broadly dispersed global difference. Or, as Sonja Dümpelmann describes the evolution of the garden in the age of empire, "as entire cities and regions were turned into gardens, and the types and styles of gardens diversified, the Western world also became increasingly uniform."[52] What authors and readers saw when they looked out at their city streets, private gardens, and country hedgerows was ever more imbricated with plant life imported from abroad in ways both inextricable and irreversible. Environmental historians have called many nineteenth-century landscapes propositional and hybrid in ways familiar to scholars of fiction. As Pawson explains, these "hybrid landscapes . . . embody two of the central tensions of modernity . . . in form they are ordered and fixed, yet they are assembled from often highly mobile complexes of plants. Many of these plants are themselves hybrids, re-constituted and re-named in response to changing social and material desires. The rhododendron of Europeanised parks and gardens is no more the rhododendron of the Himalayan slopes of 150 years ago than the supermarket tomato is an Elizabethan love apple."[53] When Sherlock Holmes conceals himself in a rhododendron bush to spy on an attempted murder, or Angel Clare looks out across a garden of rhododendrons while awaiting Tess, or Margaret is kissed by Mr. Wilcox in the rhododendrons, or the Time Traveler leaves his time machine parked among a clump of rhododendrons, or when Mary Elizabeth Braddon opens *Lady Audley's Secret* (1862) with a description of Audley Court's "smooth lawn . . . dotted with groups of rhododendrons, which grew in more perfection here than anywhere else in the country," the narrative effort given to specifically naming these plants draws together a global network that includes the growing terrains of the English game hunting ground, the mountains of Western China, and the rocky slopes of California.[54] And this is emphatically not a national or species phenomena limited to the British Isles or to rhododendrons—similar efforts occur when Australian characters traverse a bush dotted with South African acacia, or a Cape Colony planted with South American prickly pear exerts significant spiritual influence on a young boy, as in Olive Schreiner's *Story of an African Farm* (1890), discussed in the fourth chapter.[55]

These overlaps between real and fictional characters proposes a third effect of colonial expansion for plants in the British novel: a formal renegotiation of the capacity of character to enter into narrative as forms multiple, singular, or somewhere in between. Simply the appearance of new and different kinds of plants had the capacity to decenter how Britons imagined their plant life more generally. Environmental historians and scientists have focused on indigenous tribal populations when noting that imported plant species "can cause a ripple effect by displacing related traditions in the cultural 'storyscape,'" defining "storyscape" as "the place-based intergenerational narrative maintained by a native society" that encompasses both "tangible (visible, practical) and intangible (internal, philosophical) traditions."[56] Yet we can easily see nineteenth-century novels and periodical writings as the "storyscape" of broadly middle-class Britons as well, and follow the ripple effect equally clearly. This is most easily accomplished by attending to the many stories locating the origins of botanical appreciation in childhood. As the Victorian gardener and nature writer Shirley Hibbard concludes, "flowers are friends that change not . . . in age, they speak to us of boyhood, and lead us back to the scenes made dear by recollections of home; year after year, as we hasten onward to complete the cycle of our being, they still abide with us, and offer solace."[57] For many, like the ruralist narrator of George Eliot's *The Mill on the Floss,* such nostalgic companionship should not be separated from a hardy nativeness; one prefers wild-growing elderberry bushes to cultivated citrus and fuchsias for "no better reason" than that the elderberry "stirs an early memory . . . it is no novelty in my life, speaking to me merely through my present sensibilities to form and color, but the long companion of my existence, that wove itself into my joys when joys were vivid."[58] Such an apparently arbitrary preference is perfectly safe, especially in a novel looking back from the 1860s to the 1820s, if one assumes that colorful foreign introductions like citrus and fuchsia have always come too late to affix themselves to the joys of a British child. When that assumption is disrupted, and the broad swath of native plants become instead cultivated singular specimens connecting to both children and adults through a form whose constraints were highlighted, the plant mnemonic shifts. Cultural storyscapes come to consider cultivated plants, parsed and measured, as new actors in the lifelong narration of a changed and global experience.

Policing of boundaries between modes of investigation into natural and scientific truths was often disregarded in the nineteenth century; novels, periodicals, poems, and nonfiction prose all carried weight in defining, describing, and revising what both a foreign and a domestic plant could be and do. Jim Endersby points out in his account of Victorian writing on orchids that "much of the work of reimagining plants" was done not in scientific journals but in "disposable fiction written for cheap, mass-produced magazines,"[59] while John Ryan emphasizes the ways that "knowledge systems" of plants emerged from sensory engagements along with regional stories, folk and formal, so that "plant epistemologies were situated, variable, self-determined, and corporeally affective."[60] Endersby, a historian of science, and Ryan, a philosopher of plant life, employ deeply distinct methodologies in questioning a nature/culture divide. But the culturally charged locations where, they argue, plant meaning can be configured—on the pages of certain kinds of fiction, or in the sense of smell possessed by a particular person from a particular locale—supports Anna Tsing's argument that human relations to plants occur through "histories of power and difference" rather than conditions of universal humanity.[61] In reading Victorian genre novels, power differentials of the spread of global empire shift the relations between human and plant when writing their intimate personal histories.

But in addition to changing the storyscape in the framework of imperial circulations, exotic plants and the renegotiated sense of second nature they created also revised more specific fictional relations between form and character. While a plant appearing in a realist novel can be taken as a strong figurative effect reinforcing realist form, to which the analysis of thing theory can be applied, a plant is also always a living thing, one that novels were not usually in the business of making up alternatives to. Though not a media technology, plants do mediate the novel's space of possibility for character as superabundant site of global exchange. Precisely because of the intersecting possibilities of plants—at once animate and inanimate, feeling and unfeeling, sentient and instinctual—they make a useful entry point to show us what gets skipped over in thinking through the novel's temporal and material formation amidst the currents of imperial circulation. The gaps between action in space and action across time took on strong significance in a century of global fiction, granting the possibility of undetected escape and return upon which many Victorian novels' plots hinged so crucially. Plants, when they appear in such globally expansive novel plots, link the distant and the near in ways that supplement the limitations of human perception, including such unsatisfactory visual technologies as Mrs. Jellyby's telescopic (and ineffectual) vision of foreign philanthropy in Charles Dickens's *Bleak House*.

In allying themselves with humans in their growth and cultivation while remaining enigmatically separate in their thoughts, emotions, and language, however, plants also link external perception with interior recognition through a composite perspective few animal and human life forms can achieve. This offers a chance to theorize plants *as* characters, admitting them into the collection of nonhuman narrating beings we wonder about when we engage in what has been termed "unnatural narratology."[62] But it also allows us to consider the terms of that admission in the first place. The swapping of phytocentric for anthropocentric interpretations is a diversion better understood within the broader "nonhuman" turn, a field of study encompassing not only environmental studies but other reconsiderations of humanistic framings. Patrick Murphy has argued, "part of the crisis of humanity is precisely the degree to which human societies and individuals do not allow nonhuman others to participate in aesthetic memory. . . . [n]or does humanism enable the aesthetic rendering of nonhuman others as formative influences, as subject—rather than setting or objects of attention—that facilitate the author and his or her human characters as 'perceiving myself as another.'"[63] Such an acknowledgment, however, does not remove the obligations of humanistic work. In their important nuancing, Dana Luciano and Mel Chen point out that the nonhuman turn should not abandon attentiveness to varieties of social location, for, as they write, "if we accept the framing of the nonhuman turn as a move 'beyond' the merely human concerns of identity and alterity, we overlook how the very possibility of making a distinction between human and nonhuman has, historically, been constructed by the kind of actions and processes that we have named dehumanization."[64] The restored terms of that perception through a phytocentrism that does not abandon the particular differentiations of race, gender, class, and nation has historical and geographical, as well as narrative, consequences both obvious and subtle that it is the work of this book to explore. Or, as Catriona Sandilands has recently proposed: "Thinking with plant life in excess of its apprehension in terms of normative anthropogenic meaning—in other words, following plants into much queerer territories of living and relating—has the potential to open life to new, 'anthrodecentric' possibilities."[65] I have chosen a range of not entirely canonical literary examples to illustrate the many versions of these possibilities that the Victorian genre novel provides.

My chapters examine these changes in plant life in rough progression from the singular to the collective and back again. In chapter 1, "Detecting the Global Plant Specimen," I use the developing genre of detective fiction to illustrate the newly heuristic activity of looking at a plant. From two specific examples of *The Moonstone*'s Ezra Jennings and

Sherlock Holmes each regarding a flower, in apparent denial of their duties as detectives, I show the ways that ways that novels made looking at plants in fact a fulfillment of such investigatory practice. The landscape of the Victorian era during the rise of detective fiction was becoming increasingly nontransparent in its infrastructure and architecture; less considered are the ways that its organic and plant life were growing ever more artificial and obfuscatory as well. This despite the fact that an affectionate connection to nature was understood to be both respite from the detective's inquiries while also representation of the detective's inquisitive power. The evolution of the detective novel's clue, I argue, signals the broader development of the intellectual and emotional discernment needed to identify individual plant specimens as symptoms of something more.

The next two chapters concern gardens, a point of tension in this project. Well-studied on their own in Victorian literature in comparison to the individual specimens I am here pulling forward, they have been taken as emblematic of the culture of nature as a collectively constituted unit.[66] But cultivated plants and cultivated gardens are not exactly the same thing, even though the latter almost always contains the former.[67] Garden historians have usually been interested in the interactions of people with plants en masse at the garden's second level of abstracted cultural remove. In this book I use the garden space as a place to think about how fictional subjectivity depends on the license of the particular organic life that grows within a novel's pages, in or out of gardens.[68] I do this in two ways. First, in chapter 2, "Strange City Gardens," I consider the urban garden. Though Victorian London was often defined by its inhospitality to plant life, fictional urban domestic space continued to arrange itself around the stunted, fallow, or dying gardens of the polluted city. The genre of the urban gothic is particularly suited to parse these paradoxically organic yet barren spaces. I read Charlotte Brontë's *Villette* as a narrative of the restoration of urban garden space but also the delineation of plant and garden-thinking as an intellectual and emotional practice and alternative to either Gothic tropes or confessional narration. By contrast, Oscar Wilde's *The Picture of Dorian Gray* highlights the lack of division between the natural and the made by attending to the submerged plant narratives that counter and undermine Dorian's descent into Gothic horror.

Chapter 3, "Strange Country Gardens," moves away from the city to an examination of gardens associated with country estates. Here I show the ways that the narrative cementings of domestic ties and land claims that these gardens once ensured are changed through the circulations of global plants and people. In Haggard's *Colonel Quaritch, V.C.: A Tale of Country Life,* regard of a Japanese chrysanthemum betokens a new absorption in flowers that unhinges organic ties to heritage estates. Instead, foreign origin is a necessary element of domestic flourishing, as Burnett's *The Secret Garden* also makes clear. Just as in the urban environment, the apparently self-explanatory bonds between human and plant are rewritten and interrogated all over again against a new background of a larger colonial world. Reaching farther forward out of the nineteenth century era, the chapter closes with attention to Du Maurier's *Rebecca,* a text retrospectively constructing a country house world of intrusive exotic plant life that cannot be understood without the global realignments that the chapter has already explained, as well as depicting a subjugation of the narrating self to surrounding organic plant life that goes further than Haggard or Burnett's earlier novels can manage.

Chapter 4, "Acclimatization Abroad," shifts the field of focus to colonial trees as sites for self-making across the spectrum of adventure and settler colonial fiction. While the oak tree makes a familiar and powerful metaphor of English selfhood in a range of fiction, acclimatized and circulating trees like the acacia, the prickly pear, and the eucalyptus held dual symbolic and practical meaning for global British fiction at the end of the century. To demonstrate the narrative weight given to colonial trees, I first read Olive Schreiner's *Story of an African Farm,* which establishes the invasive prickly pear as a crucial piece of her characters' hybrid colonial identities. I then continue my attention to Haggard's fiction as I read in succession his settler melodrama *Jess* and his attempted conclusion to the Quatermain saga, *Allan Quatermain.* These two novels, nearly contemporary to *Colonel Quaritch,* follow Haggard's environmental thinking across avenues not particularly welcoming to developing liberal modernity, but in their own way forming a modernized environmental attachment that is, for Haggard at least, also surprisingly self-abnegating. In the final section of the chapter, I turn to Rudyard Kipling and "In the Rukh"—a tale that is both the first Mowgli story written and chronologically the last story in the narrative of Mowgli's life that became *The Jungle Book.* Presenting an adult Mowgli as assistant to the colonial Forest Service, Kipling writes India's forests as managed and manageable locations of narrative development and reads the colonial subject as hybrid with his cultivated environment.

With the final chapter, "The Sentient Specimen Returns," I conclude by taking up again the global circulation and domestic return of plants and trees with a horror genre twist. H. G. Wells's *The War of the Worlds* and Algernon Blackwood's stories "The Willows," "The Transfer," and, in particular, "The Man Whom the Trees Loved," give a version of ecological connection that can be understood as neither particularly pastoral nor in any way benign. That these plants demonstrate elements of consciousness and agency reserved for human beings is obvious, but it is also important to detail the ways that these plant actors, vigorously and sometimes murderously lavishing their attentions on their human companions, resituate our understanding of plant life and purpose in radically new ways. This chapter also serves as a conclusion that opens the project into contemporary issues of plant emotion, intelligence, and communication in literature, art, and philosophy.

For my conclusion and for the study as whole, the most important consequence from the worldwide plant exchange is the increased speed with which a plant erases its own origins, shifting itself from exotic to hybrid to naturalized specimen in botany and in fictional narrative with ever-increasing ease. Most of the plant encounters I consider in this study do involve plants implied or identified to be of foreign origin, whether or not the characters involved know or care that this is true. But I also describe some encounters with plants taken to be domestic, under the argument that what I am also describing here is something fundamental about the shift in how plants were considered within daily life. I take it as a pressure point of modernity that the materiality of plants, and the consequences of their distant origins, mediated lived experience in newly expansive and networked ways—ways that the characters, authors, and readers I consider would in many cases have only the dimmest of awareness of. Following the mediations of *fictional* plants allies two parallel interventions: the transformation of reality into represented form, and the imposition of qualities of fictional setting upon human environment via the operations of a nascent ecological thinking working on a planetary scale. These elements might be termed poetics—that is, the literary and formal qualities of the plant's textual presence that bridge the content of the text and its reception, circulation, and afterlife across the territory of Britain and its empire.

When we put together my two propositions—that, in the nineteenth century, plants both become fictions themselves through acts of cultivation and importation, and that plants make the environment around them more fictional, by obscuring and remaking its substance and origins—we find connections to much larger questions of literature, environmental history, and ecological futures. To read about plants in fiction is also to consider the possibility that plants in the outside world are also fictions, living things fostered by human intelligence, as Philip Pauly puts it.[69] The poetics of the plants—that is, their ability to convert their minor appearances in fiction of the period into formal mediations of the exchanges between of nature and culture—connected fictional and real plants and made such exchanges, sourced from around the globe, a constitutive part of the local in the British genre novel.

This book I hope will be read by those who want to think more about plants—what they do, how they grow, where they appear, what they mean, who represents them and why. But this book I hope will be read also by those who don't particularly care about plants but want to think more about novels—how novels account for, fill in, skip over, sidle around those blank spots in abstract, mentally maintained concepts like the fictional, the conditional, the propositional, and the represented. In this I echo the beleaguered popular plant writers of the Victorian era: "We confess to a design of endeavouring to interest those who are not botanists, and do not pretend to any but a most superficial knowledge of plant life."[70] Laboring hard to keep up with the intersections of minor and major characters and the plot events they each encounter and endure, the reader comes across the growth of a seemingly superficial plant in her novel with surprise. How, and why, did this plant, which speaks not nor is spoken to, and may carry no particular significance for either character or plot event, claim this presence on the narrative I read? Like a Turkish rug or a mahogany chest, it declares that the author knows of a particular cultural world. But, like a bee or a cloud or a clod of earth, it declares also that the author knows of a natural world—a gesturing toward universality that is denied as much by the expansions of empire as by the particularities of the local. Despite the impossibilities of their promise, the novel makes these declarations to cultivate its own readers: causing them to read ahead of and behind themselves and consider expanded time scales, reoriented framings of place, and all the complicated multiplicities of selfhood that the cultivated plant must speak for.

« 1 »

Detecting the Global Plant Specimen

It is after we know that Franklin Blake stole the Moonstone but before we know *why* he stole the Moonstone that we first encounter the enigmatic doctor's assistant Ezra Jennings. Jennings's sudden and dramatic appearance at the close of Wilkie Collins's novel's June 27, 1868 number—"I turned round, and found myself face to face with Ezra Jennings," records Franklin Blake—prefigures the several kinds of interventions Jennings will make into *The Moonstone*'s narrative.[1] First, his actions direct the plot: Jennings gives Blake the crucial history that helps Blake piece together the disordered fragments of Dr. Candy's memory into a chronologically sensible account of the Moonstone's theft. But Jennings's appearance also offers a physiognomic intervention. His "gipsy complexion, his fleshless cheeks, his gaunt facial bones, his dreamy eyes, his extraordinary parti-coloured hair"—all these make Jennings the most distinctive example of hybridity in a text greatly concerned with the interchange between the foreign and the domestic.[2] That Jennings is crippled by an opium addiction acquired as a consequence of a painfully debilitating illness has made his hybridity all the more compelling to critics.[3]

Building on his two better-discussed plot functions—narratological and racial—we further find Jennings making a third, botanical intervention. Though Blake initially encounters Jennings at the scene of the crime, the Verinder manor house, they immediately depart for a country stroll to escape the disapproving reception that everywhere greets the socially outcast medical assistant. As they leave behind "the last houses in the town," Collins uses the natural setting to advance multiple plot strands. Blake narrates:

> Ezra Jennings stopped for a moment, and picked some wild flowers from the hedge by the roadside. "How beautiful they are!"

he said, simply, showing his little nosegay to me. "And how few people in England seem to admire them as they deserve!"

"You have not always been in England?" I said.

"No, I was born, and partly brought up, in one of our colonies. My father was an Englishman; but my mother—We are straying away from our subject, Mr. Blake; and it is my fault. The truth is, I have associations with these modest little hedgeside flowers—It doesn't matter; we were speaking of Mr. Candy. To Mr. Candy let us return."[4]

From this disjointed moment of botanical appreciation, Blake concludes "that the story which I had read in his face was, in two particulars at least, the story that it really told. He had suffered as few men suffer; and there was the mixture of some foreign race in his English blood."[5] What thus might seem initially to be a slight and easily dismissed moment in the voluminous plot of the novel thus becomes the clearest articulation of Ezra Jennings's personal history and his singular importance to the mystery's resolution. Jennings's ability to literally fill in the gaps of the meddling Mr. Candy's feverish confession is foreshadowed here by his apparent botanical completion of a partially expressed narrative of global migration. In both cases, Franklin Blake's ability to find narrative resolution relies on a presumptive reading of the other man's obscure sorrows. Jennings's responsive attachment to particular elements of the natural environment seems to satisfactorily (for Blake at least) delineate the details of his character in lieu of more traditional descriptive methods.

And yet, readers may find this explanation of Jennings's personal history less than satisfactory, given that we never even receive any useful details about the substance of his "associations" with the flowers, which could themselves hardly be more generic in their description. Indeed, their lack of naming seems a deliberate choice by Collins to critique the methods of amateur natural historians: what *The Moonstone*'s key narrator and butler Gabriel Betteredge disapprovingly calls the upper-class habit of "spoiling a pretty flower, with pointed instruments, out of a stupid curiosity to know what the flower is made of."[6] We may then see Jennings's lack of precision about the name of the flower as paradoxically the most genuine part of his story—an assessment with which contemporary reviewers agreed. The *Athenaeum*'s review of the novel concludes: "Ezra Jennings, the doctor's assistant, is the one personage who makes himself felt by the reader. The slight sketch of his history, left purposely without details, the beautiful and noble nature developed in spite of calumny, loneliness, and the pain of a deadly malady, is drawn with a firm and masterly hand; it has an aspect of reality which none of the other personages possess."[7] Lacking aristocratic privilege and blocked from professional advancement by his birth and appearance, Jennings circles the outskirts of the economic and racial boundaries of the novel's characters and readers, seeking entry through his epistemological recoveries. As Jennings's act of selection transforms the indeterminate "wild flowers" into a presentable "nosegay," we understand not only that something important is taking place but that recognition of this importance is itself an establishing mark of moral character.

Though this aesthetic transformation from flower to nosegay is also a termination (at least from the plant's perspective), the cultivations that make these roadside blooms worthy of remark imbues them with narrative significance that resonates beyond their individual life span and the novel's momentary focus on their growing conditions. In this chapter, I will use brief examples from *The Moonstone* and Arthur Conan Doyle's Sherlock Holmes story "The Adventure of the Naval Treaty" to make a larger set of claims about cultivated flowers in fiction of mystery and detection. One of the key contributions from these new fictions of detection, of which *The Moonstone* was famously deemed "the first, longest and best" by T. S. Eliot, was their renovation of narrative setting to accommodate the detective's method of reading.[8] Just as Franklin Blake sought to reconcile "the story ... read in [Jennings's] face" with "the story that it really told," readers of detective novels practiced recognizing plants and other objects seemingly hidden in the descriptive background as intermittently foregrounded objects of crucial epistemological and narrative significance—in other words, as clues. While plants are obviously only one category of many possible clue-objects present in the developing detective genre, such epistemological spotlighting of plants as clues has satisfying resonances with the larger history of Victorian horticulture. Developing alongside the burgeoning English garden, the detective novel could take special advantage of the new qualities of cultivated plants in the Victorian age: both their complex global origins and also their increasing ability to register as singular specimens with particular wants and needs.

This is in contrast to a traditional novelistic understanding of plants as generic, multiple, and domestic—all qualities uncongenial to fictional representation as foreground rather than background elements. Plants with no individual human contact made little difference to narrative, even if their presence was implicitly necessary or significant to ongoing daily life. But plants that needed or accepted cultivation—into economically, scientifically, aesthetically, or emotionally significant forms—demanded notice, in novel plots as well as in many other kinds of literature and art. Cultivation amplified meaning and significance, but it also created such meaning in the first place as it brought together human priorities with plant interests, and gave increasing epistemological weight to plants to advance such priorities (or act against them) on their own.

Thus, the assimilation of new foreign cultivars combined two equally essential elements for the environmental developments of detective fiction in general, and the clue in particular. The first requirement was the presence in readers' lives and gardens of actual exotic plants, shipped into England via glass cases designed for the nineteenth century by Nathaniel Ward and cultivated in gardens according to the advice of a rising class of Victorian garden experts like John and Jane Loudon—historical developments that I will explain in the first part of this chapter. Equally required, however, was a vocabulary of representational and figurative language necessary to pinpoint not only the color, fragrance, and ideal growing conditions of the plants but also the language of sympathetic connection found in narrative prose that could link a perceiving consciousness with an exotic specimen. The second part of my chapter, building on that environmental history of plant exchange, explains further the renovations in narrative form that granted plants a new and singular narrative significance, as clues specifically and as storytelling prompts more generally. Detective novels, intent on pulling background into foreground, helped establish and popularize this vocabulary and language in a way that more explicitly equated the ontological status of plants and persons, categories which in detective and other kinds of genre fictions now shared the responsibility of conveying the story as it was really told.

The new era of cultivation made flowers come from everywhere and be, at least potentially, for everyone, as Jennings's roadside reverie has already shown in miniature. In the final section of the chapter, I will draw together the environmental history of the first section and the explanations of narrative form in the second section to consider other flower-inspired meditations: first in Doyle's detective story

"The Adventure of the Naval Treaty" and then, moving beyond detective fiction, in H. G. Wells's *The Time Machine* (1895) and Frank Kingdon-Ward's nonfictional *The Romance of Plant-Hunting* (1924). In all of these examples, the reveries prompted by plants were mnemonic—the flowers inspired the recall of a narrative already known but forgotten or not fully understood—but also globally revisionist. The advent of imported exotics meant that these reveries now connected flower-admirers and their memories to environments around the world, even if the flower being admired is not itself a recent immigrant. The territory within which Collins, and the detective novelists that follow him, plot their stories already depends for its constitution on global specimens, meaning that all kinds of flowers given individual attention, foreign and domestic, have the capacity to prompt reflection that links local with global. And, as Collins's description makes clear, all kinds of characters connect to and are connected by the world of cultivated flowers that surround them. As I argue in the conclusion to my chapter, such connections are valuable for the global horticultural networks they create as well as for the model of environmentally responsive narrative that ecological modernity allows.

A wide survey of the varieties of horticultural influence upon fictional beings is already present in *The Moonstone,* made evident by the innovative structure Collins uses to relay the story of the jewel's unwitting theft and unexpected recovery through an assemblage of narratives from a range of characters. "Don't you see how happy I am? I'm going to the flower-show, Clack, and I've got the prettiest bonnet in London," declares the thoroughly unhappy heroine Rachel Verinder, partaking in the outward rituals of aristocratic female society despite her inward disgust with their hypocrisies.[9] The pious Miss Clack, not convinced of Rachel's propriety, scorns equally Rachel's public visits to the flower show and Rachel's mother, Lady Verinder's, private enjoyment of her apartment's flower-filled window boxes; as Clack disapprovingly narrates, "Lady Verinder was extravagantly fond of these perishable treasures, and had a habit of . . . going to look at them and smell them."[10] Clack exploits the Verinder family's sensory pleasures for personal ends, hiding unwanted religious tracts among the window flowers even as she continues to malign her relatives' irreligiosity. The transitory beauties of the flowers also signal to the reader and to Franklin Blake, the intradiegetic compiler of these stories, Lady Verinder's rapidly approaching death, a portent to which Miss Clack is as blind as she is to the aesthetic beauties of the windowbox blooms. Equally oblivious to the impermanence of floral treasure is the novel's true villain, Godfrey Ablewhite. His secret life as a "man of pleasure," possessed of all the tasteful markers of that sensational position, includes "a conservatory of the rarest flowers, the match of which it would not be easy to find in all of London"—a pleasure paid for with Ablewhite's ward's inheritance and, ultimately, with Ablewhite's own life.[11]

Most readers of *The Moonstone*, however, will best remember the professional detective Sergeant Cuff as the novel's premier horticulturalist. Indeed Cuff, unable to fully solve the novel's central mystery—"It's only in books that the offices of the detective force are superior to the making of a mistake," he wryly observes—does succeed in retiring to the countryside to take up his father's gardener profession as a leisured hobby, where he achieves what he understands to be his greatest victory.[12] "[Cuff] has grown the white moss-rose, without budding it on the dog-rose first. . . . Mr. Begbie the gardener is to go to Dorking, and own that the Sergeant has beaten him at last," relays the butler Betteredge with customary excitement.[13] Ian Ousby suggests Collins found inspiration for Cuff's obsession with roses in the real-life gardening fascination held by Sergeant Aldophus "Dolly" Williamson, who worked on the Constance Kent murder case in 1860 and was promoted to be Chief Inspector of the detective force by 1865;[14] a periodical profile describes Williamson as a "quiet, unpretending, middle-sized man . . . often with a sprig of leaf or flower between his lips. . . . His talk, for choice, was about gardening, for which he had a perfect passion; and his blooms were famous in the neighbourhood where he spent his unofficial hours."[15]

But Cuff's specific horticultural subplot also appears to be an almost direct repudiation to John Loudon's 1838 claim in his massive encyclopedia of British plant life, the *Arboretum et Fruticetum Britannicum*, that "the white moss, unless budded on the dog rose . . . will not, in general, grow well: its sickly appearance, in some situations, may often be traced to its being worked on some improper stock."[16] John Loudon, with his wife Jane probably the most influential popular horticultural writer of the early Victorian age, directed the course of Victorian connections to cultivated nature through his promotion of gardening as a cultural practice whose educational and moral effects elevated both amateur and professional gardeners alike, as Sarah Dewis has shown.[17] As a result, the effect of the Loudons's prodigious textual generation was not only to increase the number of volumes on the practice of gardening available to interested readers.[18] It was also to create and expand a category of literary production that simulated in great physical detail the prospect of an improved lived environment. The language needed to propose such alteration, and the narrative of semifuturity that his texts relied upon, provided readers with a new conceptual and rhetorical mode of imagining the world of plants that they inhabited as intimately connected to the human minds that fostered their growth.

Thus Cuff's subplot, and the text of the gardening manual it is drawn from, both make in miniature a proposition for the claims that real-life environmental manipulations had upon the possibilities of fiction, in which "sickly appearance" might be "traced" to improprieties of many kinds using scientific and professional techniques. Detective novels, like natural history writing, seem to propose the structuring assumption that plants, taken as single specimens, both convey and conceal vital information about the nature of the surrounding world. The apparent assumption of detective fiction that the inductive method was of crucial importance for epistemological regulation of oneself and one's environment matches the ongoing expectations of the amateur and professional naturalists who chiefly regarded their environment as a series of embedded stories waiting to be discovered and told.

This was, for many writers, framed as a novel development of the Victorian age and, implicitly or explicitly, understood to be the work of global circulation. The naturalist and genre novelist Grant Allen explains in his 1881 essay "The Daisy's Pedigree" that the era's "new view of nature invests every part of it with a charm and hidden meaning which very few among us have ever suspected before."[19] Assuming the dual draws of both nature's "charms" and "hidden meanings" as mutually productive qualities requires that we consider the connection between people and plants to include both emotional and epistemological priorities. This was an equation intuitive for Victorians both real and fictional, among the characters of *The Moonstone* and in the detective stories that followed. But it could not have become intuitive without the changes in the content and character of the British flower garden that occurred in the first half of the nineteenth century leading up to *The Moonstone*'s publication. While these changes have long been given structural and institutional cause—particularly through the operations of the East India Company and the Royal Botanical Gardens at Kew—environmental historians have recently demonstrated the importance of individual plant affinities and desires in addition to these broader scientific, governmental, and commercial botanical networks; "most imperial environmental transformation was undertaken by individuals," James Beattie explains.[20] As Grant Allen's end of the century identification of the suspicious hermeneutics of the "new view of nature" makes clear, forms of interpretation, extrapolation, and deduction linked to the conditions of horticultural modernity also imbued plants with the same complicated motivations as humans, and the same singular connections.

The arrival of a clue-filled landscape awaiting a detective's interpretive eye can be understood to be prepared for by heightened earlier attentions to cultivated landscape's individual elements. Supplementing traditional scholarship of the English landscape garden focused on abstract spatial claims of social, economic, and political control, recent studies of the garden by Mark Laird and others have turned their attention to the material and individual elements of the growing space's flowers, shrubs, and trees.[21] This emphasis on the "plantfulness" of the English garden is in large part an emphasis on the global provenance of the garden's constitutive elements.[22] Indeed it is difficult to separate the introduction and spread of foreign hardy exotics in this era from the rapid expansion of the British garden more generally. Alan Bewell suggests that for amateur and professional gardeners alike, "the primary value in having an empire in the first place lay in its capacity of bringing new plants to grace English gardens."[23]

This meant that even as a sense of global environment developed across the spaces of colonial botanical gardens and Pacific islands, as Richard Grove and others have shown, an idea of exotic connection and global assimilation was equally under development on the home front.[24] "Few gentlemen are without the means of procuring [foreign seeds] either from their friends in foreign settlements, or at home," J. Cushing optimistically proposed in 1814, skirting around the anxiety expressed by John Loudon that "within the last fifty years the accession to our stock of exotics has been so great, that gardeners are quite bewildered among them," a bewilderment encouraged by the nurserymen who stood to benefit from widespread adoption of such expensive and delicate specimens.[25] This adoption became a domestication in every sense of the term—"at the present day a taste for the cultivation and accumulation of flowering plants is so universal, that it appears their presence is considered a necessary appendage to the dwelling," writes the gardener Joseph Harrison in the 1833 introduction to his new magazine, the *Floricultural Cabinet*.[26]

The importation of horticultural novelties became markedly easier after the invention in 1829, by Nathaniel Ward, of glazed cases that facilitated the transport of live plants on an unprecedented scale. These cases contributed significantly to the erasure of geographical botanic variation that Collins hints at in Jennings's roadside flowers; as Margaret Darby explains, "Wardian cases became so essential to the transport of plants that they were used to bring plants to locations from which the popular imagination now thinks of them as originating: tea from China to India, rubber from South America to Malaya, and a dwarf banana from Derbyshire to Somoa."[27] Thanks to the case's protection, "native soil" could be at once everywhere and nowhere; or, as Ward puts it in his own treatise on his invention, *On the Growth of Plants in Closely Glazed Cases* (1842), "there is not a civilized spot on earth which has not, more or less, benefited by their introduction."[28] With this wide distribution of native soil came a widely expanded range of denotations and references the plant life of that soil could provide, both in actual gardens and in the many kinds of texts that gave those gardens and plants representational life. That such a process was begun well before the publication of *The Moonstone* is supported by Deirdre Lynch's reading of Romantic-era greenhouses, which argues that "knowledge of Nature depended on practices of artifice and exhibition that rendered Nature a representation of itself."[29] By the time Collins's novel appeared, the process of "botanical transculturation" that shifted imported plants from exotic novelties to culturally assimilated and physically hybridized specimens was well underway, resulting in a continuous parade of foreign plants at various stages of landscape penetration.[30]

Such transculturations do not even begin to include other plant modifications, including, of course, the novel's primary botanical transformation: that of poppy seeds into the opiate tinctures and syrups upon which Jennings (and Collins himself) depend to alleviate the pains of global modernity.[31] Circling back to the description of Jennings's roadside flowers with this partial history of horticultural transculturation in mind, we find that here, again, the view from the colonies shapes and refines the English nation. This is in keeping with Caroline Reitz's claim that detective fiction is not separate from, but rather collaborative with other kinds of domestic fiction in shaping national identity in Victorian England.[32] The associations that Jennings feels with the flowers, as well as the admiration for them that he seems to expect, operate both collaboratively and comparatively: Jennings's feelings for the flowers are intensified because, it is implied, he has encountered them in multiple geographical contexts.[33] The nosegay is, through the weight of association, made part of a much larger ecological system than the country roadside where it is currently found. Collins is, after all, "the premier novelist of a global aesthetic bent on describing transnational experience as part of an ongoing stream of history," as Lauren Goodlad has termed him.[34] In *The Moonstone*, then, exists an implied capacity of plants to make far-flung nostalgic connections that shore up domestic networks with colonial landscapes and vice versa, in support of the novel's other, more-studied, imperial circulations. Plants can do this through their paradoxically widely distributed singularity, a function not only of their reproductive complexity, as Theresa Kelley has explained, but also of the ever-increasing understanding of plant life as a global phenomenon.[35] This lets us understand Jennings's flower, apparently also blooming in a far-flung British colony, to be an example of the very large-scale environmental deterritorialization at work throughout the nineteenth century, as new modes of travel and expanding claims of empire circulated plants around the globe. Jennings, by extension, is an example of a new kind of detective—one who draws upon his colonial experience to reframe his perspective of the landscape and the people of England itself, in order to both inaugurate and recenter mystery fiction for a global era.

Elaine Freedgood has persuasively described the operations of "colonial metalepsis" to explain what nineteenth-century novel readers are doing as they are thinking about the connections of the fictional and actual British Empire. In the unity of intradiegetic and extradiegetic conditions that metalepsis makes plain, Freedgood points out that "you are living both in your own diegetic space and in fictional space at the same time."[36] In this doubling, the reader finds possible "an ontological flexibility in cultural memory, an open circuit between fact and fiction that contributes to the imagining and undertaking of the work of empire, again and again."[37] Plants make particularly good exemplars of the metaleptic effect that Freedgood describes, because they constantly invade and naturalize in all directions throughout the imperial network, pulling the novel back and forth across oceans and continents. As Allan Quatermain asserts in Rider Haggard's *Allan and the Holy Flower* (1915), a novel organized around the pursuit of a single extraordinary orchid, "And now the story shifts away to England," adding, in a parenthetical aside, "Don't be afraid, my adventurous reader, if ever I have one; it is coming back to Africa again in a very few pages."[38] That plants can move around this open circuit of empire as they do is a function of novelistic plot, but it is also, and more implicitly, a function of environment as assumed from such a plot. Reading the wide range of colonial fiction with assimilated English plants, or domestic fiction with imported plants, a reader returns to an extradiegetic frame conceptually altered to accommodate the operations of the intradiegetic metalepsis. Plants with global distribution, as we saw in Jennings's nosegay, are a form of colonial metalepsis with a possible future and past. When drawn into detective fiction specifically, they are expected to turn these pasts and futures to epistemologically-consequential ends.

In the second part of this chapter, I focus more closely on the narrative operations of the clue and the revised connections those narrative operations make with a newly emergent cultivated global plant life. Jennings's acknowledgement of shifting relationship between plants and people helps us follow those changed connections; when he notes of the hedgerow flowers that "few people in England seem to admire them as they deserve," he also reminds us that the flowers are central here, and the human admirers only contingent to them—countering, at least in miniature, the humanistic biases of the pathetic fallacy. Plants, as cultivated fictions, mediate nature and text to provide a poetics of organic life. Emphasizing the alienating work of subject formation contained in such figurative formulations as the pathetic fallacy, this poetics at the same time also prioritizes curiosity and connection across the divide of the real from its fictional representation. In so doing, they also shift narrative weight and significance away from a centrally human form. While plants rarely manage to claim narrative priority or representative singularity entirely to themselves—I'll attend to the more active plants that do manage to make such claims in chapter 5—the influences of their decentering can be registered simply by noting the points in a novel in which the narrative priority is no longer understood to be a priori human.

These narrative nudges have consequence for the environmental ontology of the narrative overall, as I've suggested in the introduction, but they also have consequence for the degree to which authors and readers think through the influence of setting, space, and expansiveness within the novel form. The detective's acts of regard—of flowers, plants, and other forms of organic life not human or animal, in particular—are key examples of this nudging; but so too are the narrative pauses imposed as more ordinary humans stop to regard a flower.

The detective novel, however, provides the most recognizable form of this regard in the narrative category of the clue—a plot element demanding a newly pronounced attention to setting and the broader environmental reference setting implies. For the genre novel, the clue is not only a puzzle piece unlocking a cascade of plot consequences, but also a key to the schema of the novel's setting, with the capacity to grant narrative logic and significance to the interactions between characters and the organic world around them, as well as to the global reaches of those interactions.

Collins's novel reminds readers that their roadside flowers had widespread origins, even as the tortured death of their human analogue Ezra Jennings at the novel's end suggests some problems with global migrations. Nils Clausson persuasively argues that "the fin-de-siècle detective story, like its close literary cousin the fin-de-siècle gothic tale, operates both to create mystery and then to give the illusion—but only the illusion—of solving it": an illusion that is equally present in the newly open global environment as it is in the expanded cosmopolitan context that Clausson describes.[39] Thus the proposition of inductive openness granted by the detective novel belied an epistemological complexity in which certain narrative roadblocks will never be opened; we never learn the name of Ezra Jennings's flowers, still less his country of origin. My emphasis here is therefore not so much on changing techniques of epistemological discovery, but rather on the recognition that attending to individual specimens of plant life was a way of making meaning that, like the clue, grew from extrapolation and conditional assertion.[40] It is no coincidence that particularly global forms—or at least forms obsessed with the possibilities of global exchange like the genre novel as well as nonfiction guides and manuals—relied especially on these strategies of clues and hints while at the same time forever forestalling their resolution.

This endless deferral exists despite, and also because, of the generally acknowledged argument that the detective novel is the genre that most clearly and carefully works out for us in narrative the epistemological form of narrative itself, with the clue's emphasis on the relationship between character and setting chief among those developments. The development of the clue is, for Franco Moretti at least, the detective novel's most singularly distinguishing narrative feature.[41] As Moretti describes it, a clue is a story element that becomes ever more precisely present and absent at the same time—an object or occasion in the environment of the story that is there for the noticing but remains unnoticed. Clues, in Moretti's and others' accounts, constantly generate possible narratives of both the past and the future: How did a freshly painted door frame come to be smeared? Where will a missing jewel later be taken? These analeptic and proleptic narratives multiply and collapse over the course of the novel until, of course, the final solution forestalls all but a single possibility of past and present, if not future. Moretti points out, largely as a means of taxonomic differentiation, that most detective novels contain a vast number of clues scattered across the landscape of the story with no apparent meaning, or, rather, with meanings that make sense in another narrative that we as readers may never know. We can, following Moretti, divide the stages of the detective novel's development based on the environmental function clues provide. But even those not approving of this winnowing can agree with Frank Kermode that "even in a detective story which has the maximum degree of specialised 'hermeneutic' organisation, one can always find significant concentrations of interpretable material that has nothing to do with clues and solutions and that can, if we choose, be read rather than simply discarded, though propriety recommends the latter course."[42]

Discarding large chunks of story material, of course, is not a recommended practice in other forms of fiction. The formal attributes of realism—its unities of space and time, its assumptions that these unities have narrative consequence, its accommodations of subjects and agency as events made sensible on the scale of the human, and more—lend themselves to detective fiction, and yet classic detective fiction can never be understood to be properly realist, precisely because such detective fictions must take special pains to emphasize the epistemological weight of their own narrative elements. This is especially true in the case of the clue. As a figurative device that takes material and sometimes even living organic form, the clue does denotative work in narratively significant ways that vary given the clue's substance. Plant-clues in particular, with their range of social, cultural, and psychological associations, extend the clue's range not only forwards and backwards in the narrative but inwards and outwards from the page to its surrounding world. A living plant's transformation in a detective novel from natural element transparent of purpose and meaning to associated, denotative, referential, and fictional object thus marks a more startling shift than when an already artificial china plate, for example, undergoes that same transformation. Looking at a plant, then, helps us see more clearly a consequence of the clue-driven narrative evolution of the detective genre that Moretti did not explore: the pressure placed by that type of narrative on novels to possess settings hospitable to clues in the first place. The architecture and landscape of the detective novel genre must alter as clues gain strength and complexity; certain kinds of narrative settings—object-filled country houses, crowded city streets, and even landscapes filled with new and non-native plants—need to proliferate to allow the presence of the clues the mysteries demand.

Jennings's nosegay, giving a clue to the character of the effective detective, shows a subtle version of this. But blunter treatments abound. See, for example, "The Talk of the Town," an 1903 installment of L. T. Meade's detective series *The Sorceress of the Strand,* featuring a diabolical female villain. Detective Vandeleur, adversary of the titular cosmetologist/master criminal Madame Sara, discovers that the palm "of peculiar grace and size droop[ing] its finger-like fronds over the table" where a lecturer will stand is in fact far from benign: "'Look here!' said Vandeleur, and he pointed to the fine tips of one of the leaves. 'This plant never grew. It is made—it is an artificial imitation of the most surprising skill and workmanship.'"[43] Thus is foiled the plot to murder the hapless lecturer with poison gas delivered through the hollow metal tubes of the palm's branches. Resolution of the case, once the plant is reclassified from living "tasteful decoration" to artificial weapon, comes speedily if unsatisfyingly: "Only one human being could have planned and executed such a contrivance. If we can trace it to her, she spends the night in Bow Street," declares Vandeleur, his conditional phrasing reassuring readers that Madame Sara will certainly not be traced and her serialized string of thrilling crimes will continue.[44] But the irresolution, in light of this chapter's focus on the function of the clue, is interesting on its own merits. Vandeleur's friend and Watson-analogue, Mr. Druce, explains the dead end of inquiry.

> The plant was taken to Vandeleur's house. The florist who had supplied the decorations was interviewed. He expressed himself astounded. He denied all complicity—the palm was certainly none of his; he could not tell how it had got into the hall. He had come himself to see if the decorations were carried out according to his directions, and had noticed the palm and remarked on its

grace. Someone had said that a lady had brought it, but he really knew nothing definite about it.

Notwithstanding all our inquiries, neither did we ever find out how that palm got mixed up with the others.[45]

That Druce and Vandeleur continue to refer to the artificial metal contraption as a "plant," one that is classified with "the others" in the decorative scenery of the story, suggests the difficulties of articulating the increasingly active function of plant life within the progress of urban life. The interviewing of the florist, as a particular kind of urban professional most invested in the simulacra of natural—and, given the palm fronds, a by this time rather old-fashioned tropical—life, gives proof to the conversion of organic form into commodity décor. But the idea that lecture halls might be decorated with plants at all, still less that lecture halls would be settings for murder attempts, is equally a sign of floral estrangement. That is, the kinds of mysteries that alienate plants, native or domestic, from their ostensible viewers—particularly those defined as their keenest and most perspicacious viewers—assert themselves especially in this transformation of the natural world in the global nineteenth century. The detective novel, which admitted many kinds of nonhuman elements to register meaning and exchange information through the operations of the clue, is a form where plant cultivation is both emblematic and constitutive. Plants formed a representational background that could quickly turn into an operational foreground, as this story shows through particularly dramatic if heavy-handed example. The slipperiness that prevents consistent identification of domestic origin is in keeping with Meade's more general narrative sleight-of-hand, which constantly revises class and gender identities through Madame Sara's costume changes, makeup applications, and other acts of performance and disguise.

The image of the false palm malevolently shadowing its victim, or even the bunch of flowers growing by the roadside awaiting Jennings's assemblage of them into a nosegay, demonstrates the final aspect of the cultivated exotic plant relevant to this discussion of detective fiction. As I have suggested, these fictions elevated the plant's narrative status so that it became, if not equivalent to a human character, at least character-adjacent, both in its singularity and specificity of form. John Loudon explained in one of his first manuals on managing exotic species that "a flower in the open parterre, though beautiful and gay, has yet something less endearing, and is less capable of receiving especial regard, than a plant in a pot, which thus acquires a sort of locomotion; and becomes, as it were, thoroughly domesticated"; this idea of "especial regard" warranted by imported plants befits their commodity value, of course, but it also speaks to the bonds of human connection that, moving about in their pots, they are able to form.[46] In the final section of this chapter, I consider several incidents of intimate plant regard that prompt the recollection and allow the completion of the story as it is being told. These plants were not themselves always the cosseted exotic specimens in greenhouse pots that Loudon was describing in 1824, but their influence on the humans who shared their "thorough domestications" was equivalent to that of the botanical imports of earlier eras. Such plants made private, intimate connections with the people that regarded them, thus showing how Victorian selves gained self-definition in acts of plant recognition. These apprehensions help readers understand the plant not as a taxonomic specimen but rather as an affective and emotionally meaningful individual form.

"The Adventure of the Naval Treaty" (1893), the last Sherlock Holmes story published before Doyle's attempt to rid himself of the character in "The Final Problem," finds the great detective grappling both with the theft of key diplomatic documents capable of starting a European war and with a surfeit of clues—seven, by Holmes's assessment. As with most Holmes stories, the process of eliminating the wrong clues works fairly mechanically, and Holmes's explanation of the mystery is equally mechanical. As Watson narrates: "'The principal difficulty in [the] case,' remarked Holmes in his didactic fashion, 'lay in the fact of there being too much evidence. What was vital was overlaid and hidden by what was irrelevant.'"[47] But the unfolding of the "Naval Treaty" does have an odd distraction during an initial discussion of the case with Phelps, the unlucky diplomat suspected of stealing the documents. This conversation, in which the reader, having been already told of the proliferation of clues to come, is on the lookout for clue-like specimens, frustrates both those expectations and the expectations of the story's characters. While considering the (as usual ineffective) police involvement in the affair to date, Holmes dissolves into a curious form of musing, which Watson naturally relays to the readers of the *Strand*:

> "The authorities are excellent at amassing facts, though they do not always use them to advantage. What a lovely thing a rose is!"

He walked past the couch to the open window and held up the drooping stalk of a moss-rose, looking down at the dainty blend of crimson and green. It was a new phase of his character to me, for I had never before seen him show any keen interest in natural objects.

"There is nothing in which deduction is so necessary as in religion," said he, leaning with his back against the shutters. "It can be built up as an exact science by the reasoned. Our highest assurance of the goodness of Providence seems to me to rest in the flowers. All other things, our powers, our desires, our food, are all really necessary for our existence in the first instance. But this rose is an extra. Its smell and its colour are an embellishment of life, not a condition of it. It is only goodness which gives extras, and so I say again that we have much to hope from the flowers."

Percy Phelps and his nurse looked at Holmes during this demonstration with surprise and a good deal of disappointment written upon their faces. He had fallen into a reverie, with the moss-rose between his fingers. It had lasted some minutes before the young lady broke in upon it.

"Do you see any prospect of solving this mystery, Mr. Holmes?," she asked with a touch of asperity in her voice.

"Oh, the mystery!" he answered, coming back with a start to the realities of life.[48]

This extended act of floral appreciation seems particularly puzzling for a man like Holmes, whose attention to plants as anything other than weapons appears minimal. Watson's initial catalogue of Holmes's skills in *A Study in Scarlet* concludes that the great detective's knowledge of botany is "variable"; he is "well up on poisons generally" but "knows nothing of practical gardening."[49] Equally, Holmes's well-known suspicion of the pastoral, voiced most memorably in "The Adventure of the Copper Beeches," grows from his suspicions of the ability of the "smiling and beautiful countryside" to conceal wrongdoing both through physical isolation and through the false sense of security proposed by the pathetic fallacy.[50] This is a dangerous yet common misprision also warned of by the omniscient narrator in Mary Elizabeth Braddon's earlier sensation novel, *Lady Audley's Secret* (1862): "We hear every day of murders committed in the country . . . sudden and violent deaths from cruel blows, inflected with a stake cut from some spreading oak, whose very shadow promised—peace."[51] These surface-level misreadings that mistake the evil for the innocent are not the point here, especially because the rerouting of murderous intent forces the countryside and the oak into the epistemologically diminished position of red herring. Instead, Doyle's focus returns us to the rose, and, inexorably, to the human frame that limits accurate plant perception to a few choice observers such as the great detective himself.

Reaching through the same window that will later be breached with murderous intent by Percy Phelps's soon-to-be brother-in-law, Holmes here draws attention to the scant protection a home provides from the threats of the outside world. Audrey Jaffe has pointed to the ways that, in the realist novel, windows and doorways and other "material and spatial constructions that simultaneously invite and exclude" become themselves "seductively 'real'-seeming ideological forms."[52] For Doyle, and for the detective story more generally, the window frame offers an especially seductive space between the cultivated sufficiency of the domestic and the intrusive effects of the murderously inclined. As early as *The Sign of Four*, the boundary marker of the window flowerbed is used to feign a horticultural security between domestic interior tranquility and foreign vengeance that is easily and openly sundered, as typified in that novella by the window appearance of the "wild fierce face" of the murdering colonial returnee Jonathan Small.[53]

Yet in addition to hinting at the general vulnerability that the rose outside the window proposes, Doyle also pursues in the "Naval Treaty" a second area of the flower's significance, uncharacteristically prompting Holmes to proclaim Providence's superabundant virtues. In insisting that "we have much to hope from the flowers," for they are both "an extra . . . an embellishment of life, not a condition of it" and thus "our highest assurance of the goodness of Providence," Holmes demands that we preserve the gap between the requirements of basic life and the operative actions that convert those basic needs into beliefs and practices, reflectively constitutive of life's meaning. Though the window rose does not operate as a traditional clue, the insistence on this gap equally distances it from the living world; so too does Holmes and Watson's designation of the rose as a "thing" and the more ontologically puzzling "natural object." Thus while it is possible to understand this moment of reverie as evidence of Doyle and Holmes's adherence to an already outdated understanding of intelligent design, in which the flower exists only to signal the invisible working of Providence, to do so is to ignore the genre's abiding interest in objects as the determinant conduits of character and intention.

Considering the moss-rose as an object that, however briefly, takes over the burden of analysis from the detective, thus allowing him to complete his story, also helps explain the extraordinary amount of time Holmes's reverie adds to the story's telling, or *suzjet*, in deferment of its solution, the methodical isolation of the thief and would-be murderer allowing the documents to be found and the crime resolved—since it is a deferment that also allows for a further proliferation of objects. The "Naval Treaty"'s *suzjet*, that is, even for a short story, is greatly disproportionate to its *fabula*, the chronological chain of events making up the crime of opportunity and coincidence that the story relays. Readers of Holmes's adventures are already well accustomed to the many Watson-sized stretchings of the *suzjet* that Doyle imposes to lend suspense to the retrospective present-tense narration, moments when we must tarry with Watson and the beleaguered victim away from the scene of investigation and unaware of the doings of the great detective until the final triumphant reveal. In the "Naval Treaty" Watson (as usual) purports to find these pauses "painful," and describes his failed attempts to divert Phelps to the broad-ranging terrain of the British Empire: "In vain I endeavoured to interest him in Afghanistan, in India, in social questions, in anything which might take his mind out of the groove. He would always come back to his lost treaty, wondering, guessing, speculating, as to what Holmes was doing" until Watson himself is infected enough to stay up half the night "brooding over this strange problem, and inventing a hundred theories, each of which was more impossible than the last."[54]

At stake here, then, are not just the rates at which different interested parties—Watson, Holmes, and the reader—arrive at the proper conclusion about where the documents have gone. It is also the other time scales that overlay this rate of solution—the time it takes for a rose to bloom, a man to heal from an illness, and a particular naval treaty to gain or lose significance for the course of European geopolitics. The reverie with the moss-rose is notable in that it brings together the principal characters in the *suzjet* with those in the *fabula* to consider the mystery at the same time and in (as is later revealed) the same location as the missing treaty itself, rather than sending Holmes back to his more customary repose with pipe and slippers in the privacy of his own lodgings. Thus the frantic multiplications of cause and effect performed by Watson, Phelps, and his fiancée are set against Holmes's efficient elimination of extraneous detail with the increasingly abstract moss-rose as a broker between the two. Environmental setting's suspension of narrative progress mediates the unwinding of the plot, as plant temporality in the bloom of a rose coincides with the course of geopolitics.

By allying plants with clues I have made a proposition about the way an approach to a plant consciousness might be narrated without the framework of anthropomorphic agency. Here we have nothing but the evidence of Jennings's and Holmes's reveries to stand in for any information that the plants themselves might offer, and, indeed, we finish each story without any supposition that *The Moonstone*'s hedge-side flower or the "Naval Treaty"'s moss-rose—or, for that matter, the rhododendron bush that shelters and disguises Holmes as he waits to apprehend the naval treaty's thief—have any interest in the conclusion of each human mystery. However, by admitting flowers and other organic specimens into the realm of inutile clues—that is, objects of focus in the *suzjet* but not of consequence in the *fabula*—a suggestion about the agency of plants is allowed. Plants, especially named novel plants, alert readers to the fact that they are at an interconnecting node of *fabula* and *suzjet*, in which the particular materiality and temporal persistence of the narrative's setting also gains consequence in the narrative's telling. For plants, unable to move, speak, or reason on their own, such a penetration from one layer of narrative to another is the evidence of their consequence as it appears at the limits of the human. The question of how to imagine the thoughts of plants is not proposed as possible, but here it is enough to imagine the thoughts of humans whose thoughts are reflected from the plants they regard.

Holmes's window reverie is therefore a reminder that the connection between an individual human and a single plant, particularly a single flower, was not in itself a natural or necessary one, but rather a connection that needed to be demonstrated repeatedly to assert its meaning and power. Such singular relations were commodity linkages, of course, but they were also epistemological connections—establishing the bounds and limits of functional human-plant analogies. In the new global environment, the forms, colors, shapes, and sizes of plants that drew human reference needed to be defined anew. To commune in this way with a stem would be preposterous in the world of the novel, likewise if Holmes uprooted an entire plant to fuel his reverie. So the dissolution and reconstitution of the flower itself through the time frame of Holmes's monologue becomes especially important for the operations of the exchange. Initially a "dainty blend of crimson and green," the color fields of the flower resolve themselves into a single "moss-rose" only when considered as a part of Holmes, held between his fingers as he drifts into a reverie in a pose reminiscent of his grip on other material supplements to his intellect like his tobacco pipe or his cocaine needle. As he holds the flower in his hand, a synthesis is achieved that licenses the breaks and gaps in the story—what intradiegetically are considered his intuitive leaps, and extradiegetically fall into the same category of plot trickeries that Conan Doyle himself later complained against.[55] The movement to isolate the bloom of the rose alone, here and in countless other works of prose fiction and nonfiction that proposed an associative epistemology to unlock the mysteries of the world, depended on a mutual understanding of those boundaries. Plant fictions could come to be, that is, to exactly the degree that living plants could have discrete and singular characters of their own, as organic characters—which, by extension, could denote a broader further association of fictional things. Other objects can and should be considered for the similar work they can do, but only plants have the deictic ability to connect to their present-day environment while also recalling their distant origins in living, and amendable, organic form.

Singular plant character, therefore, was premised on a globally constitutive set of evidences and obfuscations. Although "Naval Treaty" tells a story nearly entirely confined to a London office and the bedroom of an English country house, its implied influence and consequences spread across Europe and into the global empires that European nations controlled. Detective fiction, and the spy fiction treading on Doyle's heels, aimed to make sense of local environment as world environment. As Yumna Siddiqi has explained, "in Conan Doyle's mysteries . . . the uncovering of a plot which is the moment of detective fiction, frequently occurs within an imperial framework. . . . Read in this way, Conan Doyle's stories yield a veritable imaginative topography of Empire."[56] Even in such relatively Eurocentric competing detective series as Morrison's *Martin Hewitt, Investigator* (1894), Guy Boothby's *The Prince of Swindlers* (1900), or L. T. Meade's other detective series, *The Brotherhood of the Seven Kings* (1899), imperial and settler colonial props, from diamonds to opium to tse-tse flies (used as weapons of horse-murder) all featured prominently. More notably, the immensely popular inheritor of *The Moonstone*'s generic innovations, Fergus Hume's *The Mystery of the Hansom Cab* (1886), concerns itself especially with the colonial circulations that built both the population and the public and private gardens and parks of Melbourne. Other thrillers, including Grant Allen's *An African Millionaire* (1897), *Miss Cayley's Adventures* (1899), and *Hilda Wade* (1900), though focusing (especially in the latter two titles) on investigation as a product of individual retribution rather than professional obligation, also take the world-circuit of the globe-trotter as their natural setting. But in all of these cases, the end of the century Victorian detective's concern with global flows in general and colonial returnees in particular signals the accommodations that narrative fiction, short- and long-form, was making to the causal ecologies of empire, including plants, material objects, and people, as well as forms of knowledge that each of these explained. Even for novels that did not follow detective fiction's exaggerated impulse to resolve interruptions or diversions in these circulations, the plant's interpolation into narrative carried with it the history of its global exchanges and compelled narrative changes as a result.

This could be true even in romances that took up such circulations metaphorically, fantastically, or both. Take, for example, H. G. Wells's *The Time Machine* (1895). In addition to the novel's other, better-known temporal revisions, Wells uses flowers to break the frame of the retrospective narration after the Traveler's return from his harrowing encounters with the Eloi and the Morlocks. Meeting with his waiting professional friends who seek material evidence of his journey, the Traveler breaks his story to dramatically place "two withered flowers" from the far future upon the table for his listeners to observe as he recounts the fate of poor doomed Weena, who, earlier in the story but far later in human time, picked those flowers to put in his pockets, which she understood as "an eccentric kind of vase for floral decoration."[57] This flower presentation is the only pause in the Traveler's continuous narration of the tale, and Wells used italics in the original publication to mark out the interruption. At the close of his story, aware of the skepticism of his audience, the Traveler relies on the flowers to keep his connection to his own experience: "'To tell you the truth . . . I hardly believe it myself . . . And yet . . .' His eyes fell with a mute inquiry upon the withered white flowers upon the little table.'"[58] If ultimately the majority of the listeners are not convinced, neither are they able to identify the proper botanical place of the mysterious white flowers—"But I certainly don't know the natural order of these flowers," muses the Medical Man.[59] The narrator's suggestion that the flowers are "not unlike two very large white mallows"—a species of bloom occurring around the world—equally leaves the blooms forever poised just on the other side of epistemological recognition.[60] While the evidence of the flowers is not ultimately sufficient to prevent the Traveler from embarking on a final journey without return, the sympathetic connections they provide outside of the "natural order" signal the persistence of affective connection that I have detailed throughout this chapter in a variety of fictional forms. Even this very partial resolution to the disconnect between the Traveller's telling of the story and the basic chronology of the story's events demonstrates that regard of and for flowers revises narrative temporality—the flowers bloom and wither by a reckoning that prioritizing the reader's experience over a grander global narrative.

But these connections were not limited to scientific romance. In a reversal of the borrowings from nonfiction form by earlier genre fictions, the plant hunter Frank Kingdon-Ward's "Dream of a Plant Collector" closes his 1924 narrative *The Romance of Plant-Hunting* with an ostensibly nonfictional plant reverie overtly fantastic in its theme and form.[61] Kingdon-Ward was deeply interested in the many rhetorical varieties of plant description, being the author of more than twenty-five volumes over his career recounting his explorations in Asia, his botanical discoveries, and, above all, the flowers that drew his practical and aesthetic interest as a plantsman who considered himself, ultimately, a public servant. This "Dream," presented with little context, distills these themes of his decades of writing into a single striking narrative that makes rough parody of the narrative innovations underway in fiction of the time. It begins with the unnamed plant collector traversing an unidentified foreign country in search of specimens, and encountering at last a plant that he calls "God's masterpiece" and like "no flower ever seen."[62] As he continues, he grows obsessed with the possibilities of the plant's distribution: "A moment of mad possession seizes him. 'It is mine! mine! mine!' he cries to the wind and the rocks; 'I will enjoy it alone.' Then, as the stupefying loveliness of the plant—his plant—ceases to be an absolute physical pain to him, sanity returns . . . he shouts suddenly, 'All the world must see it and be glad.'"[63] The hallucination then makes the surprising turn to the Chelsea flower show, where the plant hunter overhears the buzz of conversation surrounding his discovery: "everybody has it," the voices gossip, concluding that "it will be in every garden in England presently."[64] The confidence of the conversants is undercut by their geographical ignorance—"Where does it come from?" "Oh, it's one of those Chinese importations—or is it African? I always forget! *Do* people find flowers in China?"—but ultimately such origins do not matter.

> Over the bent inquiring heads of the people he could see the glowing bank of blossom that was the offspring of his discovery, of the little plant, perfect and solitary, that he had worshipped on a bleak hill side, five minutes—or was it years?—ago. It grew on other hills now. 'Quite hardy,' the man had told him. Then it must be growing all over England....
> Presently tired men would come home from overseas, and, having missed the loveliness of England, would wander out of doors on a spring evening to where his plant poured colour on the stones... and they, not knowing whence this flower had come, would only say as they stood content before its beauty, 'It's jolly good to be home.'[65]

Through the archaic device of the dream-narrative, a modern encounter between plant specimen/commodity and consumer gardeners can be written. Acutely conscious of the narrative consequences of his story of plant acculturation, Kingdon-Ward grants his fictional plant the power to generically assume the capacity to simultaneously establish and dismantle an affective human relationship with the organic world. Significantly, the plant's precise characteristics are never specified—which both facilitates the varieties of expanding narrative made possible by a more expansive plant life and also forestalls stable connections between particulars of plant and place. But most of all this narrative, a not-unsurprising excursus of lyricism on the part of the frequently showy Kingdon-Ward, depends heavily on things readers have learned from genre fiction for its devices to take place. The magical transport from one space to another, the shift to the imagined soldiers and their hypothetical collective yet unified discourse, even the dissolution of the plant form into the "fields of color," all overwrite the transactional economy of plant hunting at the dawn of the twentieth century into a self- and nationally constitutive trance whose origin story must be told and retold. In doing so, Ward erases the vast apparatus of domestic support and financing that had since at least the eighteenth century supported colonial botanical collectors and bioprospectors in their work.[66]

Kingdon-Ward's reverie, then, reiterates the lessons we have learned in other ways from the detective fiction forms that were the main focus of this chapter. The individual instance of the flower, "perfect and solitary," both requires isolated attention for its perpetuation and refuses those singular limitations. One part of the story of Victorian plant life is its repeated identification of the individual connections between people and the imported and domesticated plants they adopt; another, inseparable part is the constant duplications of those individual linkages. Britons found their plants, again and again, and found in them proof and resolution of their own personal and national story. Considering what Holmes means when he claims we have much to "hope" from the flowers, then, demands entrance into a tacit conversation with—as much as about—the plants. The more general ontological problem of making narrative out of such seemingly impossible conversations recurs throughout the novels of the era and is termed coincidence, faith, hope, or any such language indicating resignation or acceptance to incommensurate conditions of being. These irreconcilabilities both marked the Victorian era as modern and troubled the self-narrative of the path to that modernity. In the introduction, I suggested some ways that the cultivation of imported plants emphasized that development within the organic and natural world. A body of detective literature scholarship has shown the manner in which clues and the nature of evidence for the Victorians evinced the need for new methods and epistemologies to accommodate those methods.

This chapter has pointed out the confluence of plants as clues in order to underline the accommodations that interpretation must make when making literary these gaps. But clues, of course, are not the only device that the literature of the waning nineteenth century used as narrative structure to bridge these breaks; and, in particular, bridge the breaks forced open by particular wedges of assimilation, acculturation, and other kinds of global entry. In addition to the secrets and lies of spy fiction and the metaphysical mysteries of gothic and fantastic tales, the hints and directions of the nonfiction guidebooks and guides for living that populated Victorian bookshelves also relied on this process of inferred completion. As plants came closer through personhood through cultivation's attention to their naming, genealogies, and otherwise singular, individual status, their function as singular beings also reformed the operations of rhetorical cause and effect, as well as the part/whole relations of clue and narrative, and hint and practice. Despite not ever being able to know the thoughts of the flowers, the domestic operations of flowers could be, at least in their outcomes, made both clear and connected within a literary world. In the next two chapters, I will turn to the ways this plant life, when found in city and country gardens, revised the self-narration and progressive development of the humans who lived with those gardens.

❦ 2 ❧

Strange City Gardens

When the mysterious and sunburned Tartar of Charles Dickens's *The Mystery of Edwin Drood* (1870) declares of his London garden of flowering window-boxes that "I thought I'd feel my way to a command of a landed estate, by beginning in boxes," the pleasantness of the scene demonstrates more than authorial approval of the sailor's good stewardship.[1] Tartar's flower boxes, like his shipshape quarters in general, come to operate as a fantastical yet functional space of urban and novelistic retreat and a fairy-tale counterpoint to the opium den that shadows *Edwin Drood*'s central murder mystery. A "garden in the air," a "country on the summit of the magic beanstalk," Tartar's flower-bedecked apartment decorated with souvenirs of global travel rejuvenates a narrative space oppressed by confinements, even as both confinements and rejuvenations share globally sourced origins.[2] But window boxes did not always lead to Tartar's upward mobility. Arthur Morrison's novel of urban poverty *A Child of the Jago* (1896) puts its window flowers to very different uses amid its darkly deterministic approach to slum fiction. During a violent neighborhood street brawl, residents literally convert the substance of their surroundings into weaponry: the apartment-dweller "Pip Walsh, who affected horticulture on his window-sill, hurled down flower pots" from his upper-story window.[3]

These window pots, whether wounding or restorative, had definitively global origins. Popular fiction reminds us of this when Edward Malone, not yet arrived in the hostile prehistoric Lost World of Arthur Conan Doyle's 1912 novel of the same name, finds happy familiarity in the flowers of the Amazonian jungle that surround it: "It was pleasant to see the convolvulus, the passion-flower, and the begonia, all reminding me of home, here among these inhospitable rocks. There was a red begonia just the same colour as one that is kept in a pot in the window of a certain villa in Streatham upon the antediluvian plateau in South America—but I am drifting into private reminiscence."[4] Malone's pleasant reminiscence of a London suburb, uniting Streatham with South America in a shared horticultural present-tense time frame, also inverts the routes of botanical exchange. The Amazon is said to be familiar because its plant life is like London's, but, as we have seen, much of London's plant life has, now and previously, come from the Amazon or other growing grounds remoter still.[5] I'll discuss further the operations of the foreign landscape in novels of adventure and resettlement in chapter 4; in this chapter, despite Malone's deflections, I will continue to linger on the villa window in Streatham.[6] But rather than looking outward, as we did with Holmes in the previous chapter, I will look inward, from the efforts and failures at cultivation in the city and its environs to the interior life they surround and, often, fail to support. The urban garden was for many Britons the predominant form of nature they encountered; likewise, the fictional urban garden became an increasingly important signifier of imagined biological life as well.[7] While in the previous chapter we saw the ways that cultivation made intelligible and directive the function of plants in the narration of environments, in ways particularly enhanced in the detective novel but relevant to a far broader range of works, here too cultivation makes meaningful—and its absence makes obscured—the narratively transformative garden spaces of the city. These garden spaces, allied with both private and public spheres, revise the novel characters, major and minor, who enter them, realigning these characters' relations with the surrounding urban world and disrupting their narration of a stable, unified, and singular self. It is worth listening to Malone's profession of private reminiscence to recall the intimate connections plants made with readers in genre novels. His transport from the jungle of South America to the streets of Streatham recalls the reveries inspired by plants in the previous chapter. But the gaps and disjunctions imposed by pauses for plant regard in the urban gothic novels taken up in this chapter differ from detective fiction's clue-directed musings as darker diversions from which one does not so easily return. If gothic fictions in urban environments repair some of the most obvious ruptures, the lingering effects of the damages render the overall coherency of domestic life more fragile. Plant recuperations may not always be enough.

The main focus of this chapter will be the urban and suburban gardens that, through organic decay or symbolic suspension, direct the generic production of end-of-the-century imperial gothic novel. The Victorian gothic romance, which Cannon Schmitt terms a "paradoxical and even parasitic entity," shadows mainstream novels to represent their social and spatial worlds while also revealing ways those worlds go astray into darker psychologies and sexualities.[8] Nancy Armstrong has argued that gothic novels and gothic interludes in realistic novels make "a tear or hole in the fabric of realism" that impedes the unifying work of "normative perception."[9] Armstrong identifies this dissolution of realism in fractures that divide "consciousness from biological being"; I suggest that the plants in the strange garden site also offer a space for gothic interpolation of a nonanthropomorphic consciousness that indicates gap, absence, or damage in realism's smoothness.[10] In telling the stories of urban gardens and the strange plants they contained, these gothic narratives are not simply acknowledging a space of urban insufficiency in a rapidly expanding imperial metropole marked by astounding economic and social inequities, although they are doing that as well. They are offering an explicitly drawn formulation of the concessions, alterations, and other transformations required to support and maintain the garden's simulacra of the stable and bounded human.

Gardens, no matter their state of cultivation, only exist when recognized as such, and come into existence on point of recognition.[11] For this reason, the frequent appearance of half-cultivated, fallow, or untended gardens in sensation and gothic novels throughout the century speaks to not only an internal and private disarray, but a confusion of self-constitution from a public and outer perspective. Cultivating the plants in an urban garden—or, alternatively, drawing attention to the absence of a cultivated urban garden as buffer space—emphasizes novelistic fictions of the urban organic world, fictions that invariably revise existing conventions of the pastoral, the rural, and the native. This tense engagement is present in gardens outside the city as well, of course; as John Dixon Hunt and Michael Leslie have noted, "the garden is typically a place of paradox . . . created, and subsequently experienced, as commentary and response: a focus of speculations, propositions and negotiations concerning what it is to live in the world."[12] But urban gardens, especially gothic urban gardens, take as an operative premise the obfuscating, contrived, denaturalized conditions of such a cultivated space. In so doing they make the implicit global returns of the plants they contain an integral part of the making of the city space, but they also premise the urban space as, from the outset, a site of lack. The modernizing city is a place defined as a place that lacks a garden and, as recompense, requires plant supplement even if artificial and partial.

In both Charlotte Brontë's *Villette* (1853) and Oscar Wilde's *The Picture of Dorian Gray* (1890), the two novels I consider most carefully in this chapter, the main characters' antagonistic methods of self-making depend on the support of plants for the revisions of their selfhood. But these personal plant relations can be understood especially through the traditions of gothic fictions that shape each novel's manipulations of the stability of both the individual self and its surrounding organic world. By revisiting and parodying older gothic conventions within a newly expanded global environment, *Villette* posits plant relations that engulf the main character, while *Dorian Gray* extends end-of-the-century gothic horrors, and the consciousness of their terrors, to the plant life that ornaments the domestic lives and personas of the novel's characters. In order to give context to the revisions of the natural that these two novels pursue, the first part of this chapter reviews the history of city gardening in London generally and considers the place of artificial organic environments like the Wardian case and the hothouse more specifically. Recognizing these trends in horticultural history undergirds a reading of the cultivated, or uncultivated, spaces of other fin-de-siècle imperial gothic fictions and the gaps and disruptions they tear in the coherence of the city space.

John Claudius Loudon began his first massive compendium of world gardening knowledge, *An Encyclopædia of Gardening* (1822), with a list of the range of reasons and locations where gardening may be practiced. These include "for private use and enjoyment, in cottages, villas, and mansion gardens" as well as in the more public spaces of parks, scientific gardens, royal grounds, and commercial nurseries.[13] A small but significant alteration to this list came in the 1835 revised edition; gardening is now practiced for private use and enjoyment in "*town, suburban,* cottage, villa and mansion gardens."[14] In admitting the prospect of urban and semi-urban gardening to a body of works previously focused on the design and management of extensive country estates, Loudon reflected a broader shift in the theory and practice of organic cultivation. Loudon's writings, by bridging the gap between eighteenth-century aesthetic treatises on the landscape and the mid-Victorian explosion of practical manuals for management of self and garden, narrate for us the move toward a broader diffusion of horticultural practice among the middle classes and, at the same time, a fragmentation of the cultivated landscape into smaller pockets preserved within metropolitan bounds. Flower, culinary, and apothecary gardening in towns had always formed an essential component of daily urban life, but Loudon's specific inclusion of city gardening among sites designed for "private . . . enjoyment" indicates a changed methodology for writing and thinking seriously about the natural world from the perspective of the metropolis.[15] If spatially compressed to fit within the bounds of the semidetached row house, it was also figuratively vastly expanded, incorporating plants from around the globe with the help of new technologies of architecture and cultivation. Above all it was personalized—divested of the staff of hundreds needed to maintain a grand country estate, the town garden was held to more precisely reflect the character of its owner and cultivator in a direct rather than synecdochal relationship. As Loudon's works following the *Encyclopedia* show—these include *The Suburban Gardener, and Villa Companion* (1838) and *The Suburban Horticulturalist* (1842)—his early and comprehensively global sense of the allure of gardening became increasingly expressed later in his career through the small-scale examples of urban and suburban gardening practice.

Yet while city gardening was practiced, and written about, as a personal reflection of individual tastes, its primary challenges came from increasingly severe, and collectively caused, polluted environmental conditions, as Jesse Oak Taylor has comprehensively explained.[16] Thomas Fairchild was in the eighteenth century already giving advice to London residents in *The City Gardener* (1722) so that "every one in *London,* or other Cities, where much Sea-Coal is burnt, may delight themselves in Gardening."[17] Over a century later, the garden writer Shirley Hibberd also warns of the dire consequences of bad air on the organic life of the city in his guide to city horticulture, *The Town Garden* (1859), using a metaphor not yet available to Fairchild. He writes: "Thousands of beautiful plants are every spring and summer brought from the nurseries round London, and sold in the City to undergo the slow death of suffocation—dying literally of asphyxia, from an absorption of soot in the place of air, their demise being accelerated by copious supplies of water at improper times, or the withholding altogether of the refreshing element. The wonder is, not that such plants perish miserably, but that they last so long, when plunged, without hope of relief, into such a 'Black Hole of Calcutta.'"[18] The reference to the infamous "Black Hole," by the mid-nineteenth century a foundational event and myth of British

Empire, is unsurprising in a Victorian text appearing just after the so-called Indian Mutiny of 1857 had refreshed the tropes of foreign tortures in domestic minds.[19] Somewhat more surprising is the implied identification of the torturers with Londoners themselves, and the city of London as the scene of such storied cruelty. Combining environmental pollution with the gardening incompetency of city dwellers, it is the floral immigrants that claim readerly sympathy, not just for the economic or aesthetic losses of their deaths but also for the painful sufferings such deaths entailed. Plants, too, had private enjoyments curtailed by the byproducts of human industry; it remained the job of humans to constantly return those plant enjoyments to the broader British Empire.

Hibberd offers the instructions of his own manual as a solution to the "inexcusable and disgraceful" urban spectacle of "sooty gardens run to seed," but additional alternatives existed.[20] In addition to the large-scale conservatories and greenhouses accessible to the richest of city dwellers, protection from urban pollution was available on a smaller scale through the same Wardian cases that had transported many of these flowers to England in the first place, as described in the previous chapter.[21] Ward recounts in an autobiographical sketch that his plan for his protective boxes arose from a childhood ambition "to possess an old wall covered with ferns and mosses," an ambition frustrated by "the volumes of smoke issuing from the surrounding manufactories.... My plants soon began to decline, and ultimately perished, all my endeavours to keep them alive proving fruitless."[22] His personal vision for the future applications of the cases is both comprehensive and deeply impracticable. "These cases form the most beautiful blinds that can be imagined, as there is not a window in London that cannot command throughout the year the most luxuriant verdure: indeed, by means of their instrumentality, London, or any other large town, might be converted into one vast garden," he writes hopefully, proposing that a Wardian-case based economy may develop around the manufacture (by the lower classes) and collection (by the middle and upper classes) of these window terraria, "*tableaux vivans* of the highest interest."[23] The disguise and obfuscation that Loudon imagines fits with the gothic structure of novels to come, even as the ornaments he imagines filling these decorative tableaux are themselves examples of native gothic architecture.

Ward's vision of nature posits the urban garden as fundamentally contradictory to its surrounding built environment. As *Household Words* explains, "to all who preserve a healthful and natural feeling, the 'Ward

Case' will afford varied and continual pleasure, reminding them of vegetation of larger growth, and of scenery more expanded and majestic."[24] That is to say, the Wardian case itself seemed to serve as a touchstone to enable the sensory and epistemological production of the empire, so that a city-dweller "in the midst of smoke-evolving sugar-houses and factories . . . might enjoy the luxuriance and seclusion of a tropical jungle."[25] Ward's creation of a "new era in horticulture," as director of Kew gardens William J. Hooker terms it in a testimonial, is repeatedly emphasized as one most useful in an urban setting.[26] In this even Loudon saw value; as he writes in his *Gardener's Magazine,* "the success attending Mr. Ward's experiments opens up extensive views as to their application . . . in preserving plants in rooms, or in towns; and in forming miniature gardens or conservatories, either in rooms or on the inside or outside of windows, as substitutes for bad views, or for no views at all."[27] Loudon's shift from the abstract to the material understanding of the word "views" here suggests the ways that Ward's cases linked the theoretical to the concrete and the global prospect view to the local scene visible from the window. Both could, and should, be altered, as aesthetic, and, of greatest importance to Ward, moral conditions required.

British gardens private and public, as locations where cultural ideals of nature could be worked out, gained much new territory to process and display in the era of colonial expansion. Likewise objects of domestic display, sourced ever more cheaply and more distantly as the century progressed, occasioned a new discourse on the material substance of the British interior space. Ward's cases, at least as Ward originally envisioned them, offer a fascinating connection between the two. If every London home truly had replaced its window blinds with Wardian cases, we might imagine a wholesale transformation of the function of the natural within the urban environment. In fact, the transportive effect of the Wardian garden site, while gesturing at a physical and territorial rootedness, disavows the imagined rural scene as the self-evident landscape of British identification. Instead, the case proleptically stands in for a denaturalized cosmopolitanism in which the city—any city—forms the necessary frame-space to a version of the natural assembled without physically locatable referent. In Ward's own writing, the ideal conditions of nature can indeed only be achieved when the native environmental situation is removed, and this continues to be true when human-sized glasshouses, rather than Ward's small and sealed terraria, are considered. Such a removal may be liberating: "The glasshouse helped the

British public envisage alternative worlds and ways of living," argues William M. Taylor, tracing the ways that glasshouses and other garden structures both preserved the natural world and made symbolic human perception and recognition of that world.[28] But for the most part its consequences are devastating. Jesse Oak Taylor has found the glasshouse's denaturalization emblematic of environmental relations in the moment of industrial modernity, writing that "plants—whether hybrid, grown out of season, or cultivated far from their native habitats—could be removed from nature and yet continue to live. The glasshouse literalized the abnatural as a condition in which nature exists apart from itself, the quintessential habit of the Anthropocene."[29]

I agree with Taylor's conclusion that Ward's most significant legacy was neither the physical object of the glass case nor its particular scientific, economic, or aesthetic value, but instead its abstract ability to connect those elements in a deterritorialized state of nature—a state vital to the epistemological making of empire. However, I want to tease apart in more detail the process with which the abnatural could be made literal—in fictional or organic terms—and the population for whom such literalization occurred. John Ryan has found such abstractions to be evacuating, arguing that "the enframing of plants entails their removal from the cultural influences that determine their conditions, as significantly as biological or ecological factors."[30] Yet, as Ward's writings suggest, the glass case and hothouse, and, by extension, the urban garden more generally, are their own conditions of cultural influence, even if, following Taylor, the conditions are those of the abnatural. In this way, the ruptures and repairs that gothic fiction performs have an important place in narrating the possibilities of the abnatural organic environment—particularly the organic environment of a setting as alien and hostile to growing conditions as the Victorian city. When Charles Darwin asks at the end of his Beagle diary, "Who from seeing choice plants in a hothouse can magnify some into the dimensions of forest trees, and crowd others into an entangled jungle?", he is questioning how to appropriately scale outward from the frame of the hothouse to the foreign landscape of Brazil, which he likens to that of another planet. This model of scalar expansion undergirds the global premises of whole-earth imaginaries, from Gaia to the idea of the Anthropocene, as Benjamin Morgan has explained.[31] But Darwin's plaintive "who" also suggests a different set of questions, tied not to "magnifications" but to the human bias implicit in "choice plants." These questions ask how the abnatural world of the glasshouse produced new kinds of people to go with these newly imported hothouse plants. In the frayed, abnatural world of the gothic garden, plant lives make recourse to their own artificialities as much as to a restorative but unachievable originary wild nature.

Dominant paradigms of nature and narrative have not usually emphasized the truncations and shortcuts implicit in such acts of scaling and framing. Instead, the proliferation of records of native organic minutia in England, as Amy King has argued, are the often unacknowledged heart of both Victorian natural history and the Victorian realist novel; her call to "reorient our critical accounts of Victorian literary realism to their purely discursive aspects—to those moments of proliferating description made up of inductive details, rather than the architecture of plot or structure" reconnects the novel of everyday life with the close observations of natural details that characterized natural theology as a Victorian practice.[32] Thus the multitudinous particulars of the natural world, including the rose Sherlock Holmes called "our highest assurance of the goodness of Providence," have been marshalled in support of the realist novel's proliferation of detail as the additive, productive work of meaning-making. Likewise, the Victorian garden is understood to be a work of culture that symbolically constitutes its meaning through representative organic elements into a unified whole. This has been held to be true even of the urban garden, an organic space at a still further level of remove from wild nature than the gardens of the country that I will discuss in chapter 3. While the symbolic recuperations of the city gardens have worked in different fashions—botanical gardens like Kew signify breadth of both British scientific knowledge and imperial claims, royal palace grounds mark national unity, and public parks betoken civic sociability, while private gardens reconstitute the individual through respite and retreat—all of these variations on positive representations remain largely (though certainly not entirely) restorative.[33]

Yet more often in genre fiction of the era, the opposite is true. The domestic urban garden, a formal if not material analogue to the hothouse in its isolation and symbolic value, and the plant life the urban garden contains, are not taken as constitutive, unified, and restorative spaces and specimens. Sherlock Holmes's rose, as I argued in chapter 1, equally revealed the threats to domestic and national securities even as it realigned human-plant relations; other urban and suburban gardens go further in making narrative from the garden's failures of unity and reconciliation. This, I propose, is inextricable from the development of what Patrick Brantlinger influentially identified as the "imperial gothic," a fin-de-siècle eruption of the gothic genre that connects foreign invasion, domestic degeneration, and the occult into a fictional confrontation of real and deeply felt horrors.[34] Imperial gothic shares the historical gothic tradition's broader generic hallmarks of preoccupation with space; in it, the particularities of architecture and setting become psychologically revelatory details. But instead of the complexities of castle dungeons or monks's cells, the gothic's tortures emerge in the imperial metropole's alleyways, opium dens, and strange and fallow urban gardens. In these city gardens of late-century gothic novels, plants could be tortured too, often precisely because of their forced associations with humans. The consequences of this returned to narrative not only as an additional reference point in the spectrum of recognizable pain felt by humans, but also as an expansion in the range of pain that could be recognized to arise from modern conditions of global imperialism.

In a moment that anticipates Hibberd's vision of plants trapped in city torture chambers, Wilkie Collins's early novel *Basil* (1852) links the imprisonments of its violent narrator to the plants that surround him: looking out at his "London garden," he explains that it is a "a close-shut dungeon for Nature, where stunted trees and drooping flowers seemed visibly pining for the free air and sunlight of the country, in their sooty atmosphere, amid their prison of high brick walls."[35] Meditating on a similarly undefined episode of "strangely opaque syntax," Rachel Ablow has found in Thomas Hardy's *The Woodlanders* (1887) a possible projection, via "unmarked free indirect discourse," onto the surrounding organic life, indicating Hardy's authorial resistance to drawing lines of distinction between the pain of trees and the pain of minor characters.[36] The difference, in a city setting, is that the confined plant life grows or withers at the command of the human builders, who establish and remove gardens as fits the expansions of the city: "here, one side of a new street; there, a large solitary public-house facing nowhere; here, another unfinished street already in ruins," Dickens writes of a "toy neighbourhood" in the developing countryside south of London in *Our Mutual Friend* (1865).[37]

Thus, even as scientific botanical gardens like Kew were emphasizing regularity, precision, and classification in their plant life, the range of urban gardens growing alongside these institutional settings, in both real life and in novels and other fictions, were demonstrating the contrapuntal tendency of the urban garden to run riot, to die from smog, or to dissolve into weedy formlessness. While cultivating these city gardens was the work of professional and amateur gardeners, in fact and in fiction, the ongoing imaginative maintenance of the garden space as a mental refuge that both contradicted and reinforced the idea of "nature" to city dwellers was understood to be everyone's conceptual work. In an era in which the urban metropole was defined by its avenues and public spaces, hybrid locations of setting like semiprivate gardens retained important influence on the antirealist novel's assault on the permanence of civic and social structures. Breached windows, open back-courtyards, and otherwise transgressed domestic spaces have often been subsumed solely into the violations of the bedroom, when in fact more commonly such trespasses meant moving from an entirely public space to a semipublic, semiprivate space like the garden. The plant life that these gardens contained, whether or not it was explicitly labeled as exotic, received the doubled attention of the era's emphasis on cultivation in general and the city's challenges to cultivation in particular. This spotlight gave urban plants a heightened singularity that was also the chief token of the exotic.

Although Charlotte Brontë's novel *Villette* (1853) predates considerably most of the other works considered in this book, it makes an important foundation for the thorough denaturalizations of the garden and its plants in genre fiction of a later vintage. *Villette,* continuing with gestures to earlier gothic tradition that *Jane Eyre* (1847) also pursued, equally instructs the reader in gothic conventions even as it mocks their blind spots. *Villette*'s double-edged use of the gothic is only one of its many disruptions; it is a novel full of, as Mary Jacobus influentially assessed it, "incoherencies and compromises, inconsistencies and dislocations," not the least of which decenter the stability of the narrator, Lucy Snowe, herself.[38] Lucy, a Protestant and Briton teaching at a Catholic school in the titular French-speaking city of Villette, has been read as the thinly veiled fictional counterpart to Charlotte, also once a teacher at a Catholic girls' school in Brussels and, like Lucy, attached intellectually and emotionally to her older male colleague during her tenure. Such biographical parallels, however, and indeed even the warrant to claim "Lucy Snowe" as a subject with defined capacities of self-recognition and world-making expressed through first-person narration, have been called into question by a series of readers of the novel. The discontinuities of the novel's voice have been explained by feminist critics as reassertions of authorial power or eruptions of sexual desire by an isolated woman writer who, during the 1851–52 period of *Villette*'s composition, had recently endured the loss of all of her siblings but not yet entered into her short-lived marriage.[39] Narratological analysis has more recently proposed that *Villette*'s protagonist can be better understood as "a heterogeneous product of narrative's tactical operations, diverse and often fragmented processes that generate or perform a self" than as an autonomous person, a dissolution compelled in part by the "structures of traumatic experience" through which the novel is retrospectively narrated.[40] Giving context to these interior explorations are explanations, via the Brontë family's vast library, of their reading knowledge of world horrors, in particular the slave trade. As Cannon Schmitt has suggested, these readings provided for the sisters "an avenue for engagement with another strange world conceived of as a reservoir of intensity and irrationality, an outer rather than an inner world: the other country."[41]

The copious plant life of the novel has not been considered as a part of this, although it clearly joins in such engagements, particularly in the gardens of the school where Lucy becomes a resident and teacher. While the plot significance of the school's garden is obvious to every reader of the novel, since it makes the central scene of surveillance in a novel obsessed with the varieties of visual and emotional control, the participation of this garden and the plants it contains—as either symbolic or literal forms—in Lucy's narratorial fragmentation have not been widely considered. From the start, however, the introduction of the garden to the novel is unusual. First, it is introduced twice, in words that initially seem near-identical: "Behind the house was a large garden, and in summer, the pupils almost lived out of doors amongst the rose-bushes and the fruit-trees. . . . All this seemed very pleasant," Lucy narrates in chapter 8, before muddying the waters with rapid shifts in the frame of the temporal perspective by explaining "thus did the view appear, seen through the enchantments of distance; but there came a time when distance was to melt for me."[42] This melting, we learn, is professional and architectural as well as conceptual; Lucy descends from her attic bedroom to gain employment as a teacher in the school in an advancement that the reader learns about in part through specific dialogue and in part through Lucy's generalized retrospective narration—a retrospection we have already learned to consider with some suspicion for its lapses. When we return to the garden in chapter 12, we see it again for the first time, but with the benefit of further consideration on the perils of detachment: "Behind the house at the Rue Fossette there was a garden—large, considering that it lay in the heart of a city, and to my recollection at this day it seems pleasant: but time, like distance, lends to certain scenes an influence so softening; and where all is stone around, blank wall and hot pavement, how precious seems one shrub, how lovely an enclosed and planted spot of ground!"[43] As is typical of her, Lucy here denies her reader any happiness of retrospect by violently exercising the effects of comparison beyond their natural bounds. A blooming garden may seem a pleasant respite, but when that garden shrinks to a single shrub, the pleasures of nostalgia look more like willful self-delusion or mania, in keeping with Lucy's general assault on her reader's reliance on conventional narrative and fictional tropes. After detailing the gothic history of the (possible) former convent—"something had happened on this site, which, rousing fear and inflicting horror, had left to the place the inheritance of a ghost story"—Lucy reveals that among the garden's "convent-relics" of "old and huge fruit-trees," one "Methuselah of a pear tree" in particular is held to grow from the bones and tomb of a young nun buried alive.[44]

The continuity of the pear tree, spanning from the past "unconfirmed and unaccredited" legends of the Middle Ages to Lucy's present, precisely detailed story of sensory garden engagement, recenters the garden species as tokens of narrative continuity, unity, and stability even as they produce gothic horror. As with detective fiction, plant life is given the responsibility of taking over narration from human observers. Here the story that the plants continue works at odds with human gothic perversion. "Independently of romantic rubbish . . . that old garden had its charms," Lucy insists, detailing the verdant turf, "sun-bright nasturtiums," shady acacias, and vines of jasmine and ivy in verb tenses of habitual engagement. "I used to rise early" and "linger solitary" in the garden, Lucy recalls, and while her human recollections shift between a broad description of her usual movements and the specific memories of a particular night alone in the garden, the memories of the garden plants make no such differentiation.[45] Indeed, the garden further encourages Lucy's embrace of temporally nonspecific habits as she describes her connection to *"l'allée défendue,"* the hidden walk between the main garden and the protective exterior wall dividing school and garden from surrounding metropolis. "Carefully shunned" by others, the border walk and its seclusion and gloom are nevertheless attractive to

Lucy: "For a long time the fear of seeming singular scared me away; but by degrees, as people became accustomed to me and my habits, and to such shades of peculiarity as were engrained in my nature—shades, certainly not striking enough to interest, and perhaps not prominent enough to offend, but born in and with me, and no more to be parted with than my identity—by slow degrees I became a frequenter of this strait and narrow path. I made myself gardener of some tintless flowers that grew between its closely-ranked shrubs."[46] The connection here between the engrained naturalism of Lucy's own "shaded" manner and the dark walkway which she frequents gains heavy emphasis as the garden space directs Lucy's efforts at self-making. Lucy's shadings, defining her nature by negative contrast, habituate her as a frequenter and then gardener of this hidden path. Her restoration of this defunct space of "tintless flowers"—a bizarre adjectival phrase peculiar to Brontë—allows her a refuge from Catholic religious ritual, but it also clears space for active surveillance and manipulation conducted by human and non-human characters alike. After her chance encounter with a love-note tossed over the garden wall by an unknown hand, the plants themselves achieve independent perceptual power: "the eyes of the flowers had gained vision, and the knots in the tree-boles listened like secret ears," Lucy explains, and the half-simile of her description matches her intermediate status as both surveiller and surveilled of garden life.[47] This alteration is a frequent dilemma for Lucy, extending even into her work as a gardener. Later, describing her attempts to protect Dr. John from Madame Beck's oversight, she explains of the unattended garden: "Some plants there were, indeed, trodden down . . . which I wished to prop up, water, and revive; some foot-marks, too, he had left on the beds: but these, in spite of the strong wind, I found a moment's leisure to efface very early in the morning, ere common eyes had discovered them."[48] Whether these common eyes are those of flowers or of humans, or, indeed, whether Lucy's work of watering and propping-up is ever completed, her conditional syntax does not reveal; we only understand her efforts by negative relation to the formal boundaries the garden itself presents.

Lucy continues throughout the novel to present her movements in the garden as their own kind of necessarily plant-supported thinking. "While walking in the garden, feeling the sunshine, and marking the blooming and growing plants, I pondered the same subject the whole house discussed," she comments by way of introduction to the long-developing, late-in-the-novel crisis of Ginevra Fanshaw's elopement: one of only a number of narrative moments in which Lucy's garden ambulations is presented as constitutive to logical thought.[49] This layering of physical and cognitive activities—walking, feeling, marking, and pondering—does more than to suggest Lucy's ambulatory consciousness. This strategy of "marking" the plants also provides readers with an important methodology for reciprocal engagement with particular botanical specimens that is of a piece with a more general kind of plant-thinking. This marking is a particularly urban cognition—not the overabundance of stimuli that would result in an attempt to "mark" each bloom in a countryside stroll in a novel by Thomas Hardy, for example, but a strictly controlled natural engagement denoting the revised ecology of a delimited urban plant life.

Significantly, there is another gardener against whom Lucy's smoothings are presented in contrast. The older teacher and object of Lucy's passionate admiration, M. Paul Emanuel, secretly destined to the "nursing of the West-Indian estate" on the island of Guadeloupe, devotes time away from his instruction of the schoolgirls to nurture tropical and desert specimens in the school's garden.[50] As Lucy observes, waiting for him to begin her promised instruction, this devotion comes at the cost of human connection.

> M. Emanuel had a taste for gardening; he liked to tend and foster plants. I used to think that working amongst shrubs with a spade or a watering-pot soothed his nerves; it was a recreation to which he often had recourse; and now he looked to the orange-trees, the geraniums, the gorgeous cactuses, and revived them all with the refreshment their drought needed. . . . There were many plants, and as the amateur gardener fetched all the water from the well in the court, with his own active hands, his work spun out to some length. The great school-clock ticked on . . . Day was drooping. My lesson, I perceived, must to-night be very short; but the orange-trees, the cacti, the camellias were all served now. Was it my turn?
>
> Alas! in the garden were more plants to be looked after,—favourite rose-bushes, certain choice flowers.[51]

Lucy, deprived of instruction, conversation, or even particular visual regard by the "keen beam" of M. Paul's gaze, finds in the cultivars a jealously observed alternative to her longed-for connection. Even as

M. Paul avers that "my book is this garden; its contents are human nature—female human nature. I know you all by heart," suggesting that he is using the flowers merely as a screen for his surveillance of the female pupils, his continued attention to the flowers themselves belies this human attachment.[52] Or, at minimum, it proposes that Lucy is herself a kind of plant or tree, whose maintenance and tending within the confines of the urban environment requires particular care. While Villette does not seem to suffer from the urban pollution that troubled London gardeners, the constant thirst of the garden plants speaks to the persistent hostility to life the hot city stones impose, made more evident by the clearly nonnative origins of many of M. Paul's garden favorites. The fatigue evident in Lucy's "I used to think," moreover, links this activity to others in the novel that remain temporally open-ended. What has replaced Lucy's belief in the restorative work of gardening? As long as Lucy controls the narrative, the reader cannot and will not know for sure, but the evidence of the garden's continued vitality suggests the suppressions of labor that the book depends upon. Neither Lucy nor M. Paul are the garden's professional caretakers; for each, the garden is a site of performance of self ungrounded in the unending physical labor of actual care.

A crucial expansion of the terms of this performance comes with the prolonged and deeply strange opium trance that occurs near the novel's denouement, a signal but not a resolution of the novel's gothic preoccupations. Lucy's disassociated narration throughout this interlude draws together the dual efforts of "marking" and "fostering" that her previous garden ambulations implied. This begins with her description of the disguise she chooses to afford her liberation: "There, in the corridor, hangs my garden-costume, my large hat, my shawl. There is no lock on the huge, heavy, porte-cochere; there is no key to seek.... I wonder as I cross the threshold and step on the paved street.... It seems as if I had been pioneered invisibly."[53] Granting her the release to "pioneer" largely unremarked through the nighttime festival of Oriental spectacle overwhelming the expected tranquility of the park, this garden-costume also enables Lucy to transform her self-narration into a permanent present progressive, repudiating through narrative other characters' more temporally fixed characters as she moves around the edges of their perceptual registers. The episode culminates in Lucy's arrival at a "canopy of entwined trees" where she overhears Madame Beck and others finalizing the plans to send M. Paul to Guadeloupe to cultivate its land, in return for an "Indian fortune" for them and, for him, the young bride Justine Marie.[54]

Elisha Cohn has argued for a reading of Lucy's withdrawals of narration as pauses of agency beyond "critical ethos" and the diegetic frame, suggesting that the "persistence of affectively charged tone without consciousness gives that affect an in-between, suspended status—it belongs neither to Lucy nor to the reader."[55] Lucy's recovery from the shock of hearing of her devastating imminent separation from M. Paul leaves her in just such a state of suspension, but with a crucial boundary. "With my head bent, and my forehead resting on my hands, I sat amidst grouped tree-stems and branching brushwood," Lucy recalls. Her individual seclusion within the trees matches the general primacy of trees over people in this part of the park, "a quarter where trees planted in clusters, or towering singly, broke up somewhat the dense packing of the crowd, and gave it a more scattered character."[56] If consciousness belongs neither with Lucy nor the reader here, it exists at least in part with the trees, which, through the very unnaturalness of their presence in the stony metropolis, also indicate the possible outer limits of where consciousness can be located.

Like Methusaleh the pear tree and the "deep hollow, near his root," where Lucy buries the jar of her private letters, the plant life of the city, isolated and often alien, absorbs the costs and consequences of interactions with humans into a botanical diegesis to which characters and readers have only limited access. While the novel began with a more traditional figuration of the gothic garden as a definitively human-built space confining tintless flowers and watchful trees within its walls, by its end the architectural structures of the garden diminish in significance as the plants themselves gain importance in marking out the boundaries of human-plant collusion. "He rose up, dim and gray, above the lower shrubs around him," Lucy says of Methusaleh, as she hides the textual evidence of her girlish affections, the packet of letters from Doctor John that have attracted the surreptitious scrutiny of her employers, in the pear tree's half-hidden hollow that is at once treasure chest and grave.[57] In a direct inversion of Ward's glass plant cases discussed earlier in the chapter, the tightly sealed jar preserves human artifacts, while the plants—ivy, creepers, shrubs, and pear-tree—surround and observe the glass jar and the human who is drawn to mourn it. Alison Milbank has identified Brontë's renovation of older, *Blackwoods*-inflected gothic modes with a progressive and liberatory energy; in *Villette,* she argues, given "Lucy's desire to connect her violent and agonistic inner life with some external validation of her existence . . . [she] must first install herself inside a Gothic narrative in order, paradoxically, to be liberated from its controlling structures."[58] The deactivation of gothic machinery in *Villette* is usually linked to the unveiling of the mysterious ghost nun haunting the former convent garden as merely a disguise facilitating Ginerva Farnshaw's affair and escape, but Lucy's opium-stupefied embowerment amid the trees of the city park also marks a termination of the limits of human imprisonments. In preparing the way for other ecogothic fictions, Brontë undoes eighteenth-century narrative convention to propose a revised nineteenth-century literature of global terror.[59]

Villette's enigmatic and tragic conclusion, which implies M. Paul Emanuel's death by shipwreck on his return voyage from the West Indies to claim not Justine, but Lucy, as his bride and intellectual companion, has been widely discussed for its refusal to provide expected kinds of narrative closure. Among these can also be included its horticultural open-endedness. Lucy begins the brief final pages of the novel's conclusion: "And now the three years are past: M. Emanuel's return is fixed. . . . My school flourishes, my house is ready, I have made him a little library, filled its shelves with the books he left in my care: I have cultivated out of love for him (I was naturally no florist) the plants he preferred, and some of them are yet in bloom. I thought I loved him when he went away; I love him now in another degree; he is more my own."[60] For nearly the last time, she again offers the reader a baffling temporal range in her narration. Only a few paragraphs later, readers learn of the "destroying angel of tempest" that has, we extrapolate, demolished M. Emanuel's vessel, giving the present and present perfect tenses that she employs a dark future: neither school, house, library, nor plants will ever be seen by M. Emanuel, nor will the degrees of love that Lucy measures ever be registered. But, with no actual termination given, Lucy's plant cultivation and domestic flourishings seem to go on forever, like the preferred plants "yet in bloom." Her parenthetical aside that she "was naturally no florist," one of a very few fully past tense constructions in this section, separates her from these flowers, rejecting out of hand a named designation for her habits. Given that "florist," in both the era of *Villette*'s writing and of its setting, already had a strongly professional and commercial emphasis, the idea that girls such as Lucy might "naturally" be drawn to plant life in this way immediately jars. But it also emphasizes the broader distinction that Brontë has made in multiple material registers throughout the novel: between a persistent self that exerts a deterministic narrative consequence and a momentary, iterative, fragmented self that appears only when placed in conversation with an exterior counterpart.

Here, as in Lucy's opium trance, the connection between the external counterpoint of the plant and the fugitive narrative consciousness that Lucy allows requires gothic ruptures to make its linkage clear. The temporality of the gothic draws from an attenuation of physical selfhood that connects the tortures of a moment with the agonies of an eternity. Similarly, the preferred plants "yet in bloom" on a narrative plane somewhere beyond the novel's villains, heroes, and even readers combine the ephemerality of the botanical moment with a tenacity of organic life to present a new kind of cultivated selfhood. It is a selfhood deeply dependent upon, and most apparent against, the artificial supports of life that the city provides as remedy to its own destructive conditions, whether those destructions are the slave trade that ferries bodies between the West Indies and Africa at the behest of European nations, or the smoke that belches from the factories driving industrial London's growth. Horticultural writers in the first part of this chapter focused their attention on the geographical variations that hothouses and other artificial conditions of urban gardening displayed. Brontë, while implicitly incorporating the profound and broad effects of geographic difference and distance, is far more interested in the assaults on individual natures that the urban garden proposes. To cultivate plants in *Villette* is to be suspended among them, and, in both cases, the manipulations of that suspension reveal to us the arbitrary conventionalities by which the self's temporal stability is preserved.

Such suspicions—of the stability of the individual self and of the readability of the urban landscape more generally—were of course to become the most basic questions asked by novels resistant to realism in the later nineteenth century; questions about the naturalness of the city garden make less obvious but still important extension of these concerns. Sensation novels of the 1860s and 1870s set in London assume that the city garden obscures and mystifies connections and intentions, and that these mystifications in turn color the paranoias and terrors of the larger world of the novel as well. A brief but telling example of this is Walter Hartwright's glimpsed awareness, in the opening chapters of Wilkie Collins's genre-defining *The Woman in White* (1860), of a cab stopped across the Avenue and of "a gentleman [who] got out and let himself in at the garden door."[61] While Collins's narrative emphasis moves on to follow the cab's next fare, the escaped asylum inmate that

Hartwright is assisting, the activities of the "gentleman" continue to quietly perturb. What is that man doing, after all, going in by the garden and not the house door? Just as, in the previous chapter, detective novel settings needed detailed singularity of plant life to support a setting multitudinous enough to allow deductions of plot mysteries, sensation and imperial gothic novels required the ambiguity of urban garden space to obscure and rupture the stability of private and domestic selfhood. Here again there is resonance between the dispersal of plant life and the genre fiction that followed empire's larger spread.

It is notable that the garden that Collins's gentleman enters is found "a third of the way along the Avenue road" leading into London, well into Hartwright's long walk home toward the city center from his mother's cottage in suburban Hampstead. This rapidly evolving interzone, between the still-rustic outer suburbs and the thoroughly built-up urban core, becomes throughout genre fiction of the late nineteenth century a space inextricably interlinked with the spread of British Empire.[62] Todd Kuchta argues that "imperialism contributed to suburbia's material and discursive formation at the same time as suburbia came to signify the empire's inevitable decline and enduring traumas," resulting in both "suburb and empire as spaces that are geographically distinct but materially and imaginatively linked."[63] This is a linkage established as much through the abject negations empire's monsters impose on the city setting as it is through the surplus of imperial things that overstuff the suburban parlor. For every Thaddeus Sholto, who, in Conan Doyle's *The Sign of Four* (1890) lives an "incongruous" lifestyle in "a third-rate suburban dwelling-house" packed with Oriental vases, hookahs, and tiger skins, there is a Marjorie Lindon, abducted by an Egyptian shapeshifter, titular monster of Richard Marsh's *The Beetle* (1897), to a "tumbledown cheap 'villa' in an unfinished cheap neighbourhood" where there is "not even an apology for a yard, still less a garden—there was not even a fence of any sort, to serve as an enclosure, and to shut off the house from the wilderness of waste land."[64] Perhaps unsurprisingly, both these novels foreground the global acts of detection—from England outward to India, Egypt, and beyond—necessary to resolve crimes taking place at home, in the suburbs that Watson calls "the monster tentacles which the giant city was throwing out into the country."[65] Sholto fills his house with the material stuff of empire, while the Beetle, an imperial returnee bent on sexual and racial vengeance, conversely takes advantage of the emptiness of the garden space to advance a reverse colonial invasion. The linkage that each provides between London and the distant site of colonial wrongdoing, however, is equally strong.

Significantly, it is not the outermost edges of the city that ally themselves to strange garden spaces, despite (or more likely because of) the closeness of these edges to wilder nature. Along those outermost urban streets, as a wanderer in Arthur Machen's gothic horror assemblage *The Three Imposters; or, The Transmutations* (1895) explains, the road is "was lined with houses of unutterable monotony, a wall of gray brick pierced by two stories of windows, drawn close to the very pavement." Only after a long walk *into* the city center *away* from the countryside does the character find he "noticed an improvement: there were gardens, and these grew larger. The suburban builder began to allow himself a wider scope."[66] While this directionality goes against the geographical progression of nonfiction guides to city plant-keeping like Shirley Hibberd's *The Town Gardener*, which moves from the inmost London districts outward to the "small plots of garden-ground in the fronts of suburban residences, where bank-clerks, thrifty traders, agents, actuaries, poor authors, and *hoc genus omne*, seek evening repose with their families," Machen and Hibberd align in making varieties of male professionals the specific anchor of these urban garden spaces and the beneficiary of the screens of respectability they confer.[67] "No doubt people take far more interest in the fronts of their London houses than they did ten years ago, whatever they may do with their backs," comments another manual on city gardening, with some sarcasm.[68] The sufficiencies of global capital to complete the forward-facing facades of domestic British life fall away in the uncultivated rear-gardens, the same space, of course, with which the fin-de-siècle urban gothic is most concerned.

Thus the genteel screening that a suburban garden plot or window flower box may provide, is, as we have seen, often insufficient against urban and imperial incursions. Yet the lack of such protective garden spaces, registered in *The Beetle* and elsewhere, is deeply felt enough to wield even more serious effects. The area that divides Dr. Jekyll's respectable house from Mr. Hyde's backyard laboratory is described as "a yard which had once been a garden," and the loyal servants like the butler Poole still refer to it as a "garden" in their dialogue.[69] This is not a question of external appearance; from the outside of Jekyll's compound, as another character in Robert Louis Stevenson's 1886 novella observes, "it seems scarcely a house. . . . somebody must live there. And yet it's not so sure; for the buildings are so packed together about that court, that it's hard to say where one ends and another begins."[70] The dereliction of the former garden that divides Jekyll from Hyde and the "kitchen offices" from the "building which was indifferently known as the laboratory or the dissecting room" speaks to the many violations of heterosexual domesticity that the novella proposes.[71] And yet the organization of Jekyll and Hyde around a central space that maintains a ghost of domesticated power disallows any complete disentanglement of those personae or locations. Expanding urban space meant that self-definition, from the boundaries of fictional character to the constitution of personhood as a liberal subject in real space, took place through setting and also disrupted the expected time frame of that setting.

This temporal disruption is especially clear in utopian and time-travel fiction of the era, which offered another path for environmental revision by plant life. These texts, including William Morris's *News from Nowhere* (1889) and Richard Jefferies' tellingly-named *After London* (1885), imagine a future in which the urban setting is completely overgrown: "The old men say their fathers told them that soon after the fields were left to themselves a change began to be visible. It became green everywhere in the first spring, after London ended, so that all the country looked alike," explain the opening lines of Jeffries's novel.[72] Morris gives even more particular urban renewal; his time-traveling narrator is shocked to learn that the assembly of houses, each with "garden fully cultivated, and running over with flowers," where it is "of course impossible to trace the sites of the old streets," is in fact the place he once knew as Trafalgar Square.[73] To do their work of social reform, however, all of these conditional revisionings of the urban space depend on the temporal anchor of the fin-de-siècle reader to register the disjunction in cultivation evident when fields are "left to themselves."[74] Like the butler Poole in Stevenson's novella who chimes in to remind us of what the space next to the laboratory once was, these rewilded visions need a comparative perspective to reconcile human perception with organic growth and time frame. Such a recognition must be by definition solitary—the other characters, happily toiling in their future cultivations, neither need nor want to register the temporal distortions brought forward by particular plants and plant varieties. These texts depend on a docile organic life content to revert to agricultural domesticity—when given the opportunity, as Morris puts it, plant life settles into an England "that is now a garden, where nothing is wasted and nothing is spoilt . . . all trim and neat and pretty."[75] Similarly, the Time Traveler from Wells's *Time Machine,* when first alighting in the future landscape, observes "there were no hedges, no signs of proprietary rights, no evidences of agriculture; the whole earth had become a garden," but in both cases these invocations of garden space call out a prelapsarian environment notably not realized.[76] The "reinhabitations" necessary to restore an originary bioregionalism also erases the epistemological boundaries that make the designation of garden generally conceivable, a distinction clearer for Wells than for Morris.[77]

In the remainder of this chapter, I will focus not on these future regrowths but on forms of the imperial ecogothic taking place in the "nineteenth century up-to-date with a vengeance," as *Dracula*'s Jonathan Harker puts it.[78] These contested contemporary gardens rely on a narrative that gives extreme emphasis to the disjunct but overlapping time frames of the metropole and the colony, or what Johannes Fabian calls "the time of the other."[79] The concerns posed by this disjunction frequently became the distinguishing mark of character of the vengeful reverse colonizer—the Beetle, Dracula, and Ayesha all bring with them an altered, and greatly elongated, timeline of mastery and degeneration.[80] (On plant monsters that paralleled these better-known villains I will have more to say in chapter 5.) Other late-century novels of gothic horror like Stevenson's and Machen's, though less explicitly thematizing foreign invasions, also share the violent renegotiations of progressive time frame that characterize the gothic. The Victorian city, as Machen's imposter Frank Burton puts it, is "as unknown ... as the darkest reaches of Africa," restating a frequent truism of urban literature at the time with an ironic twist, given his own sadistically dark responsibilities.[81] Yet, as I will consider in chapter 4, the plant life of Africa was expected to be in fact quite familiar to Victorian readers, considering that many greenhouse plants originated from that geography.

Such modifications of the metropole's self-regulating temporality came in part through the penetrative influence of immigrants and invaders, of course, but the urban garden's built structure also demonstrates the temporal alterations of the metropole's territory. As the writings of Ward and others on the window case and the hothouse showed, such enclosed spaces gave obvious physical and visual proof of an off-set time frame, as flowers long dead in outdoor beds bloomed continuously indoors under their glassy protection. Margaret Darby links the "fantasy of nature" of "tropical hothouse plants" in decidedly nontropical England with the "magical and fantastic ... boundary transgressions, especially sexual seduction" that took place within the conservatory's glassy walls.[82] These transgressions were often violent, as in H. G. Wells's story "The Flowering of the Strange Orchid" (1904), which finds a plant collector nearly murdered by his prize specimen, a bloodthirsty conservatory-dwelling orchid, but gardens did not need to be either filled with vampiric plants or contained within glass to register a gothic disruption of stable selfhood.

Outside the conservatory walls, in the attached outdoor gardens of those wealthy enough to afford such supplementary space at the heart of the city, urban gardens offered a different kind of temporal contrast. I conclude this chapter by reading the plant life of Oscar Wilde's *The Picture of Dorian Gray* (1890) through the novel's dual forms of Decadent treatise and tale of gothic horror. While "the garden of the Decadents had always been rather crowded," as Dennis Denisoff has observed in detailing the often-ignored ecological roots of the movement, this did not mean that the plants in the Decadent's garden blurred into nonspecificity.[83] Baudelaire, Huysmans, Pater, and Beardsley gave names and, by implication, cultivated histories to at least some of the flowers that grew in their gardens; the population of these gardens was present, even if odd and artificial, sterile and perverse, and outside of conventional time and space. Following Benjamin Morgan's argument that "although decadence is often associated with a rejection of nature in favor of artifice, it is better understood as a mode of ecological thought that undermines the distinction between the natural and the made," I want to take up specifically the costs of that undermined distinction.[84] While the setting of the garden that opens the novel, scene of Dorian Gray's first taste of his subsequent insatiable desire for eternal youth, has clear Edenic symbolism, Wilde's attention to the details of the plant life present in that garden also directly links the garden to a horticultural contemporaneity in the era that the novel's characters term not *"fin de siècle"* but *"fin du globe."* Appearing for the first time in *Lippincott*'s monthly magazine in July 1890, just four months after Doyle's *The Sign of Four* also ran in those pages, Wilde's novel is replete with the effects of flowers at the borderline between the artificial and the real upon a cosmopolitan existence made (semi)palatable for a popular periodical audience. The novel's dependence on a terrible distortion of human lifespan is a famous feature of its plot and, it would seem, a contradiction of its incorporation of organic realism; as Amy King succinctly points out of the novel, "there are narrative as well as thematic consequences in dissociating bloom from its transient state."[85] Beyond the better-known costs to Dorian, which are certainly significant, the lives of plants throughout the novel, whether or not they are explicitly marked as exotic, also bear the marks of this violent dissociation.

The two examples from the novel of plant naming that emerge most readily are both moments marking out Dorian's descent into eternal youth, an "arrested aging process," according to Jed Esty, that "thwart[s] the realist proportions of biographical time."[86] First, Lord Henry's opening suasion to the young Dorian in the painter Basil Hallward's garden uses alteration between general and specifically named flower species to contrast with the transcendence of human life: "For there is such a little time that your youth will last—such a little time. The common hill-flowers wither, but they blossom again. The laburnum will be as yellow next June as it is now. In a month there will be purple stars on the clematis, and year after year the green night of its leaves will hold its purple stars. But we never get back our youth."[87] By contrast, in the second example, a Dorian already emboldened by the nonconsequence of his actions upon his human form finds botanical calendars irrelevant to his own figurative plantfulness. This is a comparison staged for us with more pronounced narrative distance: tracing Dorian's growing moral depravity, a mix of observed omniscient narration and free indirect discourse relays: "Summer followed summer, and the yellow jonquils bloomed and died many times, and nights of horror repeated the story of their shame, but he was unchanged. No winter marred his face or stained his flower-like bloom. How different it was with material things! Where had they passed to?"[88] In both cases, flowers initially seem to stand as abstract exemplars—cultivated fictions that exist imaginatively in confirmation of the novel's broader themes. This symbolic element is certainly present—the plants mentioned are all perennials, and thus possess a self-perpetuating character metaphorically employed in English poetry and prose for many centuries. But the references are also material things within the diegesis, despite the difference Dorian later insists on. We have already encountered a yellow laburnum on the first page of the novel—"From the corner of the divan of Persian saddle-bags which he was lying, smoking, as was his custom, innumerable cigarettes, Lord Henry Wotton could just catch the gleam of the honey-sweet and honey-coloured blossoms of a laburnum, whose tremulous branches seemed hardly able to bear the burden of a beauty so flame-like as theirs"—and the faint sensory evidence of its presence matches the other fleeting odors, shadows, and sounds that immerse us in this opening scene.[89] When Lord Henry assures Dorian of the consistent yellowness of the laburnum in his paean to the fleetingness of youth, is he thinking of this particular glimpse, or the qualities of all laburnums, a class of trees that, as an urban environmental manual explains, "thrive well in every part of London, some of the largest . . . being in the most smoky and dusty parts of the City and East End"?[90]

Whitney Davis has asked similar questions of Joris-Karl Huysmans's *A rebours* (1884), the infamous novel referred to in *Dorian Gray* as the "yellow book" instigating Dorian's moral decline. In chapter 8 of Huysmans's text, the main character Duc Jean Floressas des Esseintes devotes much energy to the cultivation of hothouse flowers, moving from a general interest in exotic tropical blooms to a very specific desire, framed as near-depravity, for flowers that, though actually organic and alive, rival or surpass the artificial aesthetic effects of the wire, paper, and velvet imitation blooms he has also collected. Horticulture pervades Huysmans's form as well as his content; describing the style of the book, Dorian reflects "there were in it metaphors as monstrous as orchids, and as subtle in colour."[91] Davis explains Huysmans's interest in orchids as the necessary counterpoint to Darwin's—while Darwin takes a single orchid flower "to express the historicity of its genera, species, and varieties across all their 'thousands of generations,'" Huysmans understands an orchid to exist precisely, and only, at the "point identical with the instant of human selection, with the moment (it has formal character and temporal duration in itself) of the collection of the form."[92] This is, of course, also the moment of its death, within a mode of measurement that is dependent on the lifespan of the human doing the measuring.

Though Davis does not include Wilde's novel in this comparison, the counterpoint of the human lifespan is one to which *Dorian Gray* also constantly returns. The novel's opening garden scene makes it almost impossible to determine what conditions of the garden's flowers are habitual and ongoing and which effects are momentary and perceived directly. Lord Henry's opening "glance" of the laburnum, part of a larger stream of sense-consciousness that begins the novel by depositing the reader amid a barrage of horticultural sensation, demonstrates the constant expansions of human awareness that the narrative form attempts. The laburnum's "tremulous branches," which "seemed hardly able to bear the burden of a beauty so flame-like as theirs," edge around the outskirts of a free indirect plant discourse that the multichapter garden scene continuously explores. Is the burden that the branches feel in the flowers, or in the beauty of those flowers, and is the registry of that beauty a solely human concern, or one shared by the pollinating bees "circling with monotonous insistence" in their own garden drama? As in *Villette,* the novel's circumnarration will not allow us to know what "seeming" must mean here. The novel is constantly seeking ways to find and locate a perceiving consciousness independent of the material boundaries of objects and people. Sense experience drifts between tangible objects without the reader ever being quite assured of its final location, and it is only the "subtle magic" of words, Dorian believes, that "seemed to be able to give a plastic form to formless things."[93] While Lucy Snowe, penned in by the remnants of gothic constraint, risked subsummation to the surrounding trees, Wilde suggests the plant life makes human concerns not buried but irrelevant.

Narratologists, following Robyn Warhol, have suggested that the varieties of "non-narration," which exclude swathes of possibly narrateable experience from what the text actually allows to be narrated, often have the consequence of submerging acts of human rebellion or deviancy; Helen Davis, specifically considering both *Dorian Gray* and *Villette,* identifies a subspecies of "non-narration" as a kind of circumnarration, which "talks around a subject or event rather than directly narrating it."[94] Here we might consider that *Dorian Gray* also contains variations of plant non-narration or circumnarration that modulate Wilde's novel's obsessive attentions to the gothic confinements of material form.[95] It is not only that the acts are seemingly unspeakable, but also that the setting making those acts possible is busily producing at the same time examples of other kinds of speech—alternatives that, in their expression, carry their own heavy costs. The opening garden scene gives two examples of this, both paralleling the long monologues that establish the basic premise of the novel's horror—Dorian Gray is a beautiful young man who wishes to remain that way—while also providing an alternate, if deeply submerged, attention to the costs borne by the flowers when they attract the regard of humans. This is a danger that, later in the novel, Wilde will also extend to the servants who assist these attractive flowers.

As we follow Basil Hallward and Lord Henry to the garden before Dorian Gray arrives for an extended discourse by Hallward on the inescapable and later fatal charm the younger man exerts upon the artist, we are given periodic temporal markers that anchor us in the organic space of the garden—which is proceeding according to its own, initially unrelated time frame. "The sunlight slipped over the polished leaves. In the grass, white daisies were tremulous," we learn of the setting for the bench upon which the two men sit.[96] The tremulous daisies have good reason for fear, as Lord Henry proceeds to pick apart their petals while absorbing Hallward's explanation of his own dissolution into his artwork. Examining a daisy he has plucked from the grass, Lord Henry anticipates Sherlock Holmes's pose discussed in the previous chapter three years in advance: "'I am quite sure I shall understand it,' he replied, gazing intently at the little golden white-feathered disk, 'and as for believing things, I can believe anything, provided that it is quite incredible.'"[97] He goes on, as Basil Hallward explains the cost to his soul that the painting of Dorian's portrait has incurred, to "[pull] the daisy to bits with his long, thin, fingers"—with hands that themselves are later described as "cool, white and flower-like" and possessed of a "curious charm" when he first meets Dorian.[98]

This transference of narrative independence from the self-sufficient plant agency of tremulous daisies to the "golden disks" brought into full narrative presence only by Henry's intent gaze to the scattered petals that remain after Henry has absorbed their floral integrity, makes the smallest of counterflows to the men's well-known exchanges on aesthetic philosophy. The minor work of the daisies prepares us, however, for the more pronounced botanical circumnarration that accompanies Dorian and Lord Henry in the next scene, as the latter urges the former to preserve his youth at all costs. Aghast at Lord Henry's insinuations, Dorian rushes to the garden, where Lord Henry finds him "burying his face in the great cool lilac blossoms, feverishly drinking in their perfume as if it had been wine. . . . He was bare-headed, and the leaves had tossed his rebellious curls and tangled all their gilded threads."[99] At some point in Lord Henry's lengthy exhortations to Dorian to "Live! . . . Be always searching for new sensations," the tables are turned. Lilacs no longer tousle Dorian's hair as he listens, "open-eyed and wondering," but instead:

> The spray of lilac fell from his hand upon the gravel. A furry bee came and buzzed round it for a moment. Then it began to scramble all over the oval stellated globe of the tiny blossoms. He watched it with that strange interest in trivial things that we try to develop . . . when some thought that terrifies us lays sudden siege to the brain and calls on us to yield. After a time the bee

flew away. He saw it creeping into the stained trumpet of a Tyrian convolvulus. The flower seemed to quiver, and then swayed gently to and fro.[100]

It takes the reader some moments to realize that this paragraph is in fact a renarration of the same stretch of time that has just passed in Lord Henry's monologue, but this time told from the point of view of the now-dead lilac blossom and the bee that is briefly drawn to its corpse. Dorian's physical presence in this scene is as subdued as his emotional engagement, which is dampened by the dehumanizing mental paralysis familiar to every reader of earlier gothic horrors. Yet neither Dorian's nor the reader's entry into this scene via the shared remembered experience of this debilitating terror has import for the bee, which goes about its business of pollination, or for the flowers, whose seeming quivers again propose an ecstasy irrelevant to human brains. And, after all, Dorian's floral simulacra admits no staining.

As the termination of both the lilac and the daisy suggest, however, the independent narratives of flowers face perilous ends, just as Ezra Jennings's roadside flowers did in *The Moonstone*. So too does the herby Basil, who confesses to Lord Henry of Dorian's delight in giving pain: "I feel . . . that I have given away my whole soul to someone who treats it as if it were a flower to put in his coat."[101] This fear terribly prefigures Hallward's later confrontation with Dorian upon seeing the painting after it has absorbed Dorian's crimes—"It was some foul parody, some infamous, ignoble satire," Hallward believes, while also knowing "it was his own picture."[102] As Hallward struggles to reconcile the fate of his artwork with his memory of its original beauty, Dorian Gray leans against the mantelpiece, "watching him with . . . the passion of a spectator. . . . He had taken the flower out of his coat, and was smelling it, or pretending to do so."[103] It can be no surprise that Dorian's subsequent act of "crushing the flower in his hand" precedes by only a few pages his violent murder of Basil; more surprising perhaps is the narrator's heavy underlining of Dorian's simulated act of sensory perception and the implied audience it proposes. Who is left to distinguish between real and pretended acts of smelling, besides the cut flower itself?

Dorian's coat ornament, given the hour and the occasion from which he returns, likely a wired flower, reminds us of Oscar Wilde's own signature buttonhole flower, a green carnation. The expanded mythos of the green carnation, taken as a symbol of connection by Wilde's followers and as a token of the artificial perversion of nature by those opposed to the aniline dyes producing such unnatural hues, is identified by Richard Ellman as a tribute to Huysmans, and so Dorian's wired and crushed flower also draws the reader back to the central transition spurred by Huysman's "yellow book" in chapter 11.[104] "For years, Dorian Gray could not free himself from the influence of this book," the chapter begins, and the time, space, and objects covered in this section immerse the reader in Huysman's Decadence, leaving behind the plotted fictions of the imperial gothic.[105] Dorian's resolve to perpetuate Lord Henry's charge to search out new sensations and "to teach man to concentrate himself on the moments of a life that is itself but a moment" spreads out over the lengthy course of intense engagements with rare and richly decorative material objects.[106] In pursuing the sensations these objects could represent, Dorian would "often adopt certain modes of thought that he knew to be really alien to his nature, abandon himself to their subtle influences, and then, having, as it were, caught their colour . . . leave them."[107] But despite this possible figuration of Dorian himself as a hybridized flower, the reader is warned from the outset of the impossibility of this quest. While Dorian seeks "a world in which things would have fresh shapes and colours" as the "seeming" true object of life, the narrator and reader have by contrast been joined together in a passage of second person plural narration that condemns such a fantasy world as a gothic fever dream, to be recovered from through the recognition of the imperfect presence of real material objects such as "the half-cut book that we had been studying, or the wired flower that we had worn at the ball."[108] "Wired flowers" flounder in the chasm between functional representation and failed semiosis; as in Huysmans, the distance here emphasizes the way that flowers, unlike (most) people, can have their lives unnaturally prolonged in death for ornamental effect. The ultimate disposition of flower narratives cannot be known, however, as the demands of the popular fin-de-siècle gothic novel pull us back to the operations of the human-centered plot.

But who has wired the flowers? Surely not Dorian. While in *Villette* we never attended to the workers who cared for the school's gardens while Lucy and M. Paul were otherwise engaged, Wilde gives us a faint trace of the way that the servants who surround Dorian Gray facilitate the wedge he drives between the natural and the made. As in other gothic narratives of the era, these servants participate very slightly in the novel's revisions of psychic interiority and aesthetic selfhood but very actively in the advancement of the plot events necessary to trigger such revisions. In one such instance, the theme of the wired flower is given implied gruesome expansion as Dorian conspires with the chemist Campbell to dispose of Hallward's body: his servant Francis enters bearing "a long coil of steel and platinum wire with two rather curiously-shaped iron clamps" and exits directed to go to the "man at Richmond . . . and tell him to send twice as many orchids as I ordered and to have as few white ones as possible."[109] This is both a ploy to keep Francis occupied but also a nod to the erasure of Basil's original garden as an organic point of reference for Dorian. In the dissolution of his physical form, Basil himself becomes, for a moment at least, his own gruesome kind of wired flower.

Indeed Wilde makes frequent recourse to the way that, as Andrew Goldstone explains, the "figure of the domestic worker begins to make apparent an uneasy relationship between aestheticist style and social inequality" in late-century fictions.[110] Lord Henry's cutting of an orchid for his buttonhole prompts his "thoughtless" request to "one of the gardeners" for the orchid's name. The servant's response—"he told me it was a fine specimen of *Robinsoniana,* or something dreadful of that kind"—prompts a typically Wildean dismissal of "vulgar realism": as Lord Henry quips, "The man who could call a spade a spade should be compelled to use one."[111] Underlined within this rejection of realism "as a method" is the reminder of the flower's cultivation; before the flower can be a "marvelous spotted thing" to decorate a buttonhole or a named specimen, it must be tended by those compelled to use spades.

This reminder occurs again near the end of the novel, when, as Dorian is increasingly crushed under the weight of his guilt and despair, he travels with Lord Henry to the countryside for a respite from city depravities. There, a man pursuing vengeance on Dorian for one of his many crimes is shot accidentally during a hunt; Dorian, terrified, wishes also to be dead so he may at least cease to fear death's arrival. This existential crisis takes sudden sharp form: "Good heavens! don't you see a man moving behind the trees there, watching me, waiting for me?" Dorian exclaims to Lord Henry, who replies with a smile, "Yes . . . I see the gardener waiting for you. I suppose he wants to ask you what flowers you wish to have on the table to-night. How absurdly nervous you are, my dear fellow! You must come and see my doctor, when we get back to town."[112] In this brief interchange is a compressed history of British gardening. While visiting the country estate, Dorian has returned to a landscape ideal in which an aristocratic landowner structures his relationship with the organic productions of the estate he owns through the metonymic display of flowers on the table. Gardener and trees blend together and operate as one, both functionaries of a genteel claim upon flowers and all other living things to serve as either useful objects or ornaments at the behest of the property owner. But when Dorian's paranoia replaces this general elision of servant and landscape with (an accurate) terror of personal vengeance, he undoes that arrangement's premise of mastery. Dorian's mistake, in the country as well as in the city, is to understand only a singular, private relationship between external conditions and the sensations, seeming or real, that those conditions provoke. The city garden can be seen by bees and lilacs as well as Dorian, Basil, and Lord Henry; Dorian's servants find a "splendid portrait of their master as they had last seen him" and a withered dead man with a knife in his heart when they finally enter his secret room. That is, the singular personal relations held with plants in detective fiction discussed at the end of my first chapter here betray their own inadequacies, as the competing claims of the plants themselves, and the holistic organic visions they perceive, are (at times) allowed to appear more clearly.

This represents only a small counterpoint to the general premise of much of this chapter: that while the feeling and affection for the plants is personal, the labor required to maintain them is not. The gardeners that are preserving these gardens are, in most Victorian fiction, unseen and elided from the fantasy of selfhood and self-creation. This, as Wilde, at least, does not let us entirely forget, is a denial of organic coevalness that comes with a cost paralleled by trends in horticultural practice. Forbes Watson, a "medical man" and amateur landscape critic, gives a typical dismissal of the roughly mid-century Victorian practice of "bedding-out" in his *Flowers and Gardens, Notes on Plant Beauty* (1872). Of that immensely popular style of gardening, which relies on the rotating transplantation of flowers to achieve a garden in constant bloom, Watson complains that it prevents "considering the plant as a living and growing thing. A living plant fastens firmly upon the soil, and evidently belongs to it. . . . When plants are made movable their personality is half destroyed, and by confining attention to them exclusively at the time of flowering, we complete the mischief. The plant is never old, never young; in fact, it degenerates from a plant into a coloured ornament."[113] Beyond this familiar critique of a fading trend in garden design, however, Watson's broad denunciation of plants attended to exclusively "at time of flowering" performs the same elision that *Dorian Gray* has also winkingly drawn our attention to. These flowers—whether in Labassecour, Basil Hallward's studio in Kensington, or Richmond—are not left alone; rather, they are tended to by a range of servants whose labor belies the fantasy that flowers and human souls can operate in functional equivalency or exchange. That we choose to believe they cannot is a point of weakness that allows other delusions to insinuate themselves into the narrative.

Wilde is not the only author to point this out; self-tending flowers appeared in other end-of-the-century fantasy fictions with varying degrees of sinister import. Without the device of Dorian Gray's attenuated life span, however, these fictions often more explicitly depended on child-centered fantasies. Plant life rendered these more narratively complex because it showed more explicitly the parallels between human and horticultural development. Indeed we do not need to move far from the possible location of Basil Hallward's studio in the area near Holland Park, the "most prestigious address" among the desirable locations for artist studio-houses in London, to find these fictions.[114] J. M. Barrie's *The Little White Bird* (1902), the novel that introduced Peter Pan, a boy possessed of an extended and arrested youth to rival Dorian Gray's, also gives partial life to the trees and shrubs of the nearby Kensington Gardens. There, the runaway child Maimie, intruding into the nighttime life of the garden, discovers a "magnolia and a Persian lilac" off for an awkward walk, made jerky by their "crutches": the narrator explains, "The crutches were the sticks that are tied to young trees and shrubs. They were quite familiar objects to Maimie, but she had never known what they were for until to-night."[115] The Peter Pan stories as a whole depend on the mystification of material practice as a marker of the child psyche's depth and distance, and Maimie's sympathetic efforts to assist the unpropped plants so that they too may enjoy a park walk go along with this schema. Her polite acts of assistance, "setting their leg right when it got too ridiculous, and treating the foreign ones quite as courteously as the English, though she could not understand a word they said," are a fantasy of adult sociability that also remove entirely the physical labor required to maintain that social and civic space. For Maimie, the adventures in the garden end safely after an escape from the fairies with an assist from Peter Pan, but not so, Barrie reminds us, for all other children done in by exposure or worse in the public garden space, whose dead bodies Peter buries: "I do hope that Peter is not too ready with his spade. It is all rather sad," the narrator concludes.[116] Being prepared to use a spade, in a tragic extension of Lord Henry's assault on prosaic taxonomy in *Dorian Gray*, reminds us that the sorrows of infant mortality shadow the flights of fantasy's imagined escapes.

H. G. Wells's short story "The Door in the Wall" approaches the death of childhood fantasy through a different but no less punishing horticultural perspective. The fiction was published first in *Everybody's Magazine* in 1906 and republished in his story collection *The Country of the Blind* (1913), where "The Flowering of the Strange Orchid," Wells's cautionary tale of vampiric plant attacks in the conservatory, also appeared. In "The Door in the Wall," as in *Dorian Gray*, the seemingly ordinary narration immediately unsettles the reader with news that what she is actually reading is not the life of London politician and strange dreamer Lionel Wallace, but rather "the facts of his death."[117] Wallace, we learn from the story within the story, discovered the titular green door as a five-year-old boy on his way to school and, upon entering, "came into the garden that has haunted all his life."[118] This "enchanted garden," filled with "weedless beds on either side rich with untended flowers" along with friendly yet magical animals and people, seems to stretch out forever; "Heaven knows where West Kensington had suddenly got to," Wallace muses to his listener.[119]

That this retold tale of a visit and forever-deferred return to a fairy space must end badly is unsurprising to any reader of *The Time Machine*, or indeed of any of Wells's other early romances, which all traffic in a regretful internal nostalgia played out against the violent operations of the natural world. Here, however, the violence is not the barbarous devolution of human and animal life that so horrifies the Time Traveler and his listeners, but rather the intervening distractions and ambitions of adulthood that prevent the grownup Lionel Wallace, a successful politician, from ever again—save perhaps the final time—opening the door to the garden. The story's bitter conclusion in the discovery of Wallace's body at the bottom of a "deep excavation near East Kensington station . . . made in connection with an extension of the railway southward," an excavation shaft protected by a door left carelessly unlocked, makes a neat summary of the destructive forces of encroaching industrial modernity: railways devour fairy gardens, just as adults forget their childhoods.[120] And yet the narrator's persistent distress at the simplicity of this solution, as well as the suspicious sophistication with which five-year-old Wallace noted the garden's "spikes of delphinium" and "little Capuchin monkey," prevent this easy resolution.[121] What has actually destroyed the garden, or at least Wallace's entry to it, is his effort, as a child, to read through the garden's central book—a storybook that depicts his own life from its beginning up to its present moment. Upon turning the page to see the future, however, Wallace is expelled forever, and a bias against the chronological iteration of life experience confirmed. This chapter has continued the work of the first chapter in showing the ways that genre fictions allow plants and gardens to take over the narrative reins. But this chapter has also shown the ways that plants and gardens resent, and sometimes actively avoid, this distribution of duty.

Wells's story retains the fantasy of the garden-space, acknowledging the preposterous notion of "a Cabinet Minister, the responsible head of that most vital of all departments, wandering alone—grieving—sometimes near audibly lamenting—for a door, for a garden!"[122] The near-audible grief for a garden that cannot be found, however, also makes an appropriate conclusion to a discussion of gardens that, by design, scramble for narrative purchase. In addition to the ways that landscape historians and other garden scholars have described the artificial and situational conditions under which city gardens are constructed, I have also proposed a faint but discernible level of plant narration which has both supported and supplanted the urban gothic novel's estranging forms. In the next chapter, I will turn to the country house to interrogate its gothic environment for the constraints and confinements it places upon the women who work within its gardens. There, the same gothic ruptures of realist smoothings that occurred in this chapter continue. However, in the landed estate setting, the greatly increased heritage responsibilities can make the loss of a door and a garden cost the entire perpetuation of a family line, as we shall see in *The Secret Garden*. Despite the impulse to read city gardens as unnatural and artificial in contrast to the country house's native grounds, the congeniality of the gothic form to both urban and countryside fictions betrays the contrivances of both. Cultivated natures, explicitly exotic or implicitly human-dependent, prevent the possibility of easy self-narration by the natural world in both the country and the city.

❦ 3 ❧

Strange Country Gardens

"I should see the garden far better," said Alice to herself, "if I could get to the top of that hill."[1] So begins Alice's entry into the "Garden of Live Flowers," the peculiarly backward place which surrounds the house in the second set of Alice's adventures, *Through the Looking-Glass and What Alice Found There* (1872). The live flowers of this garden, much like the Red and White Queens and indeed all inhabitants of Wonderland and Looking-Glass Land, seem to chiefly enter the story in order to admonish Alice's speech and appearance, and, by extension, her self-constitution as both a girl and a narrator. Comparing Alice and the Red Queen, the flowers assert:

> "There's one other flower in the garden that can move about like you," said the Rose. "I wonder how you do it—" ("You're always wondering," said the Tiger-lily), "but she's more bushy than you are."
>
> "Is she like me?" Alice asked eagerly, for the thought crossed her mind, "There's another little girl in the garden, somewhere!"
>
> "Well, she has the same awkward shape as you," the Rose said, "but she's redder and her petals are shorter, I think."
>
> "Her petals are done up close, almost like a dahlia," the Tiger-lily interrupted: "not tumbled about anyhow, like yours."
>
> "But that's not *your* fault," the Rose added kindly: "you're beginning to fade, you know—and then one can't help one's petals getting a little untidy."
>
> Alice didn't like this idea at all.[2]

Carroll leaves to his readers the decision whether Alice didn't like the idea that her petals were untidy, or the idea that she couldn't help that her petals were untidy, or perhaps the idea that she was assumed to have petals and to be a flower in the first place. The blurring of referential form is characteristic of Carroll's narrative play, as the Red Queen, like Alice herself, is both plant simile ("almost like a dahlia") and intrinsically botanical (possessing petals "done up close") at the same time. Even the chapter heading, asserting that the garden contains "live" flowers, inverts reader perceptions by claiming as notable a fact they believed they already knew. Though these narrative fancies build on a tradition of Victorian children's fairy stories that granted speech to simpering garden flowers also parodied by J. M. Barrie in *The Little White Bird,* discussed in the previous chapter, Carroll's proposition is more challenging. The flowers' embedded antianthropomorphism, framed within a more familiar anthropomorphism, forces the reader to think out the thoughts of flowers thinking out a girl, with the attendant efforts of "always wondering" that that entails. This resituated ontological weight explains why Alice's attempts to perceive the garden without reference to its central house are doomed to constant failure—"I never saw such a house for getting in the way! Never!", she declares in frustration—until Alice heeds the flowers' advice to move in the opposite direction of any point she is trying to reach.[3] Like ontological self-recognition, the layout of house and grounds is also inverted; one can only see the garden when one seems to move towards the house, just as one can only understand linguistic and social rules of Looking-Glass Land when apparently acting in defiance of them.

In this chapter, I will consider the ways that the country house, and its attendant novel fictions of historic domestic and national arrangements, "get in the way"—through mystery plots, gothic disruptions, and ontological crises more generally—of the development of the globalizing garden, its assimilating specimens, and the renegotiated local and global arrangements the garden and its plants stand for. Focusing on H. Rider Haggard's *Colonel Quaritch, V.C.: A Tale of Country Life* (1888), Frances Hodgson Burnett's *The Secret Garden* (1911), and Daphne du Maurier's *Rebecca* (1938), the chapter follows attention to plants foreign and domestic in novels reliant on the same disruptive structures of gothic narrative explored in an urban context in the last chapter. These country house novels substitute girls and women for the plant life that surrounds them, and vice versa; in so doing they embed (potentially) dark interruptions in the very schemes of inheritance and family development that the garden arrangements themselves propose. This is not in itself a new linkage. As Beverly Seaton, Ann Shteir, Amy King, and Elizabeth Campbell have in different ways argued, the nineteenth century, following Continental trends in the "language of flowers," endorsed "an almost universally agreed-upon botanical code that not only equated women and flowers, but also linked the two to love, courtship, marriage, sex, and reproduction."[4] In this chapter I build on those metaphorical matchings of girl and flower to explore the ways that both are altered in the changing novelistic setting of global environmental modernity. In the country as much as in the gothic fictions of the city discussed in the previous chapter, novel plots found themselves depending on a reconciliation of the domestic pasts and global futures of characters in legacy-landed estates using the botanical transculturation, assimilation, and hybridization of the estate's gardens. This process was already well underway by the late-century era that I consider; even in Carroll's nonsense garden, the rose and the lily represent varieties of domestic English flowers already supplemented in the English garden by Asian cultivars.

While not as subject to outright pollution and attack as the urban garden, the landscaped country garden of the Victorian era was equally a deeply artificial space, presented in marked contrast to the natural wildernesses that surround these houses and gardens. In the beginning of this chapter, I suggest that Haggard's novel *Colonel Quaritch, V.C.* introduces the globally sourced contents of the estate garden and hints at the dangers these fascinating new species could bring. The chapter continues by examining more closely the connections between young women and exotic plant life in large country gardens. For, in addition to its biological diversity, the country garden of the Victorian novel was also a site constantly existing in hypothetical relation to its potential alteration and improvement or overgrowth and destruction; as the Red Queen points out, "though you say 'gardens,'—*I've* seen gardens compared with which this would be a wilderness."[5] It has been the work of many successions of English garden histories to describe the difference between "wilderness" and "garden" for an era whose defining texts of landscape design included William Robinson's *The Wild Garden* (1870), and for most the Red Queen's relativist logic has prevailed. The gardens of the late-nineteenth-century countryside were impossibly charged with the simultaneous expression of a historical English nativeness, demonstration of the geographical reach of Empire as well as, of course, manifestation of individual taste and aesthetic preference. The permanence of these gardens, their expanded scope and scale, as well as their proximity to the wilder parts of England, all required a more precise, or, failing that, more voluminous, articulation of the distinction between the plants contained in the gardens and the ones that grew unsupported beyond its walls. As Carroll reminds us, this was a division drawn largely situationally; a garden and the plants it contained was a garden, unless it was a wilderness.

For some, this was a visible divide—their own plantings, and those of their fellows, gave opportunity to wrestle daily with these questions of cultivation. For many more, not possessed of land enough to plant the drifts of rhododendron and azalea and stands of oak and elm that gardening tastemakers like Robinson and Gertrude Jekyll advised, the divide was crucially one made plain through text's representations, in novels and nonfiction alike. While I briefly review the contributions of those popular nonfiction authors at multiple points in the chapter, I also take up more extensively John Ruskin's eccentric botanical treatise *Proserpina* (1875–86) to consider how his taxonomy of botanical affect contributes to the self-making of Victorian lady gardeners. Ruskin's frequently frustrated efforts in *Proserpina* to write out the place of plants in the hearts and minds of the young women who were his imagined readers demonstrates the difficulty in linking affective plant taxonomies to scientific and other standardized systems of plant identification and description. In the final parts of the chapter, I return to novels and their fictional treatments of the often gaping gulf between these ways of thinking and writing about plants. The gothic country house plots of *The Secret Garden* and *Rebecca* show the destructive cost to feminine self-constitution that such renderings of plant life also incur.

This chapter, then, builds on the investigation of gothic narratives of buried plant lives discussed in chapter 2 as well as the relations of clue and setting that were discussed in the first chapter. As genre novels concerned with crime and its punishment increased greatly in number, authorial attention to the site of the garden—itself a thoroughly constructed and artificial narrative space—increased. The presence of a range of plants sourced from growing fields around the British Empire and beyond, contained in a cultivated, managed, and walled garden that surrounds a country house is a constant element in sensation and detective novel genres, supporting both their narrative structures and broader cultural references. In this cultivated garden could be mediated the fallible self-construction predicated on implicit and omnipresent crimes, colonial and domestic. *Lady Audley's Secret, The Woman in White, The Moonstone,* and *The Hound of the Baskervilles* (1902), among many others, all feature gardens functionally useful to the plot: dead bodies are hidden in their wells, unsuspecting victims wander unprotected down their distant paths, overheard conversations on their pathways prompt confession and suicide, and, most of all, forced entry of the vulnerable house itself is eased by their ample flower beds and climbing vines. Equally inescapable are the roots these gardens have in imperial expansions and circulations. The newly renovated Baskerville Hall, "first fruit" of its owner Sir Henry's "South African gold," is only the most obvious example of a piece of architecture whose colonial funding gains organic figuration within the already hybridized natural scene of the estate grounds—and, too, only one of many examples in which the ill-advised over-display of that colonial wealth demands bloody recompense.[6] Haggard's *Colonel Quaritch,* like the later Doyle novella, draws together a globally informed garden setting with an ancestral estate in need of both domestic and imperial support to resolve its social and economic crimes. But Haggard, more interested than Doyle by far in the practicalities of tending to plant life, can be much more specific about the particular exotic specimens that populate the estate's dangerous grounds.

Though published within a only few years of Haggard's early successes *King Solomon's Mines* (1885) and *She* (1887), *Colonel Quaritch* remains an obscure piece in Haggard's canon. This is due most likely to the lack of Allan Quatermain as a character or Africa as a setting, but also perhaps from Haggard's own disgust in the novel as a literary product; he describes it as "a tale of English country life which Longman liked—it was dedicated to him—and Lang hated so much I think he called it the worst book that ever was written. Or perhaps it was someone else who favoured it with that description."[7] In addition to disabusing Haggard of ever after reading his reviews, the novel's publication also marked the end of a period of extraordinary productivity for Haggard and, as such, makes the domestic coda to his extended narrative mediation on the value of English manhood both at home and abroad, as well his evocation of the spaces that sustain that manhood.

Quaritch begins with "a soldierly-looking man" (the titular Colonel) "who, on the particular evening when this history opens, was leaning over a gate in an Eastern county lane, staring vacantly at a field of ripe corn."[8] As we soon learn, however, this seemingly vacant stare in fact visually reviews the Colonel's layered personal history. While looking at the English countryside, "the image of a woman's face rose before his mind as it had continually risen during the last five years," most notably during the battle of El Teb, where Quaritch served in the British army supporting the Egyptians against the Sudanese.[9] There, "it happened that stern necessity forced him to shoot a man with his pistol" and, as he watched the man die with a combination of gruesome fascination and revulsion that the narrator spares no pains in describing, "even then, over that ghastly and distorted face, another face spread itself like a mask, blotting it out from view—that woman's face."[10] Rather than being allowed the directly apprehended pastoral pleasures of ripe corn, then, Haggard makes clear from the start that the Colonel's "rather recondite reflections as to the immutability of things and impressions" will involve an inextricable mix of foreign and domestic life as well as subliminal interplay between the racial enemy and the ideal female love-object and potential mate.[11]

The woman whose face blots out the dying Sudanese, we soon learn, is Ida de la Molle, daughter of the current Squire and, due to the heavy costs of maintaining the ancestral estate bankrupting her father, a woman deeply vulnerable to the predatory advances of men more accustomed to the work of banking than of imperial soldiery. Quaritch, like so many of Haggard's heroes, hews close to the autobiographical bone; the Colonel's alliance to the narrator's inveiglements against the current professional generation who only "sings the song of capital" makes it easy to read the novel as a undiscerning anti-Gladstonian invocation of traditional English manliness grounded in the English countryside and proven overseas. As John Miller has argued, however, Haggard's environmentalism "simultaneously resists and encourages the determinations of capital," making the author's "incorporation of an ecological sensibility into a discourse of global capital [illustrate] the intractable problem of the imbrication of mainstream environmental thought in precisely the world order it appears to contest."[12] The texts in which this integration is made most plain are Haggard's agricultural and horticultural writings, which he considered the pinnacles of his authorial achievement. These include the two-volume *Rural England* (1902)—"the chief cornerstone [in] the labour of a life that has not been idle," as he calls it—as well as the life-records *A Farmer's Year* (1899) and *A Gardener's Year* (1905).[13] All of these writings, in the most personal and direct of terms, decry the imbalances global trade imposes on economic sustainability in the countryside without critiquing the possibilities of global environmental exchange that such world commerce also encourages. Haggard's interest is, in his fiction and nonfiction alike, in narrative action, both at home and abroad, but this does not preclude his understanding of plants as a category of life with which it is possible to exist in deep companionship and mutual regard. *Quaritch,* as an example, is a novel that considers in multiple complex ways the exigencies of the English cultivated landscape—both in its plot, which concerns the fate of an ancestral property, and in its characters, who are flower-fanciers, timber-harvesters, farmers, hunters, and other manner of admirers of the second nature that surrounds them.

Through both plot and characters, the novel constantly brings together the past and present in the setting of organic cultivation without rejecting the necessity of either. Quaritch, returning after a long absence to claim an inherited property once part of the larger de la Molle estate, observes that all that remains of the Castle were "two great towers. . . . The space within, where the keep had once stood, was now laid out as a flower garden."[14] While the novel's more modern and troublesome characters delight in the improvements of the garden landscape, Quaritch and the Squire, both traditionalists, regard these developments with suspicion. In particular the strange garden gazebo, built by Quaritch's aunt to highlight and protect her antiquarian prize of a large pit, makes unwelcome adornment to the cultivated space of what was once the de la Molle estate. This pit, known sinisterly as "Dead Man's Mount," is alleged to be the former dwelling of some ancient peoples, and attempts at bringing it into the modern era through fashionable adornment are mocked from the opening pages: as "it was found necessary to pave the hollow with tiles and cut surface drains in it, the result did not clearly prove its use as a dwelling place before the Roman conquest. Nor did it make a very good summer-house. Indeed it now served as a store place for the gardeners' tools and for rubbish generally."[15] In this we hear echoes of the other narrative mockeries of fake-gothic adornments, from Jane Austen's *Northanger Abbey* onward.

It is not the case, however, that Haggard engages in the fantasy rewriting of landscape to exclusively urge a return to pre-1066 biotic nativeness, despite his comedy with pre-Roman rubbish pits. Indeed both his nonfiction and fiction alike revel in the global circulations that bring new plants to the English garden. This is perhaps most obvious in his appreciation of orchids, which take up much of his narrative and gardening energy (as well as financial reserves, it would seem) in *A Gardener's Year,* and from which he would later earn fictional recompense through *Allan and the Holy Flower* (1915), a tale of white women in peril that also makes extensive use of Haggard's familiarity with London orchid auctions.[16] Like orchid collectors more generally, Haggard has little interest in the claims of originary bioregionalism for such show flowers, writing: "It would almost seem as though Orchids were especially intended to be grown in greenhouses; at least, those that I have seen there are certainly disappointing in their native haunts. Thus, in riding through the vast and gloomy forests of Chiapas, one perceives, high up on some great rib-rooted tree, a little patch of colour. It is a flowering Orchid, but its beauty and perfume can be appreciated by the birds and insects alone. Remove it from that tree and set it in a greenhouse, and it becomes a delight to man."[17]

Such delights also return in *Colonel Quaritch,* when the novel's villain, Edward Cossey, a wealthy banker with the power to relieve the Squire's cash crisis but who expects Ida as compensation for such relief, visits the de la Molle greenhouse with Ida to discuss in private the bargain they will strike to exchange mortgage deeds for marriage vows: "Edward Cossey, who had a curious weakness for flowers, asked her if she would show him her chrysanthemums, of which she was very proud. She consented readily enough. They crossed the lawn, and passing through some shrubbery reached the greenhouse, which was placed at the end of the Castle itself. Here for some minutes they looked at the flowers, just now bursting into bloom."[18] Throughout this difficult conversation, Ida attempts to hide her discomfort through flower management, "br[eaking] off a Scarlet Turk from its stem, and nervously beg[inning] to pick the bloom to pieces," but unlike Lord Henry's disassembly of the daisy petals in *Dorian Gray,* which transferred their botanical vitality to his human form, Ida's efforts seem to reveal her inadequacy as either gardener or garden object, despite the pride she takes in both positions. Though Ida is "affecting to busy herself in removing some dried leaves from a chrysanthemum plant," Edward can in fact see "her shoulders shake and a big tear fall like a raindrop on the pavement": a strained natural metaphor revealing not only the distress Ida feels as she is forced to support her father's future, but also the apparently insufficient protections of these greenhouse plants, flowering in the paved artificial garden of the greenhouse and dependent on human prunings and waterings for their survival.[19] That the chrysanthemums are "just now" bursting into bloom, of course, reminds us of the asynchronous place the chrysanthemum plays in the temporality of the garden, beginning to bloom only after other flowers have died back, but also underlines how out of sync both Ida and Edward are with a natural order of things.

But perhaps the reader should not so quickly assume that it is the chrysanthemums that are out of place; after all, as Haggard's musings on greenhouse orchids point out, some blooms must attract human attention to gain meaning and relevance sufficient for Haggard's narrative purposes. Cossey's "curious weakness" for flowers underlines the compelling presence of these greenhouse blooms in general and the chrysanthemums in particular, reflecting contemporary horticultural trends that highlighted the popularity of such intensely cultivated plants. The chrysanthemum (a variety of which was even named after Haggard himself) had first been imported to England sometime at the end of the eighteenth century and had existed as a popular garden plant in Britain throughout the nineteenth century, with a divergence between Japanese and Chinese forms that grew more pronounced as the century wore on.[20] The terms of this divergence were notable in that it was the so-called "Chinese" form that was taken up by middle-class flower fanciers and cultivated to alleged grotesquely extreme sizes, while the "Japanese" form retained the markers of natural perfection—making the domestic British debate over floral naturalism a contest between two exotically foreign varieties.[21] Philip Pauly points out that the degree of "naturalistic artifice" demonstrated by Japanese cultivations of the chrysanthemum forced the "open question [of] whether Europeans could understand, much less surpass, Japanese high culture."[22] Haggard weighs heavily on the Japanese side of naturalistic artifice, making no secret of his distaste for the overcultivated Chinese version of the flower with its "sameness" and "heavy and unnatural" blooms; "if anyone could grow a Chrysanthemum with a flower as large as a red Cabbage, he might make a fortune; but I would not give him a shilling for cutting. Such is my personal, and possibly misguided, taste," he concluded.[23] These enlargements were inevitably linked in the gardening press to both class and gender problematics in language that amplifies Haggard's criticism of unnatural flowers. Garden magazines complained of biased standards for show chrysanthemums that would have the floral equivalent of "the fat woman of the penny show at the fair . . . take the place of the Venus de Milo," while also complaining that more generally that the "common people . . . under any circumstances, prefer the highly-cultivated flower to the simple one, just for that one quality of bigness and plumpness" just as "most vulgar people admire great red-faced women."[24] Yet beneath these predictable snipes is a more radical revisioning: by the final decades of the nineteenth century, all appreciation of cultivated chrysanthemum flowers is global floral appreciation. Even the vulgar admirers of overcultivated chrysanthemums are still engaged in a responsive ecological connection that in general terms is to Haggard's liking; absorption, even overabsorption, in an exotic flower is, for Haggard, a potentially beneficial consequence of a world where plants bloom for the benefit of human enjoyment and financial benefit combined. It is a rejoinder to Sherlock Holmes's delight in the rose as an "extra"; Haggard understands that even such horticultural pleasures still have cash value.

Thus Haggard, far more than Doyle or other urban novelists, insists on making narrative an understanding of proper stewardship that combines urban and rural horticultural appreciation to yield aesthetic enjoyment and economic profit. The outcome of Cossey's next encounter with the garden chrysanthemum gives us some example of what happens when pretenders to such stewardship appear. The banker, now firmly intent on claiming Ida as recompense for restoring the mortgaged de la Molle manor but entangled in a subplot of past romantic affiliations, appears at the house of his ex-mistress, Belle Quest and her husband, when, just at the same time, Colonel Quaritch, finished with snipe-hunting, pays a visit, bringing along his new hammerless gun. And, again, at this crucial moment, Cossey is distracted by a novel chrysanthemum:

> Edward Cossey slowly sauntered towards them. When he was about nine paces off he too halted, and stooping a little, looked abstractedly at a white Japanese chrysanthemum which was still in bloom. Mrs. Quest turned, as the Colonel thought, to put the gun back against a wall. The next thing he was aware of was a large explosion, following by an exclamation or rather a cry from Mrs. Quest . . . he glanced towards the place where Edward Cossey stood, and saw that his face was streaming with blood and that his right arm hung helpless by his side.[25]

I will not describe further the fate of Edward Cossey, though the long unraveling of the forced marriage plot into a more satisfactory distribution of riches and affianced partners which follows this moment of chrysanthemum appreciation would take precedence in a conventional narrative summary. Of greater interest to this chapter's argument, however, is the way that Cossey's banishment from the plot to make way for its happy resolution occurs, in this moment at least, seemingly at the bidding of the Japanese chrysanthemums and abetted by the up-to-date technology of the sportsman's efficient new gun. The plants, not domesticated enough to lose the Japanese adjective that designates their difference yet hybridized enough to grow successfully in the open air of the garden, lull Cossey into a misreading of how a transfer of the de la Molle estate can occur. His mistake is not so much to become absorbed in the flowers but to imagine that his momentary absorption can supplant the attentions of a character like Colonel Quaritch—a character both intimately engaged in both the cultivation and appreciation of the gardens and fields that surround the house, and also personally familiar with the cost in blood required to defend such countryside on foreign battlefields.

It is in no way surprising, then, that the plot allows Quaritch to claim his proper rewards by marrying Ida and redeeming the estate through the discovery of its legendary buried treasure. Yet even this treasure, once discovered, is not the antiquarian preserve it was fabled to be. The garden gazebo atop Dead Man's Mount does not in fact hide a trove of gold dating back to the days of earliest English royalty, as first appears, but rather contains a cleverly forged simulacra of such an archaeological site, complete with wired skeletons artfully arranged; no insular nativeness survives disbarred from modern influence. The novel that Haggard calls "a tale of country life," then, describes a landscape equally imbricated with the global flows of plant life as it is with the pastoral traditions of days past. Yet this new kind of country life, not surprisingly, works differently for its male characters than for its female ones. Early on in the novel, declaring herself human token of the buildings of her father's estate, Ida exclaims "I am *in pawn!* . . . You see this place? *I* am security for it, I *myself* in my own person."[26] While Ida can appreciate the flowers that she grows and the estate life she represents, she cannot control their ultimate disposition. Ida's liberation from Cossey's attentions is achieved largely by forces beyond her control, even if her novel-closing marriage repairs the (literal) hole in the landscape which the extraction of the buried treasure has imposed, and the children she will produce with Quaritch will reunite the once-separated parts of the estate. This kind of symbolic resolution of the fears of ancestral haunting that the novel has intermittently raised via Dead Man's Mount of course matches the work that female cultivation is held to do more generally in repairing the discontinuities of the globalized environment. The novel's opening lesson—that only by virtue of his devotion to Ida's image

Quaritch could, if not replace, at least superimpose his present vision of the English countryside over his earlier memory of the colonial atrocities he perpetuated—is one that Ida herself will never be able to see.

Yet while the curtailment of Ida's abilities to seek escape or self-fulfillment through her gardening is recognizable if not troubling to Haggard, other nonfiction garden texts flesh out the duties of the female gardener while touching more complexly on her constraints.[27] Though lady gardeners were not expected to complete the heavy manual labor that a large landscape garden required, a range of guidebooks, encyclopedias, histories, and periodicals directed these women to a mental and physical engagement with the garden held to be reciprocally beneficial for the woman, the plants in the garden, and, by extension, the nation. Beginning with Jane Loudon's *Instructions on Gardening for Ladies* (1840) and John Lindley's *Ladies' Botany* (1834–37), a range of writings gave further textual form to the description of an English garden and, more specifically, written representation of the mutually produced, shared subjecthood of lady and plant in the cultivated garden.[28] This alignment of woman and the organic life in the garden she tended occurred in multiple ways. It often involved synchronization: Jane Loudon's *The Lady's Country Companion, or How to Enjoy a Country Life Rationally* (1845), like many other women's garden writings, was arranged around the calendar of a year to provide necessary structure—not for plants, assured in their own timelines, but for the perhaps otherwise unregulated ladies. The arbitrariness of the human-designated frame was precisely the point; these calendars reminded the ladies that the plants were possessed of their own timelines, however much human cultivations succeeded in rewriting those chronologies. The reconciliation also nearly inevitably proposed reproduction. That the plants were a lady's children was an inescapable trope throughout the texts, with some interesting variations: "To live in London and to possess a garden in the country is to be in the position of an Anglo-Indian mother whose children are in England," writes Mary Ansell in 1912.[29] Nor, of course, was this trope limited to female gardeners; William Drury's manual "for the amateur" acknowledges that "How shall I stock my garden?" is a question just short of "How shall I educate my son?" in its capacity to produce anxiety, while William Robinson calls the garden "a beautiful book, writ by the finger of God" and its flowers "overdutiful children: tend them but ever so little, and they come up and flourish, and show, as I may say, their bright and happy faces to you."[30] Such obligations were, of course, double-edged; disregard of the plant calendar or the plant children's needs was an ever-present potential dereliction made more likely by disregard of floral metaphors.

Certainly, the moral responsibilities proposed by tending children in a book written by God had deep import for the lives of Victorians attentive to the religious and spiritual responsibilities of caring for organic beings. That this moral responsibility fell especially to women is widely familiar, but particularly in John Ruskin's famous lecture "Of Queen's Gardens" (delivered in 1864 and first published in *Sesame and Lilies* in 1865), which, among its other guiding principles for feminine purity, makes metaphoric use of garden flowers as the stage for social action within and beyond the home.[31] Ruskin encourages girls to bring their love and attention to a range of "flowers," including "flowers that could bless you for having blessed them, and will love you for having loved them;—flowers that have thoughts like yours, and lives like yours; and which, once saved, you save for ever . . . far in the darkness of the terrible streets,—these feeble florets are lying, with all their fresh leaves torn, and their stems broken—will you never go down to them, nor set them in order in their little fragrant bed, nor fence them, in their trembling, from the fierce wind?"[32] Kate Millett famously identified this lecture as "one of the most complete insights obtainable into that compulsive masculine fantasy one might call the official Victorian attitude" and these broken flowers as the "scabrous menace" of prostitution, to be repaired and tended by the right-thinking "daytime lady."[33] Most studies of Ruskin's lecture, including those that, like Millett, place it in contrast with John Stuart Mill's more reasoned *The Subjection of Women* (1869), take the horticultural engagements of both works as solely the operation of metaphor. Mill's example of the confining hothouse, like the bindings cramping Chinese women's feet and other metaphorical structures of restriction he employs, are considered no more materially real than Ruskin's gardens, whether the happy garden that shelters the "tender and delicate" girl he instructs, or the disarrayed and diffuse garden of the larger world beyond the wall.[34] And yet despite Ruskin's obvious objections to the kinds of materialist readings that would seek tangible referent for these "feeble florets," his frequent recourse throughout "Of Queen's Gardens" to particular named flowers returns us to the problem of mutually created and recognized cultivated agency. The varieties of flowers named in *Sesame and Lilies*, as Joanna Tapp Pierce points out, "are not wildflowers—these flowers' natural habitat is the garden," as Ruskin's idiosyncratic reading of Alfred Lord Tennyson's poem "Maud" within the lecture makes further clear.[35] Pierce reads this as a "self-perpetuating cycle of flower-to-gardener, where the girl is raised like a flower, with constant tending, and is then turned loose in the garden to cultivate her own young flowers"; it is a highly limited freedom revealed as all the more ineffectual when in considered in conjunction with *Through the Looking Glass*'s "Garden of Live Flowers." Carroll's text, with its quest for queenhood amid torn and scattered flowers, is clearly satirically responsive to Ruskin's call, and equally dismissive of its ends.[36]

When the flowers of "Of Queens's Gardens" are paired with Ruskin's much longer and stranger *Proserpina* (1875–86), his uncompleted study of plants initially begun as a grammar of botany for young amateurs, this cycle of constrained and ineffectual cultivation becomes even more complicated.[37] From *Proserpina*'s opening lines, written in 1868, Ruskin makes obvious with what semiotic entanglements he approaches the work: "It is mortifying enough to write,—but I think thus much ought to be written. . . . In three months I shall be fifty years old: and I don't at this hour—ten o'clock in the morning of the two hundred and sixty-eighth day of my forty-ninth year—know what 'moss' is."[38] The effort of finding out would in some measure consume the rest of Ruskin's life—"I *will* know what moss is, if possible, forthwith" he resolves, a resolution whose immediacy is painfully elusive.[39] (A footnote to an entry near the end of the work reads: "Date of year needless. My seal-motto of 'Today' seems changed now into one long yesterday.")[40] The consequences that investigation carried for his later-in-life spiritual crises and his ultimately inconclusive efforts to seek a synthesis of art, nature, and moral spiritualism made *Proserpina* "a book on botany [that] is pre-eminent among his final acts of defiance," as Dinah Birch has argued.[41]

Though Ruskin presents the work as an effort of scientific taxonomy, he actually creates a study of affective plant life focused around the discovery of singularly personal questions such as "what 'moss' is." Despite efforts at guidance by Kew and Cambridge botanist Daniel Oliver, *Proserpina* continues in silent struggle with the major scientific work on botany underway during the 1870s and 1880s, especially Darwin's groundbreaking works on botany including *On the Movement and Habits of Climbing Plants* (1875), *The Different Forms of Flowers in Plants of the Same Species* (1877), and *On the Power of Movement in Plants* (1880).[42] Even Alexander von Humboldt's earlier considerations on phytogeography published in his

Personal Narrative (1814) enrages Ruskin with its perceived omissions. To Humboldt's recognition of the curious similarities to be found in plant life, particularly rhododendrons, distributed in analogous climates across distant countries, which Humboldt calls the "insoluble problems of the distribution of beings," Ruskin has an intransigent answer: "And who asked us to solve it?," he replies, preferring instead to return to his own hillside shrubberies and the consolations of a hyperlocal flora.[43]

But while he forbids Humboldt's "vain science" to delimit the proper places of plants, he does not deprive himself of the same endeavor with a key difference. Earlier chapters of volume 1 have paraphrased the girls' advice book *Aunt Judy's Tales* (1859) and its instructive Q&A: "What is a weed? . . . [A] plant in the wrong place."[44] This Ruskin revises to a "vegetable which has the disposition to *get* into the wrong place," making plain his abiding interest in the immorality and mobility of plants.[45] These vegetable intruders, Ruskin admits, do not have to be evil, but most likely are so: "That it should have no choice of home, no love of native land, is ungentle; much more if such discrimination as it has, be immodest, and incline it, seemingly, to open and much-traversed places, where it may be continually seen of strangers."[46] His meditations on the unwanted excursions of plants, compounded by his charge in volume 2 to "mak[e] our gardens gay only with common flowers" while "leaving those which needed care for their transplanted life to be found in their native places when we travelled," seem to serve as a garden manual on their own, and, at least in broad strokes, fit with the botanical instructions given by manuals of country house gardening and even novels of country house life that describe the proper place and distribution of English flowers.[47]

That *Prosperina* is no colleague of William Robinson's *The Wild Garden*, despite Ruskin's inclusion of a carefully worded letter from Robinson supporting a general effort to devise an "English" naming system for plants, is evident throughout the volume's notoriously strange attempted revision of plant nomenclature to properly designate plants that are "perfectly pretty and perfectly good" or by contrast possessing "some power either of active or suggestive evil."[48] The imprisonment of its title mythological figure, and by extension the regulation of the girls and women, supposed readers of the volume, to their appropriate botanical and social realms denotes Ruskinian parameters of the social order far broader than my focus here. But Ruskin's constant inquiries into the nature and place of plant life are equally taken up as the work of fictive character. This is true whether the questions concern the true nature of the moss or the proper placements of parasitic plants, weeds with not only no right place, but no place of their own at all: "When is mistletoe, for instance, in the right place, young ladies, think you? On an apple tree, or on a ceiling? When is ivy in the right place?—when wallflower?" he asks.[49] A key difference is Ruskin's indifference to the independent animacy of plant life, or the idea of where a plant might consider its own right place to be, independent of human reference. Like fiction writers of all kinds but especially genre fiction writers, Ruskin seeks the emotional life of plants as it is revealed by their spatial and, by extension, geographical relocations.

Larger developments in nonfiction writing about English plants, gardens, and landscape reflect these concerns with less eccentricity and more accommodation to the positive influence of exotic introductions. Appraising the legacy of *The Wild Garden* in its 1904 edition, over thirty years after its original publication, William Robinson writes with concern about what he considered one of the central misreadings of the volume: "Many of the reviews of the book did not take the trouble necessary to see its true motive . . . the idea of the *wild garden* is placing plants of other countries, as hardy as our hardiest wild flowers, in places where they will *flourish without further care or cost*."[50] This is in contrast to the writings of garden designers like Reginald Bloomfield, whose *Formal Gardens in England* (1892) was defiantly the production of an architect who applied architectural symmetries to the garden's organic life and took strenuous issue with Robinson's efforts to "make the flower garden a reflex, so to say, of the world of beautiful plant-life, instead of the formal thing it has long been."[51] As Anne Helmriech has carefully shown, this was a battle of words waged through a variety of nonfiction genres, including advice manuals, design treatises, and garden histories, not to mention the book reviews and articles appearing even more frequently in serials like William Robinson's *Garden* (for wealthy practitioners) and *Gardening Illustrated* (for amateurs and the general public), as well as the periodicals *Country Life* and the *Studio,* where the landscape gardener Gertrude Jekyll first published many of her pieces.[52] Attempted resolutions to these competing styles, like art historian's Julia Cartwright's in 1892, made recourse to the personal and interior connections of the garden as linked to globally-sourced plant life: "We would lay down no hard-and-fast rules. Every garden should be the expression of an individual idea, should realise the owner's individual dream. . . . Whatever is beautiful, whatever delights the eye and gives pleasure to the senses, should find a place there, according to individual taste," continuing to concede that "we would not even banish tropical plants and hardy exotics from a garden where climate and space allow of their proper culture."[53]

Cartwright's "individual dream" of a garden integrating both local and exotic plants befits the selective work of what Gertrude Jekyll calls a "good flower eye," that is, a sensibility that takes into account both the hardy persistence of the plant as well as more abstract concerns like "gardens and garden beauty, and human delight, and sunshine, and varying lights of morning and evening and noonday"; Jekyll is grateful to both private "home growers [and] the enterprise of the great firms whose agents are always searching the world for garden treasures" for providing plants that match these categories of pleasure.[54] That gardeners might, conversely, seek plants at home and abroad that would claim as well as give pleasure is also a tenet of the garden writers, if more implicitly. Take, for instance, William Robinson's preference that gardens capitalize on "the vast numbers of beautiful hardy plants from other countries which might be naturalized, with a very slight amount of trouble, in many situations in our plantations, fields, and woods—a world of delightful plant beauty that we might in these ways make happy around us."[55]

Genre novels may be the representational form most suited to work out the descriptive and narrative puzzle of what it means to make plants happy, and genre readers among those most able to recognize such happiness when it comes. We have already seen nonfiction prose reuse the fantasy devices of antirealist fiction in the plant-hunter Frank Kingdon-Ward's "Dream of a Plant Collector" discussed in the first chapter. Grace Kehler, following Mary Poovey, has explained the ways that late-century gardening advice manuals "typically (and energetically) promote the virtues of disciplinary individualism" while revising those virtues to accommodate "the problem of arriving at ethical forms of intimacy between human and natural worlds"—a revision that usually requires a flexing of the bounds that conventionally divide those worlds.[56] For example, Gertrude Jekyll, who in her *Wood and Garden* (1899) declares herself "on closely intimate and friendly terms with a great many growing things,"[57] enters into the parasitic drama between a honeysuckle and the oak and chestnut trees it attacks in *Home and Garden* (1900). Jekyll adopts in a particularly formally showy moment the words of the oak's noble self-sacrifice: "When I die and fall, as I must within a very few years, our enemy, now held up by me to the sunlight and gaily flowering, will lie in a mangled heap on the floor of the wood, where, overshadowed by your spreading branches, he will never bloom again, but must remain content with a lowlier way of life."[58] Kehler judges these moments at the problematic outer limits of "epistemological or empirical approaches to the nonhuman, as Jekyll turns from authoritative rhetoric to engage in guesswork and imaginative relational thinking," and indeed the oak's turgid martyrdom seems to confirm power relations more human than arboreal.[59] Jekyll's aestheticized anthropomorphism, it seems, is mostly problematic because of the wrenching temporal frame it imposes, granting a conversation of minutes the effects of months or years of growth. As we have seen, an anthrodecentric acknowledgment of the incommensurate time frames of plants and humans is relied on by nonrealistic literature for both its generic form and its epistemological distinction from the deeply humanist project of realism. Moving to a more sprightly, if still fraught, narrative of the eradication of parasites both human and botanical, I now turn to *The Secret Garden*. Burnett's novel of childhood is, like Jekyll's nonfiction writing, deeply preoccupied with how both plants and people develop over time given various inhibiting or encouraging conditions, and, also like Jekyll, willing to give narrative voice to both in describing these developments.

Frances Burnett gained experience in chronicling the vicissitudes of Anglo-Indian girlhood with the novel *A Little Princess* (1905) before she came to write *The Secret Garden,* and despite the differences in setting between the two novels, the former clearly contributes to the latter's vision of a narrative environment capable of great personal transformation. *A Little Princess* shows how its little lost girl transforms the streets and garrets of London in order to remedy incidents of urban poverty and cruelty to children, while the later *Secret Garden* studies the orphaned colonial returnee's alterations in a country context, eventually digressing entirely from Mary Lennox's story to focus on the restoration of Colin Craven as estate heir. The two novels share a sense of the serious contributions of the colonies to the imperial center for adults and children, as well as the necessity for a spatially and narratologically separate site to work out the range of these responsibilities. *A Little Princess*'s Sara is rescued and her diamond-mine fortune restored tenfold on the strength of a retold story—her own rescue fantasy, overheard through the attic window by the Indian servant Ram Dass and recounted to his British master Captain Carrisford—while later retellings of that story expand the philanthropy still farther afield, bettering the lives of many other little girls across London. Though *A Little Princess*'s attic is cultivated with "curious wadded silk" from India rather than *The Secret Garden*'s crocuses and roses, it functions equally well as a transformative location of upper-class obligation and responsibility.[60] Thus, Burnett's urban bower is in opposition to the negative urban gardens of the previous chapter, as it describes a cultivated space in which both the economic and narrative wealth of the colonies are given tangible shape by the material commodities. In both cases, the secret space of the garden or attic exists through much of the novel as a conditional and propositional space, brought to material existence through the work of narrative itself and in particular the feverish intensity of young girl storytelling. The colonially sourced objects that fill these gardens and attics create a preserve in which a national ethical and economic order can be cultivated and made visible through the discoveries of narrative. While *The Secret Garden* would seem to turn inward, away from the more expansive urban charities that *A Little Princess* provides, the novel's abstract environmental and organic repurposing of narratives of cultivation offers theoretically even broader applications than *A Little Princess*'s Cinderella fantasy while keeping the same principles at its core.

The Secret Garden therefore is, like *A Little Princess,* interested in probing the influence and effects of overheard stories about oneself and others in an intensely material setting capable of immediately reflecting those overheard stories' effects and returning them in a cycle of environmentally responsive self-betterment. The importance of these retold stories is apparent from the novel's opening lines. "When Mary Lennox was sent to Misselthwaite Manor to live with her uncle everybody said she was the most disagreeable-looking child ever seen. It was true too," Burnett begins, sardonically subjugating any assumption of the narrator's omniscience to the gossipy intelligence of "everybody."[61] This distinction, between what "everybody said" and the empirical truth, will become the focus of the novel's attention, as the story of Mary Lennox's development also becomes in large measure an attempt to retell and replace stories long held to be true. The geographical determinism of the narrator's second claim about Mary—"her hair was yellow, and her face was yellow because she had been born in India and had always been ill in one way or another"—connects with assessments of Mary's "tyrannical and selfish" nature caused by parental neglect and inadequate nurturing by the "dark faces" of her Ayah and servants to provide the reader with a familiar evocation of a colonial environment insufficient for English developmental needs.[62]

Yet when we move with the narrator to discover the first specific, rather than habitual, details of Mary's lived experience in India on that hot, mysterious morning when her Ayah doesn't come, the props of these broader equivalencies are removed. Though the narrator will later indirectly reveal the Ayah's and Mary's flighty mother's deaths from cholera, the seemingly omniscient perspective continues to be artificially blinkered as it follows Mary's movements. "She was actually left alone as the morning went on," the narrator tells us with Mary's own incredulity, "and at last she wandered out into the garden and began to play by herself under a tree near the veranda. She pretended that she was making a flower-bed, and she stuck big scarlet hibiscus blossoms into little heaps of earth, all the time growing more and more angry."[63] This initial playacting becomes deeply significant for the novel's narrative, which takes not only the appreciation and presence of the organic world but also the active management and cultivation of the organisms of that world as crucial elements of proper physical and spiritual development and growth. The novel's establishment of this particularly curious epistemological position, in which a child can use picked flowers taken from a garden to (wrongly, as we readers clearly understand) "pretend" to make a garden, pushes hard on the mutually maintained assumptions of both what pretending is and what gardens mean. But it also asks us to consider how female development, into both marriageable womanhood and decolonized Englishness, is dependent upon an ability to properly recognize what kinds of flowers belong in which kind of gardens.

Mary's mother, if she hadn't been "a great beauty who cared only to go to parties and amuse herself with gay people," should have been able to instruct Mary in how to put plants into flower beds.[64] "A taste for floriculture is spreading amongst Anglo-Indians. It is a good sign," remarks an 1855 Calcutta-published English gardening manual, and many subsequent manuals and memoirs, including Flora Annie Steele and Grace Gardiner's well-known *The Complete Indian Housekeeper and Cook* (1888), gave instructions to English women in India on the proper management and care of their colonial gardens.[65] Sara Duncan's novel of Anglo-Indian life, *Simple Adventures of a Memsahib* (1893), finds its characters seeking to preserve their homesickness, and by extension their sense of their own Englishness, through their planting of English flowers. The heroine, memsahib-in-training Helen Peachey, "could always go down and talk of home to her friends in the flower-beds, who were so steadfastly gay, and tell them, as she often did, how brave and true it was of them to come so far from England, forgetting, perhaps, that from a climatic point of view nasturtiums like heathendom."[66]

That Anglo-Indians had in general familiarity with management of an "English" garden abroad explains in part Mary's encounter with the unpleasant missionary's son Basil while waiting to depart India and take up her new life at her uncle-in-law's Yorkshire manor.

> She was playing by herself under a tree, just as she had been playing the day the cholera broke out. She was making heaps of earth and paths for a garden and Basil came and stood near to watch her. Presently he got rather interested and suddenly made a suggestion.
>
> "Why don't you put a heap of stones there and pretend it is a rockery?" he said. "There in the middle," and he leaned over her to point.
>
> "Go away!" cried Mary. "I don't want boys. Go away!"
>
> For a moment Basil looked angry, and then he began to tease.... He danced round and round her and made faces and sang and laughed.
>
> "Mistress Mary, quite contrary,
> How does your garden grow?
> With silver bells, and cockle shells,
> And marigolds all in a row."[67]

Basil's taste for rock gardens mirrors Edwardian English tastes more generally, just as Mary's heaps of earth and paths suggest a rather sophisticated evocation of landscape gardening, considering her experience and aptitude for the task. The reader finds both children's interest in the formal and artificial aspects of gardening notable, in particular the idea that Mary can "play at" gardening seemingly without any plants, even the plucked flowers of the previous example. This scene makes a semireversal of the combined plots of *Jane Eyre* and *Wuthering Heights*, in which Mary begins by rejecting the Christian missionary in India and ends up in Yorkshire, intimately (if chastely) engaged with both the wild boy of the moors and the brooding yet vastly wealthy estate heir through the site of the garden. This mirroring depends, however, not so much on the practice of gardening itself but on the accurate narration of the conditional possibilities such gardening implies. Basil's inappropriateness as a future friend or mate for Mary stems not only from his unwelcome suggestion for rockeries, but also his bullying extended abstraction of the act of gardening from actual activity to imagined rhymed representation.

Memorably, his use of the English nursery rhyme to wound her in a colonial context is revised by Mary and the narrator into a signal act of self-definition that persists throughout the book. While critics have often read the Yorkshire garden as a site in which Mary's Indian origins are shed, the operations of the book's close third-person narration, which frequently strays into free indirect discourse, insist on preserving Basil's insulting naming of her as "Mistress Mary" (and Mary's own designation of the estate heir Colin Craven as the "Rajah") through to the book's conclusion. Rather than purging the children of their Indian personas, then, the novel integrates them into the garden space through a process that is explicitly identified as the work of hypothetical, prospective self-figuration. That Mary will later attempt to find actual versions of the plants named in the dismissive rhyme—"Are there any flowers that look like bells?" she asks the rural boy of the moors Dickon when they first begin to garden together—demonstrates only one half of the kinds of repair necessary to make English gardening a repudiation of Anglo-Indian insult.[68] The other half is evident in the sentence that comes just prior to Mary's investigation of the organic equivalents of the nursery-rhyme: "Mistress Mary always felt that however many years she lived she should never forget that first morning when her garden began to grow."[69] In the open-ended and expansive time frame implied by this rather unexpectedly broad temporal perspective, interjected long before the book's conclusion, we find the Indian origins of Mary's story insinuated deep into her garden and persona, making her narrative into one of hybridization and assimilation, not substitution.

But of course the narrator can quickly dispose of Mary's future because it is not, in fact, the novel's main concern. Overwriting, and ultimately subsuming, the narrative of Mary growing into the organic forms of her nursery-rhyme epithets is the novel's adoption of the mystery narrative form so popular in fiction contemporary to Burnett to tell a story about male inheritance and rehabilitation. Once arrived in Yorkshire, Mary's developing conversion from sour Indian girl to vibrant English woman is compelled forward by her acts of detection in two related mysteries: first, of the locked secret garden and second, of the isolated and apparently crippled boy locked away in the manor, whose nighttime moans substitute for more pronounced supernatural intrusions. Though the crimes described here are gentle in contrast to those in gothic novels meant for adult audiences, the cost of not solving these mysteries threatens equally consequential dissolution.

To resolve these mysteries of origins, the novel obsesses over multiple points of character focalization, only some of which are human. In addition to Mary, the narrative takes up the perpectives of the moaning boy (later revived to be her cousin Colin), the gardening savant Dickon, and his sister Martha, the housemaid; we also, through indirect discourse, see the story through the perspective of a robin and of several varieties of plants above and below ground. Each character is interrogated for its ability to understand how it is perceived by others and how it recognizes itself through that external perception. Unlike the Wilde and Brontë novels of the previous chapter, where circumnarration largely buried plant thoughts, Burnett grants her plants direct speech, albeit easing the reader into such identification with an initial conditional description before the free indirect discourse crosses fully over into plant-thinking. Of the results of Mary's intuitive acts of weeding, the narrator explains: "The bulbs in the secret garden must have been much astonished. Such nice clear places were made round them that they had all the breathing space they wanted, and really, if Mistress Mary had known it, they began to cheer up under the dark earth and work tremendously. The sun could get at them and warm them, and when the rain came down it could reach them at once, so they began to feel very much alive."[70] These same bulbs gain further capacities as they develop under Dickon's additional cultivation, most notably a certain kind of floral xenophobia: "The seeds Dickon and Mary had planted grew as if fairies had tended them," the narrator alerts us later in the narrative, "satiny poppies of all tints danced in the breeze by the score, gaily defying flowers which had lived in the garden for years and which it might be confessed seemed rather to wonder how such new people had got there."[71] The arch tone belies the comfort of the imperial returnees in a garden deeply narratively receptive to botanical importations, while the plants' initiation into "feeling" alive recalls the live flowers of the Looking-Glass Land garden.

Throughout these scenes of Mary's gardening labor and the responsive plants and animals that benefit from that labor, the novel converts play into work without Mary recognizing it, one part of its generalized Christian Science approach to health and wellness that draws on a broadly animist spirituality.[72] Critical readings of *The Secret Garden* have usually focused (and rightly so) on following the ecodevelopmental narratives of the novel which knit heritage aristocratic land rights into individual emotional and spiritual affiliations with the land. But it is also notable that scenes of physical work in the secret garden are greatly outnumbered by scenes in which the secret garden exists only as a hypothetical garden space.[73] The characters spend at least as much narrative energy and labor figuring the garden propositionally or in its future forms as they do asserting (or, certainly, spending time in) its material reality—a reality that, arguably, is only truly confirmed by the book in its final pages, where Archibald Craven finally returns to the site of his wife's death and accepts that the piece of his property he has attempted to excise instead deserves cultivation and growth. Long after the robin has revealed the key to the garden space and Mary and Dickon are busily at work pruning and planting, they both (and especially Mary) continue to isolate the garden in a narratologically secret or separate space that exists in words rather than in living form. Significantly, Mary and Dickon's narrative work actively excludes the longer-term efforts of the estate's gardener Ben Weatherstaff, who has been crucial in maintaining the garden in a state of suspended animation, but who needs replacement when it comes to the transformations of the garden's final revivification. Burnett can do much more than Wilde to acknowledge and justify the responsibilities of the many servants of Misslethwaite Manor for the novel's transformations, but ultimately (and unsurprisingly) she, like Wilde, keeps the gardeners and maids as witnesses rather than instigators of these changes.

The plot and content of most of the book instead focuses most specifically on the children, resolving the different ways that Mary claims the secret garden—by hearing of it in a story, by physically entering it, by working with its soil, by telling others about it and showing it to Dickon, and by bringing it back into bloom. As a result, readers frequently navigate scenes like the one in which Mary makes a vivid description of the garden given to Colin on his sickbed seem like a hypothetical possibility—one which only she knows is also true. "I'll tell you what I *think* it would be like, if we could go into it," she explains disingenuously to Colin, fresh from her stint in the real garden; at this, Colin "lay quite still and listened while she went on talking about the roses which *might* have clambered from tree to tree and hung down—about the many birds which *might* have built their nests there because it was so safe."⁷⁴ The garden's existence as a space requires so much constant and repetitive narrative energy, not only because this is a children's story, but because Burnett's task in collaboratively producing a garden between an Indian girl and a British ecology via their combined consciousnesses is so laborious. By the time Colin is involved, the layers of real and fictional secret gardens would task even a seasoned adult reader to keep straight—the reader maintains through Mary, in equal measure, a sense of the real secret garden as it exists at that moment in her direct sensory perception; a shared future vision with Dickon of the real garden after their work of planting; an understanding of Dickon's metaphoric representation of the garden as a missel thrush's hiding place; a vision which she shares with Colin of a hypothetical secret garden that only she knows is also the real one; a vision of the past garden as tended by the Craven parents in happier days; and, not to mention, a narrator-assisted perception of the garden as it is seen by the robin and the flowers themselves.

Indeed, what is unexpected about the novel's dependence on the revivifying qualities of the natural world and the children's use of the "Magic" to heal Colin's psychological wound,(the only disability of his that the narrator takes seriously) is that it derives almost exclusively from highly cultivated scenes and situations. Despite frequent verbal recourse to the influence of the moor, the novel sets no scenes there and even the evocations of the wild boy Dickon's family cottage focus mostly on his family's vegetable garden. But the novel clearly prioritizes the work of plant cultivation that occurs within the boundaries of commodity exchange. Mary's work in discovering and restoring the Secret Garden of the title is accomplished with Dickon's help but, more important, with the outlay of cash. As his older sister Martha, a maid at Misslethwaite Manor, explains to Dickon via letter: "Miss Mary has plenty of money and will you go to Thwaite and buy her some flower seeds and a set of garden tools to make a flower-bed. Pick the prettiest ones and easy to grow because she has never done it before and lived in India which is different."⁷⁵

Looking at the pictures in the gardening books, the children discover the distinctions between the wild varieties and the seemingly preferable garden specimens given formal identification. As Dickon admits:

"'I couldna' say that there name,' he said, pointing to one under which was written 'Aquilegia,' 'but us calls that a columbine, an' that there one it's a snapdragon and they both grow wild in hedges, but these is garden ones an' they're bigger an' grander.'"[76] This distinction between common and formal names that Alan Bewell has termed, respectively, "ecolect and idiolect" demonstrates both Dickon's importance to the plot but also his separation from it—his intimate knowledge of nature shown by his ecolect has only transitory (though major) significance. The Secret Garden is too closely associated with Misslethwaite Manor to ever be known by Dickon as he knows the moor.[77] In staging the contrast between informal and formal so explicitly against a backdrop of expensively illustrated garden guidebook, Burnett further establishes the necessary collusion of colonial cash with domestic land rights and indigenous practice.

Burnett reminds us that, more than knowing the right names to call the plants or even having the right amount of money to buy the plants, the possession of the earth that the plant will grow in matters the most of all. Mary's negotiations with her uncle Archibald Craven for the right to work in the garden—negotiations complicated by Mary's attempt to gain permission to work in the Secret Garden without acknowledging its real existence—aim to assert new territory for ownership in a society of landed gentry that must accommodate both colonial returnees as well as the more traditional rural peasantry. But, typically for Mary, she confuses the different possible garden operations—working, witnessing, caring for and owning—when making her request.

"Might I," quavered Mary, "might I have a bit of earth?"

In her eagerness she did not realize how queer the words would sound and that they were not the ones she had meant to say. Mr. Craven looked quite startled.

"Earth!" he repeated. "What do you mean?"

"To plant seeds in—to make things grow—to see them come alive," Mary faltered.

He gazed at her a moment and then passed his hand quickly over his eyes.

"Do you—care about gardens so much," he said slowly.

"I didn't know about them in India," said Mary. "I was always ill and tired and it was too hot. I sometimes made little beds in the sand and stuck flowers in them. But here it is different."[78]

Mary's halting efforts to express in the same words the work of both caring about and caring for the garden evoke contemporary environmental care ethics, and also invokes the thorny complications of the variable scale of such ethical care. This is particularly suggested by Mary's suggestion that "a bit of earth" and "India" are correspondent kinds of places potentially worthy of care.[79] But her obligation to funnel her acts of caring through the Craven father and son, as well as to isolate her attentive care to the garden rather the broader world, severely limits her capacity to express a wider ecological ethos. Craven, haunted by his recollections of his wife's love of flowers and gardening, proceeds to convert Mary into a simulacra of his wife and as "someone one who cared about flowers," thus preparing a future marriage of Mary and Colin that will repair Archibald's alienation from the land. Mary, however, at this moment neither a reproductively mature possible bride nor a native-born Englishwoman, must constantly perform her active connection to the land. This self-perpetuating cycle renders Mary of diminishing interest to the progress of the novel, just as Dickon's steady connection to the wilder world of the moor makes him increasingly irrelevant to the final advancements of the plot.

As Mary fades from the forefront of the story, readers are given instead the rehabilitation of Archibald Craven, a transformation narrated in a very different voice and with an entirely different narrative layer. This storyline seems not meant for the child readers looking for more scenes of Dickon and his menagerie, but adult readers reclaiming solace in a particular kind of floral appreciation. The elder Craven, in Europe for much of the later Secret Garden-aided rehabilitation of Colin, and alienated from his son and his estate alike, would seem to have no reason to return to Misslethwaite Manor if not for a heavily symbolic encounter with "one lovely mass of blue forget-me-nots" in the Austrian Tyrol: "At these he found himself looking as he remembered he had looked at such things years ago. He was actually thinking tenderly how lovely it was and what wonders of blue its hundreds of little blossoms were. He did not know that just that simple thought was slowly filling his mind.... Something seemed to have been unbound and released in him, very quietly.... 'What is it?' he said, almost in a whisper, and he passed his hand over his forehead. 'I almost feel as if—I were alive!'"[80] Archibald Craven's deliverance via European wildflower appears to direct us away from the colonial origins of Mary and the imperial influences that structure her story, as well as the highly cultivated space of the

Secret Garden. At the same time, however, we understand that the European recoveries that restore the senior Craven to his proper presence as a father and as a landowner depend on the operations of Indian returnees and their flowers. This is true both in the specifics of the plot's implications that Mary's care for Colin telepathically prompts paired healing of Archibald, and also in a more general sense. If the better-known plot of *The Secret Garden* is one that preserves narrative futures and ensures that the inheritors of the landed estates know how to value in cash and in human labor the grounds and landscape that surround them, this subplot of Archibald Craven's redemption—framed as the magnanimous forgiveness of his wife for committing the sin of first falling off a tree and then dying in childbirth—depends entirely on the kinds of floral cultivations of the human that I have also been describing. Craven's "simple thought," a combined apprehension of color intensity and a more elusive loveliness, reverses the process of flower appreciation to identify the flower as the maker of figure, and the human as the figured. When the narrator briefly imposes a metaphor for this operation of mental purification—"It was as if a sweet clear spring had begun to rise in a stagnant pool"—it is nearly immediately taken away: "But of course he did not think of this himself."[81] Like Ezra Jennings regarding the nosegay, Archibald Craven both depends on the singular life of the single flower that inspires him but also erases that singularity to invoke forget-me-nots as a collective mass extending from past to present and from England to overseas, in a way he cannot narrate himself but which must instead be narrated for him.

But while these Alpine flowers can prompt recollection, they cannot complete the story's final resolution. Archibald Craven must, after a slow period of European rehabilitation, return to Yorkshire, where he discovers the Secret Garden not abandoned but filled with the lively energy of children, including his own, now-ambulatory son. Indeed, *The Secret Garden* as a book ends nearly as soon as the secret space of the garden is collectively witnessed by Cravens elder and younger, in a description that undoes its cultivated conditions and dissolves them into the same color play that Holmes once found in his rose. As they ceremonially reenter the garden, the story of the garden is renarrated again for the final time.

"Take me into the garden, my boy," he said at last. "And tell me all about it."

> And so they led him in.
>
> The place was a wilderness of autumn gold and purple and violet blue and flaming scarlet and on every side were sheaves of late lilies standing together—lilies which were white or white and ruby. He remembered well when the first of them had been planted that just at this season of the year their late glories should reveal themselves. Late roses climbed and hung and clustered and the sunshine deepening the hue of the yellowing trees made one feel that one stood in an embowered temple of gold. The newcomer stood silent just as the children had done when they came into its grayness. He looked round and round.
>
> "I thought it would be dead," he said.
>
> "Mary thought so at first," said Colin. "But it came alive."[82]

Colin's phrasing, granting as it does the Secret Garden the agency to empower its own life force, connects to his father's command to double the seeing of the garden with the narration of each the garden's still-blooming flowers. That the display of the garden takes place in autumn, rather than springtime, signals (as it did with the chrysanthemums in *Colonel Quaritch*) the transience of the estate's displayed magnificence. This is true even as the layered and confusing chronology—Craven's remembering of a past planting planned to create a future vision—diverts the garden into a looped and ahistorical present. Indeed, while it seems here that the last we hear of Mary is her misunderstanding of the garden's potential, we know from the earlier reclaiming of the Mistress Mary title that she "for the rest of her days" connects with the animate garden. This is a temporal reversion that also allows the cultivated outdoor space to work inward and revise the domestic household—as the gardener Ben Weatherstaff triumphantly declares, "There's been things goin' on outside as you house people knows nowt about."[83] In a rebuff, though not a repudiation, of *Dorian Gray*, Misslethwaite Manor admits the voices of the gardeners standing outside the grounds and looking inward, even if their recognitions are only partial ones.

The story of Mary Lennox's acclimatization to the cultivated nature of the Yorkshire garden, which parallels and supports the degothicization of the Craven manor and its inhabitants, repeats the Brontë sisters' environmental visions in *Jane Eyre* and *Wuthering Heights*, but also, in part, foreshadows the conversions enacted in Daphne du Maurier's *Rebecca* without the later novel's far darker tone. Set in the more salubrious climate (for exotic plants, at least) of Cornwall, *Rebecca,* a novel termed "highly Radcliffean" by Jerome Hogle, both makes a part of a much larger twentieth-century canon of female gothic romance but also, like earlier works from Ann Radcliffe to Charlotte and Emily Brontë, uses environmental detail as material grounds for psychic dissolution, repression, and (however limited) liberation.[84] For *Rebecca,* as for *Jane Eyre* and *The Secret Garden,* these damaging effects are narrated by a female protagonist but experienced most forcefully by representatives of English manhood attacked by a problematic alternate femininity—wild and malignant, in the case of Brontë and du Maurier, or simply physically insufficient, in Burnett's milder case. All three novels also propose a subsequent masculine rehabilitation to be accomplished by the protagonist's gentler, domesticated kind of girlhood and the cultivations of nature she brings with her—rehabilitations whose insufficiencies *Rebecca,* in particular, make stringently plain.

The fictional estate of Manderley, central to the operative symbolism of the novel's tale, gained detail and specificity from du Maurier's own memories of the real Cornwall estate of Menabilly which she rented as an adult but also visited frequently as a girl.[85] This moves du Maurier's imagined environmental reference point closer in era to the composition of *The Secret Garden.* While modernist context allowed du Maurier to treat her characters with a stronger hand, conservative genre tropes and the conservationist ecology of the great estate both put her novel in conversation with earlier novels of the female gothic and the landscape treatises that inspired them. The woods surrounding the drive to Manderley clearly realize the ideals of Gertrude Jekyll and William Robinson in their union of exotic plantings and native species, arranged in drifts, as Jekyll recommended, to capitalize on the fields of color play that were her particular landscape innovation. Brent Elliot calls the "main theme" of Jekyll's garden "the indigenous landscape, artistically managed, as a frame to carefully selected exotics."[86] Such exotics were necessary, as Anne Hemreich explains, to provide new colors for English eyes, and included newly introduced varieties like the rhododendrons W. J. Hooker had gathered in the Himalayas among other global forms.[87] These exotic rhododendrons also maintained class divisions in the garden; as Philip Pauly points out, rhododendrons "were not adaptable to small properties, and so remained the cultural property of country gentlemen."[88]

That Manderley is by no means a small property is made immediately clear by the landscape description following its famous opening line, "Last night I dreamt I went to Manderley again," but the novel's structure as a whole also depends upon the constant narration and renarration of entrance to Manderley via the exclusive main drive that indicates synecdochally the property's territorial sweep. This drive, as the feverish beginning dream sequence details, contains elements of forest, shrubbery, and more formal walled garden, which are all collectively considered a part of Manderley's cultivations. While critics have debated the symbolic division of house from its surrounding nature and the claims on these two spheres by both Maxim de Winter and his dead wife Rebecca, they have not typically probed the varieties of cultivation that further parse Manderley's elaborate spatial effects. Stanka Radović, for example, identifies the ways that the "invasive exteriority of nature" in the novel "mocks and baits the falsely naturalized aristocratic order and its representatives," employing gothic modes of haunting to make plain the permanent uncanny of the natural world.[89] But it is insufficient here to point to the divide between natural and the artificial alone. The rhododendrons that are a central part of the novel's natural invasions cannot be understood without reference to those shrubberies' larger incursions into English landscape as an acculturated species, and the nonhuman agency that the rhododendrons, more cultivated and hybridized forms than Cornish nature generally, are narrated to employ.[90] As Harriet Ritvo explains, rhododendrons, "among the most aggressive botanical invasives in Great Britain and Ireland . . . were introduced with other exotic ornamentals as part of the expansion of domestic horticultural possibilities that shadowed European commercial and political expansion."[91]

The opening dream sequence provides a crucial initial demonstration of this agency, though the organic temporal paradox of the dream means that the reader will not properly understand the story of the dream plants until the novel as a whole comes to a close. As the reader and the forever unnamed narrator continue to approach Manderley "again," the narrator is disturbed to discover "trees I did not recognize" and "monster shrubs and plants, none of which I remembered." Amid these strangers, the narrator finds even more disturbing corruptions: "shrubs that had been land-marks in our time, things of culture and grace, hydrangeas whose blue heads had been famous," that "had gone native now, rearing to monster height without a bloom, black and ugly as the nameless parasites that grew beside them."[92] Moving closer to the garden of the house, which itself still "stood inviolate, untouched, as though we ourselves had left but yesterday," the narrator finds that "the garden had obeyed the jungle law, even as the woods had done. The rhododendrons stood fifty feet high, twisted and entwined with bracken, and they had entered into alien marriage with a host of nameless shrubs, poor, bastard things that clung about their roots as though conscious of their spurious origin."[93] Though the idea of "alien marriage" is temptingly symbolic in a novel concerned with the total destruction an abusive partnership can wreak both within and beyond a human lifespan, the appeals of anthropomorphism are insufficient to describe what is happening here. For, of course, this landscape does not actually exist; it is emphatically the imaginative creation of a female mind, who, at the moment of telling, has already moved through these gardens and up this drive many times. What is our first understanding of Manderley's famous grounds is, in many ways, her last, or at least her most distant. But at the same time, it is a landscape that overwrites the narrator dreaming its existence, just as the flowers in Carroll's gardens overwrote Alice's own thoughts of self-perception. Du Maurier's narrator has a recognition of the grounds and their plant life upon which the human-figured metaphors—"gone native," "obeyed the jungle law," "entered into alien marriage"—strain especially hard with the effort of relaying the independent existence of a plant life that the narrator knows in fact needs no human referent. The fantasy that plant consciousness consists of an awareness of "spurious origins," like the fantasy that Maxim and the narrator, his second wife, had left Manderley "only yesterday," is not only patently false, but particularly demonstrative of the kinds of stories of human falsehoods that *Rebecca*'s gothic disruptions seek to reveal.

This is approached in a different way as we return to Manderley a second time, in this case through the relayed description of the estate by Max to the narrator in Monte Carlo, after he has taken her on a flirtatious automobile ride turned possible suicide attempt entirely disorienting to the then-young and innocent girl. Maxim works even more explicitly to distinguish between varieties of plants under cultivation at the estate—which also soon become apparent as varieties of female subjectivity under repression. "No wild flowers came in the house at Manderley," we learn, for Maxim "had special cultivated flowers, grown for the house alone, in the walled garden."[94] Of these, he concentrates on roses, "one of the few flowers, he said, that looked better picked than growing. A bowl of roses in a drawing room had a depth of colour and scent they had not possessed in the open. There was something rather blowsy about roses in full bloom, something shallow and raucous, like women with untidy hair."[95] Max, whose stated "earliest recollection" is of lilacs in white jars, presents a rambling introductory monologue of self-revelation via floral affiliation that the naive and frightened narrator can hardly understand. And indeed the reader, still not yet introduced to Manderley of the present, finds this relayed recreation of past Manderley's protected domestic space ominous, especially as it is underlined with Maxim's critique, recalling similar criticisms of vulgar tastes in chrysanthemums, of roses as loose-haired (and loose-moraled) women who must be contained inside walls, bowls, and houses.

While the omniscient narrator of Burnett's *Secret Garden* allowed a fantasy of direct access to the thoughts of bulbs and robins alongside Mary Lennox and Archibald Craven, here du Maurier lays bare the fallacy that the narrator can even follow Maxim's perception of the cultivated space, let alone access the flowers on her own terms. It is important to remember here too that this monologue is being delivered by Maxim as he drives his car in Monte Carlo. The insistent rhythms of Max's syntax as relayed and paraphrased by the narrator lulls the reader into understanding that the information being conveyed is that which Maxim has directly spoken—an illusion set up for the purpose of being shattered, as we soon discover. The sudden return of the "far too brilliant, far too yellow" light and sounds of the "streets of Monte Carlo" signals, among other things, the end to plant life and to the fiction that figurative language can grant a connection between the sensations of the organic world and their consequences.[96] We have been deeply persuaded, with the narrator, of the evocative force of the plant life Maxim describes. "You could stoop down and pick a fallen petal, crush it between your fingers, and you had there, in the hollow of your hand, the essence of a thousand scents, unbearable and sweet. All from a curled and crumpled petal," the narrator relates of Manderley, switching into a second person that collapses her own memory into Maxim's.[97] This switch perpetuates the fantasy that descriptive language might transitively represent the rich and overwhelming sensation of Manderley as a site outside of ordinary time and yet possessed of its own extrafecund seasons, so that its gardens may grow riotously even in the exiled narrator's diegetic present. Yet such a fantasy can only last a short time before it is shattered.

When the narrator finally arrives at Manderley and we receive the most direct narration possible in a text so heavily predicated on the failures of memory, plant life becomes ontologically indeterminate to the narrator. As Maxim and the narrator, now his new bride, proceed up the drive towards the house out of the "dark trees" and "nameless shrubs":

> Suddenly . . . on either side of us was a wall of colour, blood-red, reaching far above our heads. We were amongst the rhododendrons. There was something bewildering, even shocking, about the suddenness of their discovery. The woods had not prepared me for them. They startled me with their crimson faces, massed one upon the other in incredible profusion, showing no leaf, no twig, nothing but the slaughterous red, luscious and fantastic, unlike any rhododendron plant I had seen before.
> I glanced at Maxim. He was smiling. "Like them?" he said.
> I told him "Yes," a little breathlessly, uncertain whether I was speaking the truth or not, for to me a rhododendron was a homely, domestic thing, strictly conventional, mauve or pink in colour, standing one beside the other in a neat round bed. And these were monsters, rearing to the sky, massed like a battalion, too beautiful, I thought, too powerful, they were not plants at all.[98]

The careful design and planting of these rhododendron, like the other tasteful and aesthetic details of the grounds, is explained to be Rebecca's work. If we take the bait to read the "not plants" as Rebecca and the "homely domestic" thing as the narrator, however, we lose a level of du Maurier's intention. The fecundity of the landscape is all its own. "Speaking the truth," as much a human ontological construct as "liking," proves ultimately irrelevant to the life of these flowers, which exist not to be regarded by the narrator but to regard her. It is an engulfing reversal which the narrator can only explain by denying the plantfulness of the flowers altogether.

After the narrator has taken up residence within the house, she looks outward over the grounds to reencounter these rhododendrons "great bushes of them, massed beneath the open window, encroaching on to the sweep of the drive itself."[99] Her continuing narration emphasizes the unsettling invasiveness of Manderley's floral life: "And I noticed then that the rhododendrons, not content with forming their theatre on the little lawn outside the window, had been permitted to the room itself. Their great warm faces looked down upon me from the mantelpiece, they floated in a bowl upon the table by the sofa, they stood, lean and graceful, on the writing desk beside the golden candlesticks."[100] The overwhelming dominance of the flowers—"even the walls took colour from them"—is matched by their monoculture; not only are they "the only flowers in the room," but "nowhere else in the house did the rhododendrons intrude." With her customary blend of blindness and insight, the narrator "wonder[s] if there was some purpose in it." This room turns out to have been Rebecca's central base of domestic operations, and the arrangement of the cut rhododendrons according to the taste and directions of a long-dead woman not the signs of a haunting, as the reader and narrator are trained by literature to expect, but the perhaps equally subversive preservations of the housekeeper Mrs. Danvers. Thus the human purposes for the intrusions of the rhododendrons are made plain as the gothic plot unfolds, but the narrator's acknowledgment of the rhododendrons' entry into the confines of the house also signals the flowers' own rebellion. By contrast to the domestic entries of roses and primroses sanctioned by Max, the rhododendrons, some varieties of which were by this time already considered an aggressively invasive alien, are also possessed of a unique persistence to claim human places as their own, at least until their cut stems and petals inevitably wilt and decay. Even Mrs. Danvers's powers, which greatly outstrip other domestic workers I have considered, do not exceed the operations of the plant life itself—a token as much of general human impotence as of the privileges of economic class.

The narrator will, for the rest of the book, measure the progress of her disastrous marriage by the slow death of the rhododendrons of the house and drive: "Already they looked a little over-blown, a little faded. Next month the petals would fall one by one from the great faces, and the gardeners would come and sweep them away," she notes, still fearing the memory of Rebecca;[101] and later, as she weathers the morning after her humiliation at the costume ball, she observes that "[t]he rhododendrons were all over now. They would not bloom again for another year. The tall shrubs looked dark and drab now that the colour had gone."[102] The fear of Rebecca is for the narrator, an irrevocable descent; once discovered, Rebecca's corpse will not cease haunting Maxim and the second Mrs. de Winter even if plot developments attempt to defend Maxim's murderous actions. But it is, the narrator equally understands, a decay also irrevocable for the rhododendrons. Even if her opening dream has told a story of the "alien marriages" of the woods and garden, the battles that she imagines are already heavily inflected as the intravegetable struggles of a cultivated plant life. "A lilac had mated with a copper beech, and to bind them yet more closely to one another the malevolent ivy, always an enemy to grace, had thrown her tendrils about the pair and made them prisoners," the narrator "remembered" in those opening pages, and "there was another plant too, some halfbreed from the woods . . . marching in unison with the ivy, thrust its ugly form like a giant rhubarb towards the soft grass where the daffodils had blown."[103] These assaults by once-cultivated plants on other once-cultivated plants make the enveloping temporal present of the story—they are the first things we read about, and, in the chronology of the telling, the last images we know from the operations of the narrator's own memory—and their presence suggests that the entire narrative has been, in a way, subsumed to this entirely nonhuman growth. If scrabbling metaphors searching for purchase give the form of human conflict to this growth, that is only to reveal by limitation how far the human narrator remains from control.

This chapter has followed girls and women who have been lost or trapped in gardens without always being sure of their release from such floral confinements. In the novels of detection in chapter 1, a need for well-scattered and hidden clues demanded a concurrent development of the level of detail contained in their fictional setting and an amplification of the narrative voices of objects, like flowers in window boxes, previously left silent. Here, as in the previous chapter, the novel's burgeoning floral environment accepts gothic themes and interludes that emphasize the containment and control forced upon inhabitants of these acculturated natural spaces. But in contrast to chapter 2, I have in this chapter focused especially on the women who must both reproduce heritage land claims while also cultivating the terrain and vegetation of a greatly reshaped local ecology. The legacy crimes of landowners, often symbolized by a historical and biological English nativeness, are covered over by an organic space whose plant life challenges that assumed nativeness in its distribution and cultivation, and sometimes even in its intervention into narrative voice. (It is a resolution far more satisfying for Ida de la Molle in Haggard's *Colonel Quaritch* than for the second Mrs. de Winter in *Rebecca*.) The job of these women is indeed to make the cultural products of gardens, as many studies have noted, but it is also to attend to both individual cultivated plants in their gardens as (possibly) speaking beings and to acknowledge a more general awareness of the independent existence and even consciousness of many additional plant specimens not under individual cultivation—other flowers in the garden that can "move about like you," as Carroll's Rose and Tiger-Lily might put it.

The mountains of Western China and the Himalayas from which many of these rhododendrons, azaleas, and other exotic flowers came were also the subject of nonfiction travel writings seeking to impose scientific and narrative structure on those wilderness landscapes. Even as late-century genre fictions drew inspiration from nonfiction wilderness adventures, however, they equally depended on the operations of cultivation and assimilation abroad to give shape and scale to the colonial and imperial expansions their narratives restaged. In the next chapter I will turn to various romances of adventure and resettlement overseas to plot their interactions with the self-perpetuating cultivations of plant life abroad. Of particular interest are the assimilations of introduced plant life like the prickly pear and the eucalyptus, which vie with British settlers to make claims on the colonial landscape.

⁂4⁂

Acclimatization Abroad

In episode 6 of Grant Allen's *Hilda Wade: A Woman with Tenacity of Purpose* (1899), a text usually called a novel of detection but more accurately an episodic and adventurous revenge fantasy that takes the British Empire as its setting, the frequently thwarted protagonist Hubert, pursuing the trail of his love object, the indefatigable Hilda, travels to remote Rhodesia. There, he recounts, the "distressing nakedness of a new country confronted me. Here and there a bald farm or two had been literally pegged out—the pegs were almost all one saw of them as yet; the fields were in the future."[1] The provisional nature of this landscape, we learn, is not only agricultural, but also political—"I came here because Rhodesia seemed the farthest spot of earth a white woman just now could safely penetrate," Hilda explains to Hubert when he finally catches up with her, underlining with her "just now" the extremely recent creation of "Rhodesia" as a name for the territory administered by Cecil Rhodes's British South African Company.[2] Hubert, a single-minded lover, is little concerned with these geopolitical conditions, and the text likewise treats the Rhodesian interlude as one installment in its global survey of popular literary forms and settings that includes stops in many outposts of the British Empire. Unsurprisingly, Hilda and Hubert's short-lived attempts to pursue farming as characters in a novel of settler colonialism meet with limited success, and the interlude comes to an abrupt end after the story's villain leads an attack by the Ndebele (the text's Matabele) that forces Hilda and Hubert to flee into the next adventure of the serial. As Hubert explains, the ill-fated farm "was a dreary place, save for Hilda. The bare daub-and-wattle walls; the clumps of misshapen and dusty prickly-pears . . . all was as crude and ugly as a new country can make things. It seemed to me a desecration that Hilda should live in such an unfinished land—Hilda, whom I imagined as moving by nature through broad English parks, with Elizabethan cottages and immemorial oaks—Hilda, whose proper atmosphere seemed to be one of . . . ivy-clad abbeys, lichen-incrusted walls—all that is beautiful and gracious in time-honoured civilisations."[3] Hubert's callow attempts to register the contrasts between old-growth English forest and the "raw" and treeless southern African landscape carries forward longstanding debates over the proper landscape of those British colonies in fact and fiction: a history not of managed forests but of introduced trees, as Kate Showers explains.[4] At the same time, his imagined connection of an idealized Hilda with an equally idealized heritage if parasitic English landscape makes the same gendered associations that the gothic novels of the previous chapter each, in different ways, explained as unimaginable for fiction written in the new era of cultivation. Allen implicitly rebukes Hubert for these assumptions, posing him as a feckless and unperceptive narrator who exists mainly to showcase by contrast Hilda's perspicuity and resourcefulness. In so doing, Allen (and to a lesser extent Arthur Conan Doyle, who completed *Hilda Wade* after Allen died one chapter short of the finish) teases the ideological strictures of what adventure fiction could be in this era, in a style that Ross Forman has also identified as at work in Doyle's own *The Lost World*.[5] More specifically, Allen uses this Rhodesian farm to parody how the setting of adventure fiction made a particular contribution to the genre's fantastical restagings of the global spread of British Empire into the struggles of particular individuals. Critical consensus has determined adventure fiction to be chiefly stories of British masculinity forged in landscapes most notable for their absolute difference from Britain, but attention to the plant life in fiction from the British colonies gives another part this story.[6] The serial publication of Allen's stories, both as individual episodes within a loosely affiliated main plot and as sequential fictions, whose villains and heroes return multiple times to restage their exploits, depends on a renewability of plot incident but also of environmental setting. Despite singular catastrophic events erasing particular aspects of the landscape, a more general cultivation of the landscape could always continue.[7] This was also true in popular fiction from the colonies. Romance needed to be renewable, even if, as we shall see, the substance of that renewal comes more through plant life than the human cultivators of those plants. This gives new inflection to classic formulations of the adventure novel, which, with Jacques Rivière, assess the genre as one "borrow[ing] everything from the future." This is a mode of telling, which, as he puts it, the author, "instead of extracting his materials from the soil on which he is standing, . . . forces them up from those vast reserves where, in a jumble, await those things that have not yet received any existence."[8] When we read colonial romances with an eye to the plants they grow, rather than the materials they extract, however, our understanding of the destructive work of their forced production changes from depletion to overgrowth. The novels worry not that the plant life will be used up but that it will take over the terms of its own management.

In this chapter I will consider cultivated plants, especially trees, in texts of several kinds: Olive Schreiner's *The Story of an African Farm* (1883), Rider Haggard's *Jess* (1887) and *Allan Quatermain* (1887), and Rudyard Kipling's story "In the Rukh" (1893), part of the *Jungle Book* Mowgli sequence. The disparate genres of these writings, which range from straightforward adventure to imperial melodrama to the complicated "literary platypus" that Schreiner's *plaasroman* has been called, as well as their distinct settings, which range from southern Africa to India's northern forest reserves, do not immediately seem to ally these fictions, yet they all share a crucial attention to the impositions of plant management on literary setting that directs their form.[9] It has generally seemed contradictory to consider settler colonial landscapes, like the *plaasroman* or farm novel, at the same time as adventure landscapes, even as the two shadow and overlap each other. Adventure novels are held to adhere to a nomadism characteristic of precivilized human existence, whereas settler novels seem to be concerned with a narrowly defined sense of belonging, ownership, association, and claim rooted in a particular connection to a very particular piece of land.[10] In this chapter I argue that, in the context of the British Empire, plants cut against the implacability of this divergence. In some ways this makes stories of colonial plant life similar to novels of imperial childhood abroad, as the temperings of the bildungsroman necessary to accommodate colonial progress also adjust expectations of temporality, as Jed Esty has shown.[11] Imperial children, however, grow up only once (and even then with difficulty, as the Mowgli of "In the Rukh" makes clear), while colonial cultivated plant life, at least potentially, grows again and again—especially in the case of "alien" introductions run "wild" into the landscape.

In previous chapters I have suggested that experimental novel genres found settings populated according to their narrative needs—detective novels gained the descriptive specificity of setting necessary to accommodate both clues and red herrings, while gothic novels found organic life supported only, or especially, in locations that emphasized the artificiality of that natural existence. Colonial fictions, rather than abandoning the idea of cultivation, anchor their stories to its growths, even as they distinguish between the possible territorial claims and administrations of British peoples from the plants they introduce and adopt from that colonial territory. To take one familiar example, Allan Quatermain prepares for his diamond-hunting mission at the start of *King Solomon's Mines* by visiting Cape Town's "botanical gardens, which seem to me likely to confer a great benefit on the country, and the new House of Parliament, which I expect will do nothing of the sort."[12] Cultivated plant life thus anchors a narrative of wild adventure to its prospective future of planned cultivation, the civilizing process that is adventure's necessary flip side, while narratives of domestication always grapple with the implicit possibility that cultivated plants may hybridize and pursue their own ends, like the acclimatized South American prickly pear and Australian eucalyptus that become signifiers of southern African farm life for Schreiner and Haggard. In both cases cultivated plants propose a temporal frame of environmental reproduction and renewal that, while organic, also intersects with human chronologies. The *rukh* that adult Mowgli manages in Kipling's *Jungle Book* story is a "far cry," as Kipling puts it, from the jungles he played in as a child.[13] Plants, in specific, identifiable form, make waymarkers on Victorian empire's road to both epistemological recognition and political control. Like the pegs that mark out the outline of the future fields in Allen's *Hilda Wade*, cultivated plants identified by adventurers and settlers alike connect these human forms to the broader organic landscape. The constant recognition that the plants named are themselves interlopers, invaders, or aliens, however, underlines what is uneasy about these bonds of connection—neither these trees nor these people are necessarily meant to be in this place, even if their methods of appropriating the land register rather differently in the specific colonial locations that I consider here.

To follow how this works I want to return not to the "immemorial oaks" or "time-honoured" ivy and lichen that "seemed" to surround Hilda, but to the "clumps of dusty and misshapen prickly pears" that actually did make the vegetation of her farm. Allen, whose ongoing natural history column "In Nature's Workshop" was running in tandem with *Hilda Wade* on the pages of the *Strand* during the months of 1899, had already demonstrated his familiarity with this plant in an 1890 article on "Prickly-Pears" for the *North American Review*. There, addressing US periodical readers from a vantage point in Algeria, he used a familiar rhetorical turn: "How strange that here on this arid African hillside an American cactus, the common prickly-pear plant, should grow . . . as readily as it grows in its native Mexican desert. It is merely, like myself, a naturalized alien on this side the Atlantic, to be sure; for the cactuses are all true American citizens by birth and training."[14] While Allen's upbringing through his teenage years in Canada and New Haven likely did not occasion much cactus camaraderie, his tendency here, as elsewhere in his writing on plants, to only semifacetiously consider his plant subject as a sovereign being is reflective of both his sharp social consciousness and his generally Darwinian sense of fellowship with surrounding organic life.

The presence of the prickly pear in Allen's fiction gives the fictional plant a far more subdued agency than the tenacious specimen that was "easy enough to make . . . grow . . . the real difficulty . . . once it gets in, ever to get rid of it."[15] This dogged companionship has been confirmed and built upon by recent environmental histories of the plant's spread: "Few plants, other than domestic crops, have tracked the European diaspora as closely as the more than 120 species of platyopuntias or 'prickly pears,'" explains Lance Van Sittert.[16] In both Australia and southern Africa, the prickly pear was initially deemed helpful for animal fodder and as a kind of living fence—alternatives to the pegs that trouble Hubert with their lack of enclosed substance—but soon moved beyond those uses and independently reproduced across the broader landscape throughout the latter half of the nineteenth century. The process of reclassifying the plant from aid to threat was neither "instantaneous nor unanimous" but did remain crucially tied to the expansion and self-definition of European settlement; as Jodi Frawley explains in an Australian context, the uneven but growing designation of prickly pear as not "benign immigrant plant" but "weed" was an assessment of "'out of place-ness'" that was "a locational and relative position for a plant to find itself in . . . dictated by its transnational, migratory motion in relation to white settlers."[17] Other "out-of-place" things, of course, could also be held to include those white settlers themselves, as well as the adventurers whose fictions staged fantastic and chronotypically compressed alternative tellings of the hybridizing process of settler colonial assimilation.

The prickly pear's movements as a kind of global adventurer, therefore, had to do not only with its biological success in a new ecosystem, but with cultural and intellectual networks, including not only the knowledge nodes of the colonial botanical gardens, but also the more informal human networks of farmers and travelers and the nonhuman technologies of agricultural machinery and scientific laboratories that identified the prickly pear as an "out-of-place" traveler. As Frawley concludes, "For some time during the nineteenth century the plant had complied with a specified field of social relations as domesticated plant. As the plant became *unruly* it started to come into view. Although settlers imagined a whole range of uses for the prickly pear, the plant had other plans."[18] Although they are not named by Frawley, novels as a fictional form play a key role in both identifying things, including plants, as in or out of place and, as I have been proposing throughout this book, giving narrative indication of the "other plans" of plants. In addition to producing the developing idea of "invasive alien species" as a discourse-narrative as well as quasi-biological designation, the 1880s and 1870s were also, through the range of novels addressing the reality and fantasy of life in the overseas British Empire, an era in which the plans of fictional foreign plants became increasingly a part of both narrative's character and setting.[19] In reading British fictions of southern Africa in the following sections of this chapter I would like to modulate Margaret Cohen's question—"How might it enrich a literary history of the modern novel to undertake an archaeology of adventure fiction from the vantage point of freedom of movement?"—from the point of view of the prickly pear and other assimilated and managed colonial species. By doing this, I suggest that the freedoms of movements granted to themselves by the European diaspora's vegetable fellow travelers direct novel fictions to the same revisions of global space and character that Cohen allows human adventurers.[20]

This is, of course, not often a pleasant endeavor. No shortage of scholarship exists addressing the landscape of colonial fiction and nonfiction as a setting to be critically interrogated for its suppressions and reinscriptions of power and its violent controls on movement by any but a particular kind of adventurer. As influentially read in Anne McClintock's *Imperial Leather,* the African mountains and plains which make the setting for Haggard's novels of adventure featuring Allan Quatermain both produce the substance of European wealth, whether diamonds or gold, and obscure the violence of that wealth's acquisition.[21] Mary Louise Pratt's *Imperial Eyes* demonstrated the ways that African and South American travel narratives and other kinds of nonfiction prose evacuated the specificity of the indigenous landscape via the operations of the European's commanding, masterly gaze.[22] From the great "Anglo-explosion" settler diaspora that transformed the nineteenth century, described in James Belich's *Replenishing the Earth,* reckonings of the environmental revolutions brought by settlers to the ecologies of Australia, New Zealand, and Southern Africa are beginning to appear in studies of settler fiction.[23] These postcolonial critiques of colonial genres have allowed crucial liberations of analysis that have helpfully and necessarily transformed the field of inquiry; they have also allowed us to see the ways a breadth of generic assessment can come at the expense of setting's localism. Philip Steer points out that the fin-de-siècle romance gives us "plots of exploration, encounter, and enrichment"—or what Franco Morretti influentially explained as the adventure novel's schema of "penetrate, seize, leave (and if needed, destroy)"[24]—especially, if not exclusively, when we judge the entire adventure genre through the geography of Haggard's African narratives, as opposed to, for example, the fluid, borderless, and unstable nature of Robert Louis Stevenson's Pacific "romances of uneven development."[25]

Laura Chrisman, in also calling for further attention to the particularity of literary geographies, notes the contrast between Joseph Conrad's fantasy colony in *Heart of Darkness* (1899) and Olive Schreiner's more precisely situated, and far lesser-known, critique of colonialism *Trooper Peter Halket of Mashonaland* (1897).[26] Conrad's novella, appearing in the pages of *Blackwood's* magazine in overlapping months of 1899 with Allen's *Hilda Wade,* certainly rejects even Allen's level of biogeographical precision. Marlow, narrating his journey along the Congo River, gives a primeval and terrifying, but deeply undifferentiated, environmental vision of that journey, describing the river's "great wall of vegetation, an exuberant and entangled mass of trunks, branches, leaves, boughs, festoons . . . like a rioting invasion of soundless life, a rolling wave of plants, piled up, crested, ready to topple over the creek, to sweep every little man of us out of his little existence."[27] Conrad revised the desired commodity in the Congo from the then-ascendant milky sap of the rubber tree to the already exhausted material of ivory, presumably because, as Jeffrey McCarthy begins to suggest, it would be much stranger for that novel's ur-colonizer Kurtz to gradually turn into a rubber tree than the polished ivory he seems, for Marlow, to metonymically become.[28] Against the lush but nonspecific background of the Congo's vegetation, the ivory's metaleptic (if anachronistic) organicism grows all the more powerful.

The disavowal of a renewable and manageable plant life required for either the rootings of economic botany or the circulations of the global plant trade becomes a necessity of Conrad's fictional world, in which vegetation can be recognized as alive without concurrently acknowledging that vegetation's subjecthood or the constraining conditions of its particular form.

Conrad's evacuation of botanical specificity seems all the more indistinct when we return to the story of the prickly pear, which makes a significant early appearance in Olive Schreiner's *The Story of an African Farm* (1883). This novel, first published under her pseudonym of Ralph Iron, has for some time been considered a particularly puzzling novel in structure and intent. This perplexity has been prompted in part by the multiple plots—the novel follows, unevenly, the three children Em, Waldo, and Lyndall to partial adulthood and, in the case of Lyndall and Waldo, early death, while employing multiple narrative voices, temporalities, and perspectives to do so—and in part by the import of its location, which a contemporary review of its second edition deemed the novel's "incongruous setting of South African settler life."[29] Schreiner's own complex attitude toward colonial expansion, as well as her lack of interest in the smooth closures of traditional realist form, produces a text strongly challenging to totalizing interpretation of any kind, including postcolonial recuperation.[30] Jed Esty has recently taken up the novel's temporal incongruities, which he considers challenges to both the idea of personal development in classic bildungsroman as well as the progressive amelioration implicit in the premise of colonial expansion. Neither of these challenges are for Esty expressed particularly through the novel's landscape, which he finds primarily notable as empty, futureless, merciless contrast to the comparatively rewarding prospects of a protagonist in a mid-century bildungsroman of Dickens or Brontë.[31] By contrast, other readings of Schreiner have radically prioritized the environment of South African karoo as a "uniquely female pastoral," with which the dissolution of both Lyndall and Waldo's bodies into the landscape is "a reunion with the natural world, a co-mingling which joins rather than a domination which separates."[32] As a supplement to both of these general readings of *African Farm*'s setting, I want to propose the prickly pear as an individuated botanical reference point for Schreiner's efforts to trouble the course of human individual growth and spiritual development.

Indeed, the prickly pear appears in the first lines of the novel, which describe "a small solitary 'kopje'" (or "hill," the glossing of the "Dutch and colonial" words in the novel another linguistic marker of the fictional setting's distinction), atop of which "a clump of prickly-pears lifted their thorny arms, and reflected, as from mirrors, the moonlight on their broad fleshy leaves."[33] Only after acknowledging these plants do we proceed to the "homestead" at the kopje's foot and discover the childhood miseries of Waldo, Lyndall, and Em as they suffer under both the tyrannical hand of Bonaparte Blevins and, especially in Waldo's case, crises of spiritual growth.[34] One of the novel's many divisions is to prioritize, in its first half, Waldo's singular struggle to choose a moral and ethical life founded outside of traditional Christian structure, before shifting its attentions in its second half to Lyndall's better-known efforts to subvert patriarchal and colonial controls in the making of her life as a kind of New Woman. The early deaths of both characters marks, for Esty, a touchstone of the bildungsroman abroad: unnaturally elongated youth terminated by abrupt death marks a world unreceptive to planned and progressive futures. The insinuations of the prickly pear, deemed a "baleful plant" and "Mexican marauder" in nonfiction of the era in which *African Farm* was written, posit an alternative organic temporality: "It propagates and spreads itself with alarming readiness . . . once it attains a stronghold, it is well-nigh impossible of extermination," writes one guide to the country.[35] Imagining the farm in relation to the prickly pears, rather than the prickly pears in relation to the farm, is one token of Schreiner's comparative environmental modernity amid a white settler discourse now tending to relegate the cactus's benefits only to ostriches, the Dutch, "natives" and baboons.[36]

After this initial introduction, the prickly pear notably soon returns in a scene set vaguely in Waldo's childhood years, as he sits alone and cries on the hill outside the farm, something he "often did" in order to preserve the fact that "none knew his great sorrow, and none knew his grief but he himself, and he buried them deep in his heart."[37] Perched atop the kopje, "he turned up the brim of his great hat, and looked at the moon, but most at the leaves of the prickly pear that grew just before him. They glinted, and glinted, and glinted, just like his own heart—cold, so hard, and very wicked. His physical heart had pain also; it seemed full of little bits of glass that hurt."[38] Schreiner shifts the reader's field of perception down from the skies to the close intimacy of Waldo's own visual recognitions, but does not allow such intimacy for long. The allegiance between Waldo's heart, in its abstract or material figuration, and the leaves of the prickly pear, must be revisited more impersonally. Schreiner continues:

> With his swollen eyes he sat there on a flat stone at the very top of the "kopje"; and the tree, with every one of its wicked leaves, blinked, and blinked, and blinked at him. Presently he began to cry again, and then stopped his crying to look at it. He was quiet for a long while, then he knelt slowly and bent forward.... "I hate God!" he said. The wind took the words and ran away with them, among the stones, and through the leaves of the prickly pear. He thought it died away half down the "kopje." He had told it now.[39]

Her description both proposes a more removed view within which the reader can reconcile Waldo, tree, hill, and wind but also resists the possibility of such an abstract remove. The reflecting of the moonlight accomplished by the prickly pears of the novel's opening for the benefit of no particular human are here appropriated by Waldo to absorb his own self-conceived wickedness. Thus, what we might suppose the neutral relations of plant and landscape are made eerie and morally inflected, not only by the comparatively nonnutritive moonlight, but also by Waldo's misprised vision, which is bent on making the plant life a receptacle of his confession. Yet this secret of "hating God," carried by Waldo for over a year, dissipates upon release according to an environmental time frame Waldo cannot (yet) fathom.

Whether the landscape ever gains an interest in the secrets Waldo tells it, or whether Waldo fully understands the relevance of such confessions, is impossible to particularly determine; Waldo's later life does, however, significantly realign him in sympathetic connection to other introduced species—notably oxen and chickens—engaged in their own struggles with the landscape. The prickly pear returns one final time in the novel, at the start of the long chapter 11, "An Unfinished Letter." This section begins with Waldo's return to Em and the farm after a year and a half's absence, diverges into the long fragment of a letter Waldo is continually writing to Lyndall which also serves as a transcript of his efforts to defend the lives of animals and his own spiritual life against individual and social acts of cruelty, and then concludes with Em's revelation that the confessions of the letter are needless, since Lyndall is already dead. Before the chapter goes into complex emotional registers of that revelation, however, its initial setting once again establishes the prickly pear outside and above the farm: "It was a wild night. The prickly-pear tree, stiff and upright as it held its arms, felt the wind's might, and knocked its flat leaves heavily together, till great branches broke off."[40] The wind's return to the prickly pear, unlike the reflected light of the moon, is harshly transformative, if less devastating than the damage wrought by the storm to the human-made buildings of the farm. But it is also, by the chapter's end, exhaustible; as Em attempts to break the bad news gently, Schreiner notes that "the wind, which had spent its fury, moaned round and round the house, most like a tired child weary with crying."[41] This return to the players of the opening scene also reverses their roles: where once Waldo confessed to the wind, now the wind is become an earlier version of Waldo, the crying child. Remaining aloof, but persistently present, the damaged prickly pear stands aside, alone of organic beings "impossible of extermination."

One admirer of Schreiner's evocation of the southern African landscape was Henry Rider Haggard, a novelist equally familiar through personal experience with the mixed cultivations of southern Africa and the many adventures possible therein. In "About Fiction," his enthusiastic 1887 defense of "King Romance," he praises Schreiner's book as one of only two novels "which deal in any way with every day contemporary life" that have excited his interest in the past five years; this is largely because the novel is, distinct from "the ordinary run of manufactured books," "written from within," and owing its "chief interest to a certain atmosphere of spiritual intensity which could not in all probability be even approximately reproduced."[42] This praise was twisted into one critical jab among many in John William Watson's anonymous and vigorous attack on Haggard's writing, "The Fall of Fiction" (1888), which not only took issue with novels of romance generally and Haggard's productions specifically, but also dismissed Haggard's early-1880s career-making quartet of African novels as each the product of plagiarism. *Jess* (1887), the Haggard novel supposedly cribbed from Schreiner's *African Farm,* is now the least read of the group, which Haggard frequently boasted of composing in a single two-year span—the others are *King Solomon's Mines,* published in 1885; *She,* which appeared in serial in the *Graphic* in 1886 while *Jess* ran in the *Cornhill;* and *Allan Quatermain,* written concurrently with *Jess* and also published in 1887. The cause of *Jess*'s neglect is not mysterious: it, unlike the other three novels, is not exactly a novel of adventure (despite its ironically titled first chapter, "John Has an Adventure") and stays mostly in the settled territory of the Transvaal familiar to Haggard as himself a former colonial farmer.

Yet the novels have in common with each and with the rest of Haggard's prose a deep interest in the characteristics of the organic environment. Among Andrew Lang's many rebuttals to Watson's attacks is the absence, in Watson's assessment of *Jess*, of that novel's "excellence in the description of landscape, which (I have heard) is considerable."[43] (Lang, a friend and collaborator of Haggard's as well as author of fantasy and fairy tales, was too much of a "sensitive plant" to actually read the novel, according to Haggard's memoir.)[44] *Colonel Quaritch*, his novel of chrysanthemum appreciation published the following year, continued this attention to the details of the organic landscape, as was seen in the previous chapter, and, like *Jess*, also shares a central female character whose intermittent melancholy evokes a milder version of *African Farm's* despairing Lyndall. Whether these affinities are truly outright borrowings of Schreiner's prose, or merely resonances unsurprising in two authors closely familiar with the land and the people of southern Africa, is perhaps less interesting than the chance these novels provide to thematize the circulations of plant life against a global background and within a landscape of heightened "spiritual intensity."

As these framings suggest, *Jess* is a deeply personal novel whose settings represent scenes from Haggard's early life as a newlywed ostrich farmer in Natal. But it is also a novel that follows a more global and circulatory spatial logic, away from England and, ultimately, back again, all the while insisting on the intertwined nature of the foreign and the domestic. It is, too, an attempt to defy descriptions of Haggard "as 'a mere writer of romances and boys' books,'" as well as "a living record of our shame in South Africa" and "a bit of history put into tangible and human shape."[45] Neil Hultgren has well explained the ways that *Jess*, though often taken as an attempt at realism, in fact reflects Haggard's interest in the mid-1880s in "both opposing and rethinking the premises of realism."[46] As Hultgren elaborates, *Jess*, with its often preposterous plot twists and serendipitous narrative conclusion, joins with other end-of-the century imperial melodramas in playing out its dramatic plot within the context of British military conflict abroad. The conflict depicted in it, the defeat of the British in the 1880–81 Transvaal War and the subsequent reclamation of English farm settlements by Dutch Boer settlers seeking to establish their own republic, takes shape alongside the novel's central love triangle. This romance finds new arrival Captain John Niel drawn to both Bessie and Jess, the daughters of the older English farmer Silas Croft. Niel's work on Croft's farm Mooifontein is aided by, among others, the Khoekhoe servant Jantjé and harassed by, especially, a neighboring suitor of Bessie's, the half-English, half-Boer Frank Muller—a man whose personal cruelties suggest and stand in for what Haggard considered to be the wider atrocities of the Boers in general. The twists and turns of the plot that follow Bessie's rejection of Muller and Muller's instigation of Boer rebellion, as Hultgren puts it, allow "melodrama's providential plotting to imagine a victory for British domesticity amidst the military losses of the Transvaal War."[47] The conclusion, which yields Mooifontein to the Boers and sends Croft, Bessie, and Niel back to England after Jess sacrifices herself to murder Muller, closes this circle neatly, installing John Niel "as a land agent to a large estate in Rutlandshire, which position he fills to this day, with credit to himself and such advantage to the property as can be expected nowadays."[48]

Though both Haggard and Schreiner clearly consider the lives of plants a necessary part of their portraits of rural life, they do not share a sense of the futures of these plant lives. *Jess*'s opening lines, in instructive contrast to those of *The Story of an African Farm,* enthusiastically perpetuate a sense of global horticultural contemporaneity evident even to the inexperienced Niel. Haggard begins: "The day had been very hot even for the Transvaal. . . . Even the succulent blue lilies—a variety of the agapanthus which is so familiar to us in English greenhouses—hung their long trumpet-shaped flowers and looked oppressed and miserable, beneath the burning breath of the hot wind which had been blowing for hours like the draught of a volcano."[49] Here we can recall Haggard's insistence in *A Gardener's Year* that orchids were better grown in English greenhouses where they could gain human appreciation rather than languishing unseen in Central American forests. Niel's sympathy with the "oppressed and miserable" blue lilies, mediated by human perception, is also emphatically made possible only by the priorities of that human-centered frame. The ostrich attack that immediately follows puts Niel off from further botanical meditations for a few chapters, but Haggard's recourse here to the second person plural of "us" tellingly locates the reader at some distance from the farm life about to be depicted. Niel, a grizzled veteran coming from Mauritius via Durban, is a close character analogue to Colonel Quaritch, down to his small bequest from an aunt who, in Niel's case, finances his Transvaal investments. The reader is similarly, it seems, a close companion to the other characters of *Colonel Quaritch* and their English greenhouse enjoyments, given expected agapanthus familiarities. This is in keeping with Lang's assessment of Haggard—"he does not see the world through books, and he writes like a sportsman of genius"—but it is also just one of many indications that Haggard cannot understand character without thinking about organic cultivation, nor can he imagine characters that do not think likewise.[50] In my attention to Haggard's use of specific plant life, I follow John Miller's larger call to recontextualize Haggard's environmentalism more complexly across his nonfiction agricultural writings from England and his adventure fiction from Africa by taking into account his recognition of the imbrications of global capital in the conservations his novels advocated for.[51]

John Niel's initial attraction to Jess, developed abstractly in the opening chapters as Niel explores the landscape around the farm for sport, gains focus once he discovers Jess herself in this landscape, apparently sketching at the bottom of a "vast gulf" filled with "thousand upon thousands of white arum lilies, 'pig lilies' they call them there, just now in full bloom."[52] His approach to Jess, who as we later learn is actually asleep and dreaming her own romance of "this kloof and you," is briefly obscured by further horticultural intervention when, in the descent down the gulf, "she was hidden by a bush that grows by the banks of the streams in South Africa in low-lying land, and which at certain seasons of the year is literally covered with masses of the most gorgeous scarlet bloom."[53] The discontinuities apparent between a landscape description claimed in a permanently progressive present and the depiction of an individual woman whose life, later in the novel, will end in dramatic suicidal fashion in almost exactly this same hidden spot, are in part the effect of Haggard's rather overwhelmingly aggressive prose style. But it is also clearly part of what Haggard hopes to be his fictional project in this novel—a detailed inquiry into the roots of character prompting the specific individual actions that in turn became the collective community consequences of the Transvaal War, set against alternating collective and singular communion with plant and other organic lives both cultivated and wild.

Haggard's insistence on showing how imaginative conclusions are reached by plausible physical processes in his adventure fiction was a chief cause for complaint by his critics in that genre—"it is one of the ignominies of this hybrid species of invention ... [to be] jolt[ed] ... at every step from the naturalistic to the fantastic and back again," grouses his anonymous attacker Watson.[54] In a melodrama like *Jess*, however, referential movement between a categorical evocation of shrubbery blooming in certain seasons and the particular human body of Jess can be blurred more easily, as Jess herself is the first to point out. Her long interior contemplation, at the novel's midpoint, directly addresses the question of how self and setting may never be recognizably separate. "Was she merely a creature bred of the teeming earth, or had she an individuality beyond the earth?" Jess wonders, spurred by her general recognition of her own insignificance within the broader natural world. This is Haggard's sportsman's version of the fin-de-siècle's cosmic ennui given female voice: "But what did it matter? The sunshine would still flood the earth with gold, the water would ripple, and the butterflies hover: and there would be other women to sit and fold their hands and look at it all, and think the same identical thoughts, beyond which the human intelligence cannot travel."[55]

While the fate of her own individual life does, in the end, matter to Jess, and still more do the individual futures of other characters in the novel matter to them, the narrator of the novel is most interested in discovering how each of these individual women came to be individuated at all—a process he understands as not entirely natural, but instead beholden to the controls of the historical moment. In echo of John Stuart Mill's claim in *On Liberty* (1859) that "human nature is not a machine to be built after a model, and set to do exactly the work prescribed for it, but a tree, which requires to grow and develop itself on all sides," Haggard adds a further cultivated twist.[56] Distinguishing the development of different kinds of men as the difference between "the growth of a tree on a plain and a tree in the forest," the narrator continues: "Thus is it with us all. Left to ourselves, or surrounded only by the scrub of humanity, we become outwardly that which the spirit within would fashion us to, but, placed among our fellows, shackled by custom, restrained by law, pruned and bent by the force of public opinion, we grow as like one to another as the fruit bushes on a garden wall."[57] That this is opined in the context of a discussion of the novel's villain, Frank Muller, that sources the origins of that character's evil in an excessive freedom of development, blunts the criticism that we have learned from Mill of public opinion's pruning and bending. If it would be better to be wild and good, it is still preferable to be cultivated and constrained than wild and bad.

The operations of the narrator's figurative language here, importantly, are not divorced from the narrative incident of the novel. We have encountered both fruit bushes and garden walls within the diegesis and they have had some bearing on the development of plot and character. Even more significant has been the use to which the novel has put a different set of trees, the "long avenue" of "blue gums," or *eucalyptus globulus,* the most common variety of eucalyptus in southern Africa at the time, that line the entrance to Mooifontein.

> This avenue was old Silas Croft's particular pride, for although it had only been planted for about twenty years, the trees, which in the divine climate and virgin soil of the Transvaal grow at the most extraordinary rate, were for the most part very lofty, and as thick in the stem as English oaks of a hundred and fifty years' standing. The avenue was not overwide, and the trees were planted quite close one to another, with the result that their brown, pillar-like stems shot up for many feet without a branch, whilst high overhead the boughs crossed and intermingled in such a way as to form a leafy tunnel, through which one looked at the landscape beyond as one does through a telescope.[58]

While we understand Mooifontein has farmed plantations of both eucalyptus and acacia (or, as it was termed, "wattle"), this avenue has a cultural, rather than economic, significance for the farm. It forms a visual technology by which human perception of the landscape is both enhanced and narrowed, but it also represents a specifically British perception of the land, that, while appreciative, is also a misreading. Like a telescope, the blue gums encourage a narrowed focus that tragically overlooks a threatening peripheral context. This alliance of Britishness with eucalyptus is made more clear with the repeated emphasis on Silas Croft's displays of patriotism, flying an "exceedingly large Union Jack" from a flagstaff "formed of a very tall young blue gum, in such a position that it could be seen for miles around."[59]

It is the boldness of this display, enabled by the tallness of the transplanted eucalyptus, that proves Silas's undoing. "We are going there, and we are going to take the place: and we are going to try Uncle Silas by court-martial for flying an English flag, and if he is found guilty we are going to shoot him," declares Muller; and not only do those specific humiliations come true, but the Boer's reversal of the flag to hang upside down and half-mast shows a larger defeat: "The English government has surrendered . . . the country is given up," Muller announces, as a wounded Silas lies bleeding at flagpole's foot.[60] While Silas's efforts to ally the eucalyptus with Britain ultimately fail, the gum trees succeed in remaking the landscape on their own terms of signification; by 1897, gum trees "have become a conspicuous feature in the landscape of the veldt plateau . . . all over Matabililand and Mashonaland one discovers in the distance the site of a farmsteading or a store by the waving tops of the gum-trees," a contemporary travelogue explains.[61]

The work of the gum trees in *Jess* reflects their complex environmental status. The distribution of Australian eucalypts to South Africa (not, at the time, a country, but from the point of view of the eucalyptus a collective of distinct ecosystems linked through scientific and economic networks) was not a matter of chance or of runaway growth but rather a carefully directed and human-sponsored effort.[62] The planting of non-native trees was a priority for nineteenth-century settlers in the Cape Colonies, as it had been for explorers and traders anchoring in Cape Town in previous eras. In addition to desiring the economic benefits of timber and pulp necessary to fuel the industries of imperial expansion, nineteenth-century forestry officials sought to transform an arid landscape according to the now-outdated desiccationist theories that believed forested terrain less vulnerable to drought and erosion.[63] The introduction of foreign plants and trees would also seem to make sense for colonial landscape whose earlier missionaries had sought to alter its environment to better match the pastoral, Christian contours of the England they had left behind.[64] But the introduction of the eucalyptus tree in particular is more of a puzzle, given its antipodean origins and lack of connection to the forested English landscape that oaks and other trees readily provided. Rune Flikke has persuasively argued that, in addition to the economic and environmental interventions, we must also consider the planting of eucalyptus in late nineteenth-century King William's Town and other parts of the Cape Colony "as a public health initiative that viewed health as directly determined by air quality."[65] This clarification allows us not only to focus on the revisions the trees made to the landscape as visual landmarks or sites of economic productivity, but also as olfactory revisionings within a wider sensory world defined not only by sight and touch but also by smell. Haggard's novel does not make narrative affordance for smell, but in the long and narratively significant scene (spread over several chapters) set amid this avenue of gum trees after its first introduction as "Silas Croft's particular pride," the transitory and relayed narrating identities do strongly suggest a mutual perception linked to the trees that is not exclusively visual nor aural. Flikke suggests that the supposed healthy odor of the eucalyptus is a learned reaction, situated for British settlers very precisely in particular relations of colony and race against the miasmas and contagions of the native people and their dwellings. So too do the various narrators of the eucalyptus avenue deploy different forms of narrative voice, supplemented heavily by the omniscient narrator's own intrusions, to propose a quasi-supernatural effect created by the atmosphere of these transplanted trees. Haggard's muscular experiments with a roving free indirect discourse in this text prepare the reader for an environment in which every perspective can be taken into account—baboons and eucalyptus as well as English, Boers, and Khoekhoe.

The scene begins with John and Bessie walking down the avenue to a tree plantation where John is both "anxious to inspect some recently planted wattles" and, awkwardly, to propose to Bessie, a request she eagerly accepts despite her sense that he will be ashamed of her and her "colonial ways."[66] "Meanwhile," Frank Muller "was to be seen leisurely advancing towards the blue gum avenue" while, at the other end, "Jantjé was lurking about the stems of the trees in the peculiar fashion that is characteristic of the Hottentot, and which doubtless is bred into him after tens of centuries of tracking animals and hiding from foes."[67] Eager to avoid the violent Muller, Jantjé slips into the grass growing between the eucalyptus trees and waits: "Nobody would have guessed that that tuft of grass hid a human being; not even a Boer would have guessed it."[68] As he travels up the avenue, Muller's lengthy soliloquy shifts startlingly from his resolution to "marry [Bessie] by fair means or foul" to his revolutionary intentions to establish a "united Dutch South Africa and Frank Muller to rule it!"[69] The scene then moves indoors to follow an argument between Silas and Frank over the fate of both Bessie and the English in general, but we understand that both Jantjé and Bessie remain outside, the former concealed and the latter framed by the overarching trees. Frank Muller's angry departure from the farm brings him straight along the avenue to Bessie again, where his "agony of passion" leads to an implied attempted rape put off only by "an unexpected diversion, of which the hidden Jantjé was the cause . . . a ventriloquistic power which was not uncommon among natives."[70]

> Suddenly the silence was broken by a frightful and prolonged wail that seemed to shape itself into the word "Frank," and to proceed from the air just above the struggling Bessie's head. The effect produced upon Muller was something wonderful.

"Allemachter!" he cried, looking up, "it is my mother's voice!" .... "*Frank! Frank! Frank!*" wailed and howled the voice overhead, now on this side, now on that, till at last Muller, thoroughly mystified and feeling his superstitious fears rising apace as the moaning sound flitted about beneath the dark arch of the gumtrees, made a rush for his horse.[71]

Bessie, meanwhile, has taken advantage of the diversion to escape, missing the final terrifying prediction that Frank will "die in blood." This prophesy that does in fact later come true at the hands of Jess, wielding Jantjé's knife. Jantjé, though in this scene "shaking . . . with an inward joy" at his success in terrifying Muller, remembers the language of the curse for a dark reason: it was originally uttered by Muller's mother after discovering Muller's wanton murder of Jantjé's family after an (unfounded) allegation of oxen theft.

It is evident that the eucalyptus tree cover is as central as any human character to this scene's complex and social cultural history, which effectively presents the gendered and nationalist themes of the entire novel through the dramatic performance on the enclosed stage of the avenue. Aware of Haggard's profoundly racist worldview, we can understand his positioning of the Khoekhoe Jantjé as a broker between the human and plant worlds. This is especially apparent in Jantjé's ability to disappear into the landscape that is employed again at the novel's conclusion as, after Frank's murder, he is "gone from the ken of the white man far into the heart of Central Africa."[72] But Jantjé's simulacra of Muller's mother's voice, dispersed and recirculated by the dark arch of the trees themselves is a more complex achievement—especially given, of course, that these trees bear their nonindigeneity with pride. A large part of this complexity comes from the foregrounding of the trees themselves as operative agents cooperating with Jantjé to punish Frank as the chrysanthemum once seemed to shoot the villain in *Colonel Quaritch*. Thus, this revenge of the trees may seem obscure; no anthropomorphic operation of accusingly pointed branches singles out Muller as the bad actor. But the impossibility of saying for sure what relays the sound of a long-dead woman's voice to the ears of Muller seems to be the point. Whether supernaturally amplified, ventriloquized by Jantjé, or wafted with the eucalyptus trees' pungent fragrance, the effect for Muller is the same. Even as we are distressed by the racist dehumanization of Jantjé's subsumation among this group (reminding us of *Dorian Gray*'s gardener, lurking in the trees), we find evidence of a model that allows plant agency by not ruling it out.

There is one character not present in this central scene on the avenue, and that is Jess herself, already gone to Pretoria to clear the way for Bessie and John's engagement. Jess has established herself throughout the novel as a character particularly interested in the boundaries and terminations of selfhood, as well as the impossibility of ever, with the human mind at least, apprehending those bounds and limits. Linked strongly with the cycles of natural renewal at work in the kloof where John Niel once discovered her amid the lilies and where she will also die in his arms, Jess is out of place in the acclimatized avenue of the eucalyptus and its non-native cycles of regeneration. These restorations are neither the wild bloomings and deaths of the flowering plants in the kloof, nor the flag-raisings and lowerings of the English and the Boers, but the spreading eucalyptus's acculturated expansions, which both signal the sites of European colonial domesticities but also expand beyond and over their acquisitive claims—literally, as we saw in the case of the stands of gum trees marking out the sites of settler farmsteads for distant viewers. The global histories of travelers like the prickly pear, the eucalyptus, and the acacia record not only economic gains, but also the generative plant persistence that continues even when English settlers cannot.[73] It is a continuation that operates also across Haggard's own personal history. Writing in his memoir, *The Days of My Life*, of the era lightly fictionalized into *Jess*'s story, Haggard recalls the house he lived in with his then-wife and the cultivated setting of that domestic fantasy: "I believe that [our cottage] still stands in Pretoria. At any rate an illustration of it was published in the issue of *South Africa*. . . . The blue gums in the picture are undoubtedly those we planted; they are very big trees now, I am told."[74]

Beyond the autobiographical interest of the persistence of his own plantings, Haggard theorizes a perpetuation of human life by the lives of plants that is the ultimate recompense for the preservations human capital and cultivation have initially performed. Thinking of the trees on his Norfolk estate in *A Gardener's Year*, he writes: "The Oaks, Beeches, Limes, Walnuts, Acacias, and, perhaps, some of the Elms of certain sorts, should stand another three or four hundred years, unless someone hacks them down. It is curious, and rather melancholy, to look forward into the dim and unimaginable future, and wonder what their fate will be when one is no longer present in the flesh to protect them;

when that flesh itself, perhaps, has been transformed into hard wood and rising sap and waving foliage."⁷⁵ The fantasy of tree-becoming entices Haggard, but also puts him off enough to reduce his future self to mere "flesh," rather than more particular named form. Robert Mitchell, analyzing the "Englishness" of Wordsworth's yew tree at Morton Val, acknowledges the difficulty of finding that "vague and illusive referent" in a living tree and explains that such a representation requires "a queer, vital middle term that establishes a sense that the slow life of the tree is somehow like the liminal life of 'peoples' (that is, of human groupings that extend far beyond one's immediate relatives)."⁷⁶ Haggard's invocation of future human flesh transformed into tree life cannot be imagined as thoroughly universal, but it does offer a broader global encircling of human-plant fellowship than we might otherwise assume. Haggard valorizes Englishness, that is, but he also values the lives of trees and plants that make their own transcultural presence known. This is evident not only in his more realistic fictions, but also in the plots and settings of his fantasy stories.

For if *Jess* is a domestic melodrama that contains significant portions of adventure, the near-simultaneously composed *Allan Quatermain* is an adventure that devotes a surprising amount of time to domestic cultivation. The novel, which though only the second written and published of the Quatermain fictions (following the character's memorable introduction in *King Solomon's Mines*), is chronologically the last in the series, concerning as it does the death of both Quatermain and his Zulu companion Umslopogaas in the lost white kingdom of Zu-Vendis. That kingdom, of which Allan observes "agriculture is the great business of the country, and is really well-understood and executed," connects with other lost race genre fictions to theorize cultivation in contained or even impossible places like the center of the earth.⁷⁷ Such lost race fictions also imagine, as Angela Poon has explained, an alternate England in its feudal form that restages and improves upon the original.⁷⁸ This modulates Bradley Deane's observation that "lost world stories mark their distrust of narratives of progress and civilization by imagining settings in which time is largely impotent"; while Zu-Vendis's barbaric masculinity may be the psychic fantasy of the New Imperialism, the renewable cycle of its cultivation narrative connects the lost world to a recognizable progressive temporal frame.⁷⁹

The beginning of the novel, retrospectively narrated by Quatermain as he approaches his own death in Zu-Vendis, returns us temporarily to England, and a younger Quatermain, distraught at the recent death of his son, pacing up and down the "oak-panelled vestibule," complete with one hundred mounted trophies, of his estate in Yorkshire.[80] His lengthy meditation on the distinction without difference of human savagery and civilization that follows supports Quatermain's basic assertions that all forms of culture, whether social or agricultural, are merely a distancing from a more universal organic connection. "I longed once more to throw myself into the arms of Nature," Quatermain resolves, "not the Nature which you know, the Nature that waves in well-kept woods and smiles out in corn-fields, but Nature as she was in the age when creation was complete, still undefiled by any sinks of struggling, sweltering humanity."[81] That this is an expected goal for an adventure novel does not detract from the fact that, especially for Haggard, it is a rarely achieved one—neither the diamonds of *King Solomon's Mines* nor the caves of *She*'s lost city of Kôr remain free from humanity's struggles. Haggard's fascination with the effects of cultivation on British identity, and, equally, on the consequences of contained cultivation within systems that fail, for whatever reason, to adapt to changing historical progress, makes the study of horticultural and agricultural practice particularly well-suited to his narrative needs. In the planting and plucking of a flower, or the harvesting of a field of corn, Haggard can find models for a cultured self-sufficiency that his human characters aim for, even as they always fall short.

As an example of this, before we encounter the vestiges of civilization with the Zu-Vendis, Haggard inserts a preliminary adventure for Quatermain that has particular interest for a study of cultivated plant life abroad. Quatermain and his companions Sir Henry Curtis, Captain Good, and the Zulu warrior Umslopogaas, in search of wilderness, are shocked to instead discover the Scottish missionary Mr. Mackenzie and his family in a remote but well-supplied compound: "A gentleman, a lady, and a little girl! . . . walking in a civilized fashion, through a civilized garden. . . . Hang me if this isn't the most curious thing we have seen yet," Good observes, looking through a spy glass as blind to broader context as *Jess*'s eucalyptus avenue.[82] This civilized garden, which encompasses all the missionary buildings and doubles as walled fortress self-sufficient for four months or more, meets with Quatermain's rapturous approval—"I have always loved a good garden"—as a fantasy space of acclimatized European plant life.[83] Especially to his liking are the two cultivated gardens maintained by Mrs. Mackenzie and her daughter: "What Mrs. Mackenzie called *her* domain—namely, the flower-garden, the beauty of which . . . is really beyond my power to describe. I do not think I ever saw such roses, gardenias, or camellias (all reared from seeds or cuttings sent from England); and there was also a patch given up to a collection of bulbous roots, mostly collected by Miss Flossie, Mr. Mackenzie's little daughter, from the surrounding country, some of which were surpassingly beautiful."[84] Lindy Stiebel has called this house "in microcosm a British paradise in Africa, a British protectorate hierarchally organized and feudally arranged" while skimming over the specifics of the plants actually under cultivation in this space.[85] Quatermain's delight in the cultivated English garden, and his even more "surpassing" interest in the collection of native "roots" grown by Flossie, bears further attention, however, especially since it is in the quest for another native plant, the bulb of the rare "Goya Lily," that compels the excitements of the book's first third. Haggard devotes several pages to Quatermain's very precise description of this plant—"I have never seen anything to equal this bloom in beauty or fragrance, and as I believe it is but little known, I take the liberty to describe it at length"—while also revealing that this description collapses together previously heard accounts from "central African explorers" astonished at the flower's loveliness and Quatermain's own future observations of the flower, "which I afterwards first saw under circumstances likely to impress its appearance fixedly in my mind."[86] Unlike the floral narratives of my first chapter, in which local blooms intervened to prompt narrative recollections in detective novels, here Haggard locates narrative as generatively bound up with the floral specimen from the start. Before the plot incidents that grant the lily human relevance occur, we are reminded that the lily has already had narrative significance, just as Quatermain's death is always both before and after the textual circulation of his exploits.

The reader's narrative interest in the flower begins when Flossie sets off with only "a couple of boys" to "get Mr. Q— a bloom of the lily he wants . . . I am determined to get the lily if I have to go twenty miles for it," she writes.[87] The fears of the adults upon reading this note are amplified when Flossie fails to return by nightfall, then driven to fever pitch by the delivery of the severed head of one of the "boys" over the enclosing walls. Bargaining with the Masai kidnappers goes poorly, and the chief threatens the missionary group that "'if thy answer is late thy little white bud will never grow into a flower, that is all, for I shall cut it with this,' and he touched the spear."[88] But the nonmetaphoric flower is already safe, for within the flower-collecting basket returned to the Mackenzies as proof of life, the adventurers discover both "a most lovely specimen of both bulb and flower of the Goya lily" and a second note from Flossie averring her intention to shoot herself at dawn if no help has arrived, along with a written reminder of the girl's horticultural devotion even in the face of death—"Scrawled across the outside of [the basket] was, 'Love to Mr. Quatermain. They are going to take up the basket, so he will get the lily.'"[89]

Flossie's intrepid spirit, as well as the "double-barrelled, nickel-plated Derringer" she keeps in the bodice of her dress, foreshadow the New Girl adventures by Bessie Marchant and others that emerged in the first decades of the twentieth century, when the titular *Di the Dauntless* (1926) helped her father "graft English ways on Moroccan natives."[90] The threats to Flossie's virginity likewise continue a long succession of previous captivity narratives in which white women faced death and sexual violation at the hands of natives. But typically for Haggard's interest in the cultivations of the natural world, he, more than most writers, also insists on the intervention of the botanical specimen as a synecdoche for Flossie that brings together her virginity, whiteness, and African birth to imagine, in partial, truncated form, a feral Englishness in the African landscape as a model for settler assimilation.

In this way Flossie's character echoes, more than any other's, Quatermain's own feelings about his self-imposed exile from England, even if the girl's words demonstrate Haggard's standard sense of feminine self-regard. Rejecting a possible return "home," Flossie explains: "'Why, I should hate to be buried in a crowd of white girls all just like myself, so that nobody could tell the difference! Here,' she said, giving her head a little toss, 'I am *I*; and every native for miles round knows the "Water-lily"—for that is what they call me—and is ready to do what I want, but in the books that I have read about little girls in England it is not like that.'"[91] The critique of girls' reading material skirts around the fact that, as Kate Flint reminds us, the adventure fiction of G. A. Henty and others were among the most-read books of this era by girls as well as boys.[92] Flossie's knowledge and cultivation of African plants demonstrates her superior acclimatization to the landscape, as opposed to her missionary parents' attempt to presume Englishness as a religious and environmental enclave: growing roses and preaching sermons behind their fortress walls. In her imperious, if childish, head-tossing, Flossie seems a mini-Ayesha, white tyrant of the just-published *She,* but the epithet of "Water-Lily" also proleptically connects Flossie to a different heroine in Haggard's writing, the eponymous Zulu heroine *Nada the Lily* (1892), as well as to his own daughter Lilias. As the previous chapter explored, girls who tend to garden flowers are often supplanted by the boys and men who own the estates that encompass those gardens, and Flossie's story (despite her head-tossing) does not end differently. What is interesting, however, is the degree to which Flossie herself accommodates her metonymic figuration as an African flower, and the ready awareness with which she understands narrative, femininity, and nation to be mutually productive conditions.

By the time the reader finally arrives at the battle to liberate Flossie, it does not surprise that the escape of Flossie comes as almost an afterthought from the slaughter that leaves the Masai dead and the Englishmen "red from head to foot" with their blood.[93] The threatened danger, however, prompts Mackenzie to give up his station, despite his pride in making the place "blossom like a rose in the wilderness," and return Flossie to England, subsuming her among the other white girls.[94] A small consolation is the £1000 check that Quatermain gives her father to deposit in an interest-bearing account in order to have the funds to buy "the best diamond necklace" for her wedding day. Quatermain's insistence on giving Flossie a future interest in diamonds, a commodity whose value, Quatermain is confident, will never diminish, largely thanks to his own actions in burying much of the world's diamond reserves during the events of *King Solomon's Mines,* secures her reproductive futurity by linking it to an artificially constrained resource. Unlike the plant life that Haggard and Quatermain have both admired and cultivated as exotic imports, diamonds cannot so easily find transculturated origins. Yet whether Flossie or the Goya lily are themselves happy with this turn of events we do not learn, as Quatermain and his party depart on their adventure to Zu-Vendis soon after. Equally, we never know if the previously resistant to cultivation lily ever grows in the abandoned missionary garden. The Masai threat has in some measure come true—no Water-Lily will bloom from the little white bud in the African landscape—and while Haggard regrets the loss, he also clearly understands it to be inevitable. But if Flossie and the Goya lily do not return, both Ayesha and Allan can live on, revived again and again for further adult adventures through the sequential work of popular fiction. Invigorated by forms of cultivation that allow both endless perpetuation and constant new beginnings, the plant life in Haggard's novel informs a colonial setting that can always be retold again in England.

While Flossie's adventures, like those of other girls, must be carefully truncated, the cultivations of boys' adventure fictions link gender and environment with far less caution. A large proportion of boys' adventure novels published in both England and America at the end of the century can be understood as fantasies of present adventure yielding future economic agricultural returns. Examples include G. A. Henty's *The Young Colonists: A Tale of the Zulu and Boer Wars* (1885), whose titular protagonists travel to southern Africa meaning to establish a tree farm but accidently end up participating in the Boer War instead, or, earlier, Mayne Reid's boy heroes of *The Plant Hunters* (1858) and its sequels, which demanded readerly respect for the occupation of plant-hunting: "To his labours the whole civilized world is indebted—yourself among the rest. Yes, you owe him gratitude for many a bright joy. . . . By his agency England—cold cloudy England—has become a garden of flowers, more varied in species and brighter in bloom than those that blossomed in the famed valley of Cashmere."[95] This chapter concludes by moving from southern Africa to northern India and Rudyard Kipling's Mowgli, the adventurous boy protagonist of many of the *Jungle Book* stories who makes a complicated companion to Kim, the protagonist of Kipling's most famous work of boys' imperial adventure fiction. While Kim remains forever in boyhood, in a way that Sara Suleri linked to the frozen present of imperial time more generally, Mowgli does in fact reach fictional adulthood.[96] Or, more accurately, he begins in adulthood, as "In the Rukh," the short story which introduces the character of Mowgli as a grown-up ranger in the British Raj's Indian Forest Service (IFS), is the first written of what would become the *Jungle Book* stories. The story, however, continues to hold an uneasy status within that series, and the cultivations it depicts are equally distinct from others in the sequence.[97] The plant life in "In the Rukh," in marked contrast to that of the other *Jungle Book* stories, is definitively managed and cultivated, albeit within a much larger collective than the singular and individuated plant lives I have thus far taken up. We can read Mowgli himself as the representatively singular plant life, assimilating through European cultivation into the new space of the IFS-administered *rukh*.[98]

Composed in Vermont, "In the Rukh" first appeared in the story collection *Many Inventions* (1893) and did not appear in the initial printings of *The Jungle Book* (1894) or *The Second Jungle Book* (1895). When the story was republished in *McClure's Magazine* in June 1896 (its first appearance in a periodical), Kipling added an explanatory headnote. Seeking to reconcile the discrepancy, he indicates that "we may infer" that the events of "In the Rukh" take place "two or three years after [Mowgli] had finally broken away from his friends in the jungle" and acknowledges this story's setting to be "a far cry from Seeonee to a Northern Forest Reserve."[99] The declaration in "Tiger, Tiger," a story which concerns the young Mowgli's first encounter with human society, that Mowgli "was not always alone, because years afterwards he became a man and married. But that is a story for grown-ups" has also been used to separate "In the Rukh"'s bureaucracies from the prelapsarian fantasy of the other *Jungle Book* stories.[100]

Taking any environment of Kipling's India as pure fantasy is impossible for many reasons, not least of which that the jungle of the *Jungle Books* was, as Kipling well understood, an object of profound bureaucratic attention and management throughout the later nineteenth century. After the expanding demands of the railroad for timber made deforestation a more pressing concern, the Government of India established the Indian Forest Service in 1864. The decades of British rule in India that followed unquestionably saw profound changes in human-forest relationships, including British denials of long-held community rights to forest lands as well as significant loss of biodiversity on the subcontinent and human removals as effects of deforestation. Recent scholarship, however, has also attempted to nuance the role of IFS foresters in these degradations, pointing out their efforts to establish "participatory systems of forest management" as well as, more debatably, their spiritual appreciation of the natural forest world as a conceptual model that "encouraged the rise of proto-ecological thinking."[101] For environmental historians seeking evidence of nascent British colonial ecophilia, "In the Rukh" and its attention to "the romance of the forest" appears to be an example of literature that thoughtfully and respectfully engages with managed empire forestry in India.[102] Reading the story against the other texts in this chapter, which have placed adventure and settled domesticity as differentiated efforts of resource extraction both drawing upon forms of cultivation to modulate their withdrawals, we can see that "In the Rukh" also seeks to explain cultivation as a more complicated form of taming. Such dewildings are not commensurate with, but are indebted to, the formative tenets of Victorian environmentalism.[103] Though no single cultivated plant within this story is allowed to propose the terms of its own narration as in the examples in earlier chapters, Mowgli, as feral child assimilated into subaltern adulthood, himself stands in for the cultivated specimen and repossesses some of its power.

The long opening paragraphs of the story prepare the reader for what is to come: little plot and much setting. The story opens with a typically Kipling elliptical invocation of British bureaucracy: "Of the wheels of public service that turn under the Indian Government, there is none more important than the Department of Woods and Forests. The reboisement of all India is in its hands: or will be when Government has the money to spend."[104] What follows is worth quoting as some length as by far the most engaged fictional treatment of the operations of colonial forestry in Victorian fiction:

> Its servants wrestle with wandering sand-torrents and shifting dunes: wattling them at the sides, damming them in front, and pegging them down atop with coarse grass and unhappy pine after the rules of Nancy. They are responsible for all the timber in the State forests of the Himalayas, as well as for the denuded hillsides that the monsoons wash into dry gullies and aching ravines, each cut a mouth crying aloud what carelessness can do. They experiment with battalions of foreign trees, and coax the blue gum to take root and, perhaps, dry up the canal fever. In the plains the chief part of their duty is to see that the belt fire lines in the forest reserves are kept clean, so that when drouth comes and the cattle starve, they may throw the reserve open to the villager's herds and allow the man himself to gather sticks. They poll and lop for the stacked railway-fuel along the lines that burn no coal; they calculate the profit of their plantations to five points of decimals, they are the doctors and midwives of the huge teak forests of Upper Burma; the rubber of the Eastern Jungles, and the gall-nuts of the South: and they are always hampered by lack of funds.[105]

So far, with some significant interjections, the reader may follow along with a characterization of an imperial bureaucracy that is relatively familiar. Beginning with the impersonal "Department of Woods and Forests," next referred to as "it," and subsequently characterized by "its servants" and "they," the operations of Raj administration range across Indian geography while following a European vision to birth a productive colonial economy. "Nancy," otherwise understood to be the

Continental school of forestry where IFS employees were nominally expected to receive advanced theoretical training, directs these natural manipulations and revisions from afar. As we come to understand through sidelong reference, the interpenetrating work of Empire is everywhere here, especially in the "battalions of foreign trees" and already disproven expectations that "blue gum," or eucalyptus, can cure "canal fever," or malaria.[106] The collective cultivation that bureaucracy allows is briefly granted organization power, but nearly immediately, however, a more singular purpose emerges. Kipling continues:

> But since a Forest Officer's business takes him far from the beaten roads and the regular stations, he learns to grow wise in more than woodlore alone; to know the people and the polity of the jungle; meeting tiger, bear, leopard, wild-dog, and all the deer, not once or twice after days of beating, but again and again in the execution of his duty. He spends much time in saddle or under canvas—the friend of newly planted trees, the associate of uncouth rangers and hairy trackers—till the woods that show his care in turn set their mark upon him and he ceases to sing the naughty French songs he learned at Nancy, and grows silent with the silent things of the undergrowth.[107]

Now Nancy gives us naughty songs and the erotic human desires that confound and contest bureaucratic regulation; now the Forest Office "business" expands outward into directions that surpass the "regular stations" and becomes a deeply transactional site of exchange that is at once iterative, reciprocal, and totalizing. "Again and again," bonds of friendship, association, and care are developed extralinguistically, as nominal markers of the "execution of duty" but equally part of the Forest Officer's transformation into something not entirely human—an ecological kinship, as Kipling sees it, incommensurate with the necessary but "denuding" works of broader systems of IFS management. The "marking" of the Forest Officer by the woods that surround him, a faint reversal of the act of cultivation that allowed Lucy Snowe to mark the flowers in her Continental garden, also foreshadows the more permanent claims that trees will make on humans in the next chapter.

And now, having evacuated the possibility of human character, and subtly rebuked the reader for wanting to hear about the lusty singer of French songs rather than the silent hermit of the undergrowth, Kipling at last introduces what will pass for a character in this story.

> Gisborne of the Woods and Forests had spent four years in the service. At first he loved it without comprehension, because it led him into the open on horseback and gave him authority. Then he hated it furiously, and would have given a year's pay for one month of such society as India affords. That crisis over, the forests took him back again, and he was content to serve them, to deepen and widen his fire-lines, to watch the green mist of his new plantations against the older foliage, to dredge out the choked stream, and to follow and strengthen the last struggle of the forest where it broke down and died among the long pig-grass. On some still day that grass would be burned off, and a hundred beasts that had their homes there would rush out before the pale flames at high noon. Later, the forest would creep forward over the blackened ground in orderly lines of saplings, and Gisborne, watching, would be well pleased. His bungalow, a thatched white-walled cottage of two rooms, was set at one end of the great *rukh* and overlooking it. He made no pretence at keeping a garden, for the *rukh* swept up to his door, curled over in a thicket of bamboo, and he rode from his veranda into its heart without the need of any carriage drive.[108]

Even as Kipling throws the reader the narrative scrap of a personal surname, the rebuking of the reader's dependence on a reference frame of human character continues. Challenging those who might need a carriage drive to understand the story's transition from settled domesticity to wild remove, Kipling overlays the possessive pronoun with uncertainty. "His fire-lines," "his new plantations," and the pleasing "orderly lines of saplings" function as organic prostheses for Gisborne himself, growing and rooting his initially resistant British body into and over the choking pig-grass of the secondary cultivations. No epistemological or ontological divisions are necessary between the colonial veranda and the *rukh*'s heart.

The sweeping encroachments of the *rukh* also overwhelm the story's simple plot, which like other Kipling stories hinges on native betrayal and native loyalty as intermixed and deeply inevitable contingencies. It is the story of the attempted revenge by Gisborne's Muslim servant Abdul Gafur, whose thievery Mowgli discovers and whose daughter Mowgli woos and wins. Frequently overwriting the Gafur revenge plot, however, are the efforts by Gisborne and the German Muller to discover the true history of Mowgli's own growth and development. Though his name recalls the Victorian Indologist Max Muller, the Muller of "In the Rukh"—"the gigantic German who was the head of the Woods and Forests of all India, Head Ranger from Burma to Bombay"—seems much more likely to be a portrait of one of the three Germans who held the post of head forester in the British Raj for the first four decades of the IFS's existence.[109] These men—Dietrich Brandis, Wilhelm Schlich, and Berthold Ribbentrop—drew on European training as well as, in Brandis's case, previous experience in Burma, and, as David Arnold explains, deeply affected both the structure of the IFS through their institutions of new management practices and techniques of officer recruitment as well as, through their influential scientific publications, British knowledge of Indian woodland.[110] Kipling's Muller possesses a similarly transcendent power—"he was the chartered libertine of all the offices, for as a Forest Officer he had no equal," he writes—and shares with his real-world counterparts an interest in recruiting Indian workers to do the work of the IFS.[111] As Brandis wrote long after his 1881 retirement from the Service, "the larger the number of natives employed in responsible positions in the forest, the more forestry will cease to have the character of an exotic plant, or a foreign artificially fostered institution," matching Muller's sense that the work of forestry must be accomplished through personal cooperation, not posturing correspondence destined for the imperial archive: "I tell you der big brass-hat pizness does not make der trees grow."[112]

This sensitivity to ecological nativeness suggests one reason why Muller, more than Gisborne, initially better understands Mowgli's origins. Gisborne takes Mowgli as purely antediluvian spectacle: "'He's a most wonderful chap . . . I wonder what in the world he is,'" Gisborne thinks, and for all his sensitive attunements to the cycles and seasons of the *rukh*, can't understand why Mowgli might have calloused elbows and knees or the ability to drive horses and ungulates before him.[113] The German, closer to the government census with its records of unexplained missing children and to the stories of the "wolf boys" in Europe and India like the wild boy of Lucknow that Kipling's father, John Lockwood Kipling, described in *Beast and Man in India* (1891), has a better understanding of what it looks like to be raised by wolves: "'Normally dey die young—dese people,'" he observes.[114] For Muller, Mowgli exceeds European and Christian myth; he is Adam but he is also "older dan dot childtale, shust as der *rukh* is older dan der gods."[115] All of these possible mythologies are finally subsumed to Gisborne's practical use: "'I must get him into the Government service somehow. A man who can drive nilghai would know more about the *rukh* than fifty men. He's a miracle—a *lusus naturae*—but a forest-guard he must be if he'll only settle down in one place,' said Gisborne."[116]

Mowgli does end up settling down and working for Gisborne, an acquiescence Kipling ascribes to their shared affinity for the *rukh*. The terms of the first encounter between the two men veer between the poles of what counts, in a bureaucratic, colonial sense, and what gives feeling within the space of a domesticated Indian forest.

> "I am the warden of this *rukh*—Gisborne is my name."
> "How? Do they number the trees and the blades of grass here?"
> "Even so; lest such gipsy fellows as thou set them afire."
> "I! I would not hurt the jungle for any gift. That is my home."[117]

The two men's understanding of what it means to be "warden" of the *rukh,* despite their immediately established shared affection for the space, is consistently quite different. Gisborne asks Mowgli offhandedly "What news is there in the *rukh?*" and is astonished by Mowgli's lengthy and detailed response on the habits of the jungle animals; "I do not know this," Gisborne answers lamely. To this Mowgli continues the reproof:

> "Tck! Tck! And thou art in charge—so the men of the huts tell me—in charge of all this *rukh*." He laughed to himself.
> "It is well enough to talk and to tell child's tales," Gisborne retorted, nettled at the chuckle; "to say that this and that goes on in the *rukh*. No man can deny thee."[118]

Here, as elsewhere in this book, a conversation about the managed organic setting is also a conversation about the possibility of narrative, and of narrative's ability to recompense for what exceeds or evades direct representation or plot device. Mowgli's subsequent efforts to "prove" his knowledge and the internal logic of his own story, by driving the nilghai bull to Gisborne's veranda, achieves only in the most limited sense the narrative justification he has sought. "Does the Sahib believe now?" asks Mowgli upon presentation of this animal proof, while at the same time giving equal veridical weight to the bull's role as protagonist in the story: "Ho! ho! he will have a fine tale to tell when he returns to the herd."[119] In demonstrating these multiple ways to know the *rukh*, Mowgli provides overlapping assurances of consequence to Gisborne: "The Sahib is in charge of this *rukh!*" but also "If the Sahib needs more knowledge at any time of the movings of the game, I, Mowgli, am here. This is a good *rukh*, and I shall stay."[120] If they differ in their understandings of how to narrate the *rukh*'s managed space, however they agree on the idea that managing brings its own affections; as Mowgli declares, "It is always good to cherish young trees."[121]

Gisborne is explained to expend his salary only on "a purchase from the Calcutta Botanical Gardens, or to pay a ranger's widow a sum that the Government of India would never have sanctioned."[122] This frugality represents both Gisborne's restricted understanding of the plant and human society, both as frequently in need of external supplement through the return of scientific specimens or additive death-benefits, but also his problematic ignorance of the consequences of removing from human circulations the translated benefits of the *rukh*. Abdul Gafur's later thievery of Gisborne's untouched excess salary, kept in a bedroom drawer, is, in the servant's mind, fair recompense for the difficulties of accommodating for his master both the impositions of the *rukh,* a nearly sentient organism, and Mowgli, its sentient and ambulatory manifestation. The translation of the *rukh*'s presence into monetary consequence, is for Gafur, and even for Gisborne, a central way of organizing the parameters of the encounter between the human and the natural world. Gisborne's repeated appeals to Mowgli to serve as his assistant so that he may have the title of Ranger and a British pension reveal that Gisborne, for all his intuitive connections to the *rukh,* still understands it as a fundamentally cultivated and cultivatable site—from which proper management, whether planting, pruning, or simply correctly perceiving, will accrue not only into sympathetic connection but also a financial support, registered in foreign currency, and recurring not seasonally but at the pace of imperial bureaucracy.

> "Mowgli, if as thou sayest, thou art herder in the *rukh* for no gain and for no pay"
> "It is the Sahib's *rukh,*" said Mowgli, quickly looking up. Gisborne nodded thanks and went on:
> "Would it not be better to work for pay from the Government? There is a pension at the end of long service."
> "Of that I have thought," said Mowgli, "but the rangers live in huts with shut doors, and all that is all too much a trap to me."[123]

Muller's presentation of the *rukh* in the vernacular to Mowgli aligns more with the expectations Kipling has for Mowgli's history, but even Muller's thinking is still anchored in pensions and in Kipling's (much reviled by critics) understanding of native voluntary servitude as inspired by reverential personal loyalty: "Thy business is this,—to wander no more up and down the *rukh* and drive beasts for sport or for show, but to take service under me, who am the Government in the matter of Woods and Forests, and to live in this *rukh* as a forest-guard.... For that work there is a payment each month in silver, and at the end when thou hast gathered a wife and cattle, and, may be, children, a pension. What answer?"[124] To this Mowgli agrees—"I serve, if I serve in this *rukh* and no other: with Gisborne Sahib and with no other"—and receives in return "the written order that pledges the honour of the Government for the pension."[125] For Kipling, this honor pledge structures and contains the multiple meaning that the *rukh* carries for each of the different characters. The servant Abdul Gafur declares most simply and superstitiously: "But the devils! The *rukh* is full of devils!"[126] Meanwhile Muller sees it as both pagan space—"I remember when dere was no *rukh* more big than your knee.... Now der trees haf come back.... But der trees dey had der cult of der old gods"—and also beyond any kind of human framings.[127] "Now I know dot Bagan or Christian I shall nefer know der inwardness of der *rukh*," he finally concludes.[128] The narrator, meanwhile, ascribes to the forest a collective aesthetic power from an extrahuman perspective: "The *rukh* lay out in great velvety folds in the uncertain shimmer of the stardust," we are told.[129] As each of these relations with the *rukh* are allowed to stand, the ethical care and management pledged in "cherishing young trees" is held to overarch them all.

The tale's conclusion, in which Mowgli and the daughter of Abdul Gafur are discovered in fireside communion with Mowgli's wolf family, restages domesticity for a forest setting. At the story's end (and at the beginning, in some ways, of the same story) it is Gisborne who tutors Muller, turning aside the German's rifle before Muller has a chance to kill the wolf pack that fosters Mowgli's baby and wife "under the shade of a thorn thicket." "You were quite right about Mowgli," said Gisborne, "I meant to have told you, but I've got so used to these fellows in the last twelve months that it slipped my mind."[130] Thus has Mowgli been assured the government pension at the end of things, in acquiring the promised wife and child, and so been accounted for in an imperial reckoning, while also succeeding in partially acculturating Gisborne into the fluid consciousness of the *rukh*. Gisborne still marks time by the month, but his habituation to the *rukh*'s dwellers, we understand, is a deepening of his already responsive and benevolent management of these cultivated landscapes.

That the story ends with the conversation of two Europeans, voices that will nowhere else be heard in the Mowgli story cycle, in a place ("the Northern Forest Reserves") quite distant from the Seoni hills where the jungle in the rest of the *Jungle Books* is found, shows why "In the Rukh" does not feel like a conclusion to the story that the *Jungle Books* begin. But Gisborne's accommodation of Mowgli's multispecies and *rukh*-dependent version of adulthood is a faint anticipation of what Anne Milne has called "thinking the feral into bioregionalism," what she terms a "dynamic, lateral and reflexive way of approaching the feral not as a problem but as a participant."[131] These participants, and Mowgli, as feral child turned adult "feral citizen," can manage the *rukh* in a manner proposed by the hopeful protoecological vision of both Muller and his real-world counterpart Brandis and "accelerate or illuminate change appropriate for and reflective of the needs of that community."[132] Of course in doing this we must proceed with caution; Catriona Sandilands rightly warns of uncritical celebrations of "the idea that 'feral' means a sort of rewilded return to a state of pre-anthropogenic grace," and such is especially the case here, when Kipling's ecological fantasy is so devastatingly dependent on imperial claims.[133] But it helps us give necessary nuance to a text where readerly understanding of "wildness" often covers over the in fact highly managed terrain of the *rukh*, understood to be even more cultivated here since animal systems of law and order join with regulations of the social and natural world. Sandiland's evocation of "feral landscape" as a description that "gestures towards a view of the world that is both demonstrably a multiagential co-production . . . and continually re/subject to the biopolitical interventions of capitalism" helpfully (if anachronistically) situates what Kipling intends to leave us with at the end of "In the Rukh," and gives us an alternative to environmental histories that suggest this work as thoroughgoing ecophilia.[134] It should be clear that Kipling's intention and historical practice are far distant; as Jane Hotchkiss argues, "In Mowgli . . . Kipling has created the ideal subaltern, the native without the 'native problem,' by engendering a new Indian disturbingly divorced from Indian history, culture, and tradition."[135] That is, as John McBratney has claimed, Mowgli is "not a creation independent of imperial politics but one complicit with it."[136]

The fantasy of cultivated colonial ecology thus moves easily from the plants of the *rukh* to the person of Mowgli himself—a cultivated being with deep organic affinities who also illustrates the outer limits of the human for readers within the British Empire. Daniel Bivona, Don Randall, and Jessica Straley have all sought to situate Mowgli in relation to the domestic novel tradition of the bildungsroman with very different ends. Randall and Bivona take the stories as a textual unit, finding the saga "a narrative that discovers its resolution in advance of its elaboration" with, for Randall, "appropriately imperial resolution" and, for Bivona, "a novelistic unit of sorts: a *Bildungsroman* ... like many ... a story about a disciplinary project."[137] More recently Straley has argued against reading the stories with a fixed chronology; her argument that "*The Jungle Books* suspend the boy, the species, and perhaps the British Empire in eternal, unspecialized, heterogeneous, and infinitely powerful adolescence" helpfully extends David Sergeant's claim that "the two sides to Kipling's head, the two kinds of Mowgli and the two kinds of jungle story, run concurrently and do not cancel each other out."[138] These heterogenities of Mowgli's development set aside the different kind of temporal progression that organic cultivation implied: not a telos, but a constantly balanced development that restaged its own beginnings again and again under the benevolent care of the Forest Warden. While Kipling's romance of the Indian Forest Service has been too easily adopted as such by some environmental historians, the consequences for literature of this cultivated adult diversion from the central wildness of the young Mowgli do suggest a possible modulation of imperial romance's ends. More than the fantasy commodity of the Goya lily in *Allan Quatermain,* or even the farmed eucalyptus of *Jess,* the specifics of the *rukh*'s economic value are weighed alongside the narrative perpetuations of its organic life within the larger heterogeneity of imperial cultivations.

In the final chapter, I will consider the fate of another IFS employee, David Bittacy, otherwise known as "The Man Whom the Trees Loved." Bittacy's subsumation into an English forest still in communication with the Indian trees he once tended in Blackwood's ecogothic fantasy represents a very different accommodation of the human by the landscape than we have seen in this chapter. Faced with the increasingly ravenous demands of plant life that ever more actively seeks to assimilate people along with their setting, the colonial defenses of flagpoles, walled gardens, pensions, and other imperial systems can be toppled. As they are, assumptions about the limits of consciousness and the self-evident trappings of personhood, either in narrative or in real life, also begin to fall away and accept redefinition. It is one thing to be seem to be surrounded by oaks, ivy, and other signifiers of the English landscape as Hilda Wade is in Grant Allen's fiction, or even to roam the oak-paneled halls of an English country estate as Allan Quatermain does before advancing on his final adventure. It is quite another, as Haggard begins to suggest in his *Gardener's Year* fantasy of tree-becoming, to recognize that humans will become part of the plant life that surrounds them for far longer and far more completely than plant life will bend to the ministrations of any individual human. The spread of the British Empire is overwritten in the end by the acclimatized transplants that ride its expansion, and the adventures of the peripatetic gum tree and other colonial cultivars become the settled fictions of its landscape claims.

❦ 5 ❦

The Sentient Specimen Returns

Toward the end of John Ruskin's *Proserpina,* the critic takes issue with an "extremely learned and able" pamphlet he has discovered that asks the troubling question: "What is a plant?" The pamphlet author's survey "of walking trees, and rooted beasts; of flesh-eating flowers, and mud-eating worms; of sensitive leaves, and insensitive persons" leads to what Ruskin paraphrases as the "triumphant" conclusion that "nobody could say either what a plant was, or what a person was." This dilemma Ruskin finds "frivolous" and easily dismissed, as he explains: "A plant is a creature that is fastened to the ground by its feet, has no brains in its head, and only an imitation of them in its marrow; cannot talk with its mouth, nor see with its eyes; is not proud of being admired, grateful for being tended, nor afraid of being killed."[1] This strange definition makes sense only when read against the explanation of animals that Ruskin also provides: in his words, animals are sentient and mobile beings, "capable of pleasure and pain," and possessing qualities that most "broadly . . . and usefully" sum up the purpose of life. Though opposed in conclusion to Samuel Butler's claims for the expansionist potato in *Erewhon*—which asked of the potato's grasping tendrils, "What is consciousness if this is not consciousness?"—Ruskin's formal invocation of plant life resonates with Butler's antithetical premise: we know what plants are because they are everything humans and animals are not.

Throughout this book, novel characters have been charged with the sense that plant lives, especially foreign plant lives, might be ongoing, even flourishing, all around them, in ways that scarcely brooked human understanding, even if this flourishing was aided by human hands. The four preceding chapters of this book have largely been occupied with locating moments in which plants, emboldened by new arrangements of narrative form available in fictions resistant to realism, come forward into the narrative to hint at independent plans and ends on the edges of human perception. This was strange enough, but stranger still was the idea that plants were not only proceeding but intruding, demanding recognition (at best) and recompense in human flesh (at very much worst). This chapter takes up the most agile and agitated of Victorian and Edwardian plants to consider what happens to genre and narrative when environmental controls admit sentient and even mobile plant specimens.[2] Such specimens include the examples of man-eating trees featured in Arthur Conan Doyle's 1879 story "An American's Tale"; Phil Robinson's "The Man-Eating Tree" (1881); Frank Aubrey's *The Devil Tree of El Dorado* (1897); and Fred White's "Purple Terror" (1899)—fictions which all present vicious trees (or, in Doyle's case, murderous flytraps) in overseas locations both fecund and indeterminate. These continue the work of acclimatization described with the prickly pear and eucalyptus in the previous chapter in greatly amplified form.[3] Even more challenging to narrative norms and to the forms of humanistic thinking, however, are the reconfigurations of domestic plant life proposed in the carnivorous plant fictions in H. G. Wells's *The War of the Worlds* (1897) and Algernon Blackwood's "The Man Whom the Trees Loved" (1907). The plants in these stories gained agency not by virtue of their perceived suffering, but instead through fantasies of the suffering they could inflict and the revisions of narrative agency they could propose. Scientific writing on insectivorous plants and cryptogamic fungi advanced in parallel with fictions of man-eating trees and alien Red Weeds, with both allowing, to greater and lesser degree, the derived intentionality of the vegetable kingdom to serve as evidence of an active and directive consciousness somehow available, though in ways not necessarily evident to humans.

Victorian science popularizer John Ellor Taylor mused expansively in his *The Sagacity and Morality of Plants* (1884):

> It is only within the last few years, since botany has been studied from its biological side, that we have wakened up to understand what wonderful objects plants are. A new language has been developed in which to describe their novel relationships. Whether we believe in the consciousness of plant-life or not, this language almost implies such a belief. We speak of plants adopting this habit or that device—always and only when such habits and devices are beneficial to them—as if they did it of set and intelligent purpose. . . . Who knows—perhaps there can be no life, animal or vegetable, unaccompanied by consciousness![4]

We are not so very far away here from Michael Marder's much more recent formulation in *Plant Thinking* that plants are "agents in the production of meaning," though Taylor's intended readership of "those who take an intelligent interest in plants" may seem to be even broader than the philosophical circle within which Marder operates.[5] Of equal interest here to the proposition that plants can think, and think "novel" thoughts, however, is Taylor's agnosticism as to the location of this consciousness. Is the language describing plant-thinking, used in the "works of Darwin, Lubbock, Müller, Wallace, Kerner, Grant Allen, Wilson, and others," to name only those "particularly noticeable for this style of description," in fact developed independently by these men?[6] Or is it instead the plants themselves, whose "set and intelligent purpose" has directed these notable Victorian scientists and science writers to admit the thoughts of vegetable life? As tempting as it is to follow Taylor in brushing away the limits of anthropomorphic hegemonic consciousness with a breezy "Who knows!" Victorian novels continue to help us work through such comparisons. Marder and other contemporary scholars engaged in a "hermeneutic shift from an anthropocentric to a 'phytocentric' critical position" return us to the questions raised by Taylor, Darwin, and other Victorians concerned with what might be consciously directing *The Power of Movement in Plants,* in ways that especially attend to the assistance novels can provide in answering these questions.[7] Patricia Vieira has identified "phytographia" as a study of the encounter between plant inscriptions and written human records of those incriptions with attention to "the specific modes in which the vegetal word is embedded in human cultural productions," and Taylor's description of the dawning awareness of plant consciousness as recorded in Victorian science writing demonstrates some beginning examples of that narrative form.[8]

Following through these active plant beginnings allows us to better apprehend the Victorians' developing argument for the existence of a plant-based consciousness—or, more precisely, an idea of consciousness that does not explicitly exclude the possibility of plants. Yet the challenge in such presuppositions of nonexclusion are multiple. For one, writers of thinking plant fictions had to explain how such consciousness could be determined in the first place. For another, these fiction writers also had to acknowledge the variables of scale and collectivity when aligning consciousness with different kinds of plant life—fungi, forests, parasitic vines—that did not match anthropomorphic definitions of individual identity or ally themselves to national and imperial sovereignties. In describing the activities of "man-eating trees," "strange orchids," and "plants that fight," this fiction used these problematic cultivars and their aggression against human characters to expand beyond the limits of realism. To admit plants as narrative elements with any degree of agency is to defy the standard parameters by which we understand narrative fiction to operate, since a plant with narrative agency radically alters notions about sentience, mobility, reproduction, and representation—not the least by blurring distinctions between character and setting. At the same time, thinking of plants as nonhuman narrative actors does not preclude us from understanding them, as Catriona Sandilands argues of the "sexualized botanical horror stories" in such fictions as Wells's vampiric plant tale, "The Flowering of the Strange Orchid," as "complex queer agents that demand attention to specific entanglements of sex, gender, race, and species."[9]

These were specific entanglements of which Victorian-era writers and their successors made intermittent use. L. M. Montgomery's Canadian orphan, *Anne of Green Gables* (1908), startles her reluctant adoptive mother Marilla Cuthbert by demanding to know the "name of that geranium on the window-sill"—not "apple-scented geranium," as Marilla identifies it, the sort of name that joins it to a shared horticultural order, but "just a name you gave it yourself. Didn't you give it a name?" Anne's explanation—"I like things to have handles even if they are only geraniums. It makes them seem more like people. How do you know but that it hurts a geranium's feelings just to be called a geranium and nothing else? You wouldn't like to be called nothing but a woman all the time"— befuddles the prosaic Marilla, but is recognizably the work of subject recognition unhinged from scientific taxonomy.[10] Botany, studies of natural history, and studies of the history of Victorian plant science have for the most part overwritten the act of individual recognition with the act of naming; a specimen name still covers a collective condition. Cultivation does not separate out this collapse, but in its popular practice in fiction it much more often prioritizes the affective response to a particular specimen than the specific recognition of its name, despite all efforts by botany instructors to the contrary.

This has particular reference to the priorities of female naming, especially those most eager to distinguish themselves from being held as "nothing but a woman." One of the many black marks against Blanche Ingram, Jane Eyre's sophisticated rival for Mr. Rochester's attentions, is her mockery of the "gentle Miss Dent" during a "discourse on botany": "It seems Mrs. Dent had not studied that science, though, as she said, she liked flowers, 'especially wild ones;' Miss Ingram had, and she ran over its vocabulary with an air."[11] The cruelty of the facile review of botanical vocabulary signals not just Blanche's preening self-presentation, but a more general suspicion of female participation in the regulated taxonomy of specimen names, even as Miss Dent's general appreciation of flowers she categorizes simply as "wild" suggests her equally undesirable simple limits. Brontë's fiction is far from the fanciful animism that Montgomery, Burnett, and others drew on their novels for children, or the more erotic neopaganism that I will consider with Algernon Blackwood later in this chapter. Yet the distinction that Brontë suggests between "science" and "liking flowers" is one that has been a tension throughout the book. In explaining the connections people make with plants that are not part of botany's scientific discourse, character, temporality, agency, and other fictional devices are paramount in asserting selfhood, and, more tentatively, questioning the anthropomorphic limits of that self.

Anne Shirley's sympathetic connection to the desires of the geranium to be hailed (though perhaps not her one-sided decision that the plant must be named Bonny) befits her character in a girl's story modeling empathy as an essential component of both social order and a humane spirit. For other authors such kind-heartedness is in shorter supply and plant regard is, like many other relations, theorized as antagonistic. H. Rider Haggard, surveying the bonsai trees on display at the flower show, writes: "One wonders what *they* think of the whole business, if think they can, as, stood upon some verandah, they stare from their squat, china jars at their mighty brethren of the forest, younger, perhaps, by a century than themselves. How they must hate the creatures that planted their germs in orange skins and shaved off their lusty roots, turning them into abortions and a mockery to their kind. Or, perhaps, they are content to live, even thus, knowing, at least, that nobody will cut them down for timber."[12] The fellowship of the Japanese bonsai with the English forest is distinguished by Haggard from the Asian human "minds with a curious twist in them" that "seek amusement in the distorted and unfamiliar" by creating these dwarfed trees, as well as the global forestry economy more generally.[13] The hatred that he winkingly assigns to these specimens is, in the case of the flower show, truly aimed at the frivolous overcultivations he believes fancy horticulture demands. But he is equally willing to find natural bad intentions in plant life recognizably carnivorous. Later in *A Gardener's Year*, he considers an Sundew specimen in his collection, which he terms a "vegetable butcher."

> To my mind, its unpleasant habits show in a very striking manner how real, if subtle, is the connection between the animal and the vegetable world, for here we have a plant actually feeding on the living creatures that it has caught, and, what is more, baiting its traps in order to catch them. Is there, then, so wide a gulf between it and *homo sapiens,* who does precisely the same thing and lives thereby? We think nothing of putting this law of death—Nature's hideous scheme—in motion for our own profit, but when a wretched little plant imitates our exalted example, the effect is uncanny.[14]

The step forward made here from plant sensitivity to plant malevolence was long-anticipated, as Theresa Kelly has shown in her discussion of Erasmus Darwin's consideration of the supposedly poisonous Upas tree.[15] Haggard's move to the propositional sphere when thinking of the Sundew ("Is there, then") may seem particularly apt for a writer of fantastic fiction, but he was certainly not the only writer to wonder if the strong distinction between plant "habits" and human actions might in fact be only a perceptual construct. As Mark Chase and others point out, a full definition of the conditions of botanical carnivory has never been achieved.[16]

Haggard's interest in understanding the interests of the Sundew was not unique. Grant Allen drew on both Darwin and Swinburne in calling the plant "atrociously and deliberately wicked" in his 1884 article "Queer Flowers," written for the *Cornhill Magazine*.[17] Allen frames the Sundew's description in a larger reflection on the horrors of possible plant sentience; he writes, "There is something too awful and appalling in this contest of the unconscious and insentient with the living and feeling, of a lower vegetative form of life with a higher animated form," and "there seems to be a sort of fiendish impersonal cruelty about its action which sadly militates against all our pretty platitudes about the beauty and perfection of living beings."[18] Allen's distress over the sundew inverts customary directions of sympathy by doubly deploying "murderous propensities."[19] The sundew itself is actively cruel in seeking out its insect prey, but the sundew's cruelty is also metaphorically active, "militating" its way into conventional discourse and disrupting the familiar systems of figurative language. In both regards, the sundew, an "inconspicuous small weed" with "literary and scientific honours . . . heaped upon its head to an extent almost unknown in the case of any other member of the British floral commonweal," goes against the standards by which fin-de-siècle Victorian culture has been held to recognize conscious existence: the sundew impresses not because it suffers itself, but because it causes others to do so.[20] Counterpoised to late-century debates over animal welfare, vivisection, and vegetarianism, discussions of plant sentience now gravitated not to sympathy but to antipathy and fear. Likewise, the figurative forms used to incorporate with them within the "British floral commonweal" underlined the carnivorous engulfment such plants could perform.

The thoughts of the Sundew in nonfiction texts move fluidly to the more overtly fictional thoughts and desires of the fictional man-eating plant just as Allen's delineations of the invasive prickly pear traveled from natural history essay to globe-trotting fiction. It has been a premise of this book that such crossings should be attended to for their bidirectional explanations, following Elaine Freedgood's investigation of colonial metalepsis discussed in the book's first chapter. The narrator of Phil Robinson's "The Man-eating Tree" begins not with the exciting plot details of the Central African plant attack but with an extended philosophical reflection on the necessary correspondence between plant and animal worlds, concluding: "The vegetable world, however, has its revenges. You may keep the guinea pig in a hutch, but how will you pet the basilisk? The little sensitive plant in your garden amuses your children . . . but how could you transplant a vegetable that seizes the running deer, strikes down the passing bird, and once taking hold of him, sucks the carcass of man himself, till his matter becomes as vague as his mind, and all his animate capabilities cannot escape him from the terrible embrace of—God help him!—an inanimate tree?"[21] Kelly Hurley, exploring fin-de-siècle gothic, has proposed that Aubrey, Doyle, and Robinson, like William Hope Hodgson and H. G. Wells, use imagined evolutionary monstrosities, both animal and vegetable, to generally attack anthropomorphic priority: "The viscosity of the predatory natural world may be said to represent the suchness of matter, as it gains sentience and rises up to swallow the bounded human world," she suggests.[22] Hurley's reading is borne out by Robinson's insistence that "the sensual instincts of beast and vegetable are manifestly analogous—the world must be as percipient as sentient throughout" and, equally, by his claim that "given the necessity of . . . urgent self-interest, every animal or vegetable could eventually revolutionize its nature."[23] But Robinson's identification of the particularly terrible revenges of the vegetable world links his evolutionary fantasy not just to any kind of monster but to monsters emerging from practices of Victorian plant enthusiasms' global plant exchange specifically. The fear is not that the petted plant specimens in the kitchen garden will evolve *into* sentience, but that they possess sentience already.

For many authors, these fearful fantasies took place in a space necessarily marked as foreign. Doyle's flytraps grow in a frontier alternately identified as Arizona and Montana where "grass as hung over a chap's head as he rode through it, and trees so thick that you couldn't catch a glimpse of blue sky for leagues and leagues, and orchids like umbrellas!"[24] Roraima, the great plateau which conceals both Aubrey's Devil-Tree and the long-lived tribe that keeps the tree's secrets, contains "flora and fauna [that] flourish unchecked in the utmost luxuriance of tropical savage life," where, bafflingly enough to the British narrator, "one of the greatest marvels and mysteries of the earth lies on the outskirt of one of our colonies, and we leave the mystery unsolved, the marvel uncared for."[25] Will Scarlett, the enterprising amateur botanist and central character of White's story, first experiences the "Purple Terror" in a military expedition across Cuba, a country to which his "geographical and botanical knowledge were going to prove of considerable service to a grateful country when said grateful country should have passed beyond the rudimentary stages of colonization."[26] Cheryl Blake Price has shown in her work on man-eating trees that these stories reflect both "ecophobic reactions to the colonial environment" as well as "anxiety that the colonial wilderness . . . was disappearing through the mechanisms of colonialism."[27]

These fictional plants, of course, had no desire to remain overseas in grateful colonial wildernesses. The desires of Will Scarlett, who is lured to the "Purple Terror" both by his lust for new plants as well as his lust for a beautiful woman, compel him to abet a reverse-colonial invasion of the domestic by the foreign in a manner specific to the horticulturally enraptured Victorian era. As he views the flowers of the murderous parasitical vine, "all Scarlett's scientific enthusiasm was aroused. It is not given to every man to present a new orchid to the horticultural world. And this one would dwarf the finest plant hitherto discovered."[28] While White's story only proposes such an exchange—the orchids remain rooted in their Caribbean setting—it was also a common feature in tales of murderous plants used to describe the effects of a specimen returned to a domestic locale. These acts of botanical importation were not unique to the era, but the vast increase in the scale of the collections and the reach of the botanical collectors placed ever greater pressure on narrative and nomenclature to preserve geographical distinctions between native and non-native species. As John Rieder points out, such "fantasies of appropriation," cloaked as "zoological and ethnological acquisitiveness" unite the emerging genre of science fiction with the earlier prose of travel narrative under the logic of colonialism; given the overwhelming evidence of Victorian emotional attachment to their plants, we must also add to these appropriations the fantasy of botanical acquisition.[29]

The most famous genre fiction exploring these fantasies of plant appropriation is told from the opposite direction: not from the point of view of the colonizing invader unwittingly carrying with him a raft of invasive seeds, but from the point of view of the about-to-be colonized. H. G. Wells's *The War of the Worlds* (1898) remains remarkable for its nineteenth-century naturalization of the most alien of vegetable attackers, whose strangeness rests especially in its nonspecificity of form. Wells does not foreground the dual nature (animal and vegetable) of the Martian invaders in his novel, and in fact we do not learn of the "Red Weed," the plant that gives Mars its characteristic color and threatens to choke England in the process of doing the same, until we are far into book 2, "The Earth Under the Martians." Even then the narrator's introduction is presented as an aside during a more general discussion of the differences between life on Mars and terrestrial life. He records:

> At any rate, the seeds which the Martians (intentionally or accidentally) brought with them gave rise in all cases to red-coloured growths. Only that known popularly as the Red Weed, however, gained any footing in competition with terrestrial forms. The Red Creeper was quite a transitory growth, and few people have seen it growing. For a time, however, the Red Weed grew with astonishing vigour and luxuriance. It spread up the sides of the pit by the third or fourth day of our imprisonment, and its cactus-like branches formed a carmine fringe to the edges of triangular window. And afterwards I found it broadcast throughout the country, and especially wherever there was a stream of water present.[30]

This passage is notable especially for its dislocations of scale: between, on the one hand, the broad horticulturally omniscient description given of the Red Weed's "vigor and luxuriance," elsewhere called "Titanic" and "gigantic and of unparalleled fecundity," and the first-person narrator's limited knowledge about the weed, which initially matches exactly his limited visual perspective, trapped in a bombed house with a terrified curate and with only a triangular window framed in Red Weed to observe the horrifying progress of the Martian invaders.[31] Similarly, he tethers his account of the weed to the deflating temporal reversals of the passage, with the off-hand use of the word "afterwards" spoiling prematurely the inevitability of the invasion's failure. In introducing the weed at this point, the narrator has already cut away from a vivid description of the arrival of the fifth Martian cylinder to "add in this place certain further details which, although they were not all evident to us at the time, will enable the reader who is unacquainted with them to form a clearer picture of these offensive creatures."[32] The narrator's reluctance to comply with the rules of his own narrative condition and tell the story as it occurred here correspond with the novel's far more mysterious model of narrative agency: that of the Martians themselves, both the creatures operating the tripods and the swiftly growing fronds of the Red Weed. Here, as in the Sherlock Holmes story, the events of the story and the order of the story's telling are markedly disjunct; but the *War of the Worlds,* a mystery novel without a proper detective or a satisfyingly conclusive solution, disdains efforts to ever bring *fabula* and *suzjet* back into alignment.

As the narrator repeatedly reminds us, the British subjects involved never really know why the Martians come to Earth but must instead endlessly speculate about what the Martians' known actions say about their probable intent. But despite the lack of human understanding of Martian volition, there are multiple intentional actors here. The tripod operators are of course viciously active, but we also see that the Red Weed is itself exercising a form of mobility that appears to be intentional. This apparent intentionality on the part of this invasive plant is, in fact, of critical importance given the most central concerns of the novel. In *The War of the Worlds,* this weaker sort of derived intentionality is the only one admissible either when thinking about narrative agency or when inferring the presence of a threatening and otherwise inaccessible alien consciousness. The British waterways that carry the Red Weed and the mechanical tripods that transport the Martian creatures are both prostheses for the alien invaders, amplifying and making more legible the movements that assert directive consciousness. Though the creatures in tripods accept more readily than the Red Weed the impositions of anthropomorphism, Wells does not functionally distinguish between the two. This supports the idea that Wells implicitly advances throughout his work—that plants in general, and this plant in particular, represent an outer limit to the range of human interest in the alien. Indeed, the distinction between the two kinds of Martians is largely irrelevant: the young Martians "bud off" their parents, like "young lilybulbs" or "young animals in the fresh-water polyp," while the older Martians, lacking entrails (or any organs besides brains and hands) are sustained by fresh blood obtained "directly by means of a little pipette into the recipient canal," and, in short, act very much like a super-intelligent version of the Red Weed itself.[33] That Wells is, throughout his fiction, concerned with the distinctions between jungles and gardens is of a piece with his particular interest in weeds—the alien of plants, and the best example of the alien nature of plants. This is, of course, because as was considered in the introduction, the word "weed" is exclusively a derived and relative term—it carries meaning only in relation to some other class of "things that are not weeds"—and so to recognize a weed is to recognize an arbitrary distinction of purpose that the weed by its lively vigor aims to resist.

That the novel uses the Martians to critique, via reverse colonization, the follies of British imperialism is, of course, a touchstone of its reception and its era; in one reading, Stephen Arata has linked the Red Weed's invasion to Wells's reaction to the British extermination of the indigenous Tasmanian population.[34] And clearly the novel can and should be read as an account of a galactic version of an acclimatization society that has gone terribly wrong, as environmental historians and historians of science have done. Matthew Chew argues that the late nineteenth-century expansion and collapse of the canal-choking Canadian waterweed *Elodea* in Britain "doubtless inspired" Wells's text, while Christina Alt has linked the prickly pear's spread with the Red Weed's fictional course in an environmental history linked to the studies of assimilating plants in chapter 4.[35] But the weed also serves as another fictional investigation of global circulation that interrogates the terms by which plants can have proper names and homes. As Wells's novel seeks to demonstrate, even plants that do not survive by attacking unwitting travelers have intentions that the observer cannot register except by effect, and even then only if that effect happens to be that of causing grievous harm. Human hands—implied constants in the actions of broadcasting, acclimatizing, and transplanting—falsely imply human agency in the development of global environments, but Wells means to pick apart the mental constructs that support that false narrative of exclusively human influence on the surrounding world. At the dawn of the environmental movement, this novel offers the idea of the functionally sentient plant as an example of the way in which environments and plants can, in fact, broadcast themselves, through a directive consciousness that can both be understood to exist and yet be defiantly and totally inaccessible to our figures and narrative forms. When Wells's narrator recounts a walk through the ruined landscape where "all about me the Red Weed clambered among the ruins, writhing to get above me in the dimness," his insistently foregrounded and present-tense imposition of intent onto the plant hints at the countless other impositions and violent figurative replacements that British fictions have done to their fictional vegetable worlds.[36]

Wells's fictions of collective plant life, extrapolating beyond the singular specimen's bounds, are actually on the milder side of what such fantasies of collective horror might become. More terrifying fictions that also took up the problem of how larger plant forms could also make narrative a distributed consciousness with expansive and uncertain limits include William Hope Hodgson's "A Voice in the Night" (1907) and John Uri Lloyd's *Etidorhpa* (1895), among other fictions of fungal malice, and depend for their terror especially on the inescapable pervasiveness of the fungal spores. "The Voice in the Night," first published in the popular and influential pulp magazine *The Blue Book,* tells the story of an ill-fated pair of lovers who encounter an island where a "vile fungus . . . was growing riot. In places it rose into horrible, fantastic mounds, which seemed almost to quiver, as with a quiet life, when the wind blew across them. Here and there, it took on the forms of vast fingers, and in others it just spread out flat and smooth and treacherous . . . [t]he whole quaking vilely at times."[37] The pair's gradual realization that the fungus is growing unstoppably, not just across the island but through and around their bodies, is followed by a sudden and insurmountable compulsion to eat the growth. This desire continues even after encountering "an extraordinarily shaped mass of fungus . . . swaying uneasily, as though it possessed life of its own" with "a grotesque resemblance to the figure of a distorted human creature" which, upon grim consideration, is understood to in fact be a sailor previously marooned on this same island. In understanding and nobly accepting their future fate, the couple's narration spares the tale's shipboard listeners, who already perceive the fiancé of the pair as no more than a "great, gray nodding sponge."[38] The story's horror, then, comes not from the fear of dying on the fungus island, but of continuing to live there—albeit in a greatly transformed fashion. Fantasies of unification between plant and human continue to chill precisely because they place the resulting hybrid at the far outer limits of not only narrative, but consciousness itself. Fungi, and in particular cryptogamic fungi, had already been a subject of interest and repulsion throughout the second half of the century, especially because their spore-based reproduction resisted so strongly conventional structures of metaphor.[39] It seemed impossible to distinguish parasitic fungi from their hosts, let alone identify the singular personhood of the fungus itself.

Even more apparently discrete forms gained the ability to work in cooperation. Algernon Blackwood's 1907 short story "The Willows," appearing in his collection *The Listener,* described the near-sacrifice of two travelers on the Danube to an island of psychically manipulative willows. In the narrator's horrified realization of the evil at work, plants are made mobile and humans fixed in place: "Creeping with silent feet over the shifting sands, drawing imperceptibly nearer by soft unhurried movements, the willows had come closer during the night. . . . There was a suggestion here of personal agency, of deliberate intention, of aggressive hostility, and it terrified me into a sort of rigidity."[40] The psychological shock of managing a marooning in a place where "We touched the frontier of a region where our presence was resented. . . . We were the first human influences on this island and we were not wanted. *The willows were against us.*"[41] Though the protagonists eventually escape, spared by the sacrificial murder (apparently by willow) of an anonymous peasant, the effect of an environment apparently "on the frontier of another world, an alien world, a world tenanted by willows only and the souls of willows" shows at what cost the human world is defended against a botanical villainy far more ontologically complex than Frank Aubrey's devil tree described in his 1896 novel of the same name.[42]

Blackwood continues and builds on this environmental horror in his subsequent *Pan's Garden: A Volume of Nature Stories* (1912). These stories, and Blackwood's oeuvre as a whole, have been taken by S. T. Joshi and other critics as a part of an early twentieth-century "weird fiction" movement preceding the work of H. P. Lovecraft.[43] Yet while weird fiction is generally understood to propose a cosmic horror that constantly threatens the incursion of a soul-annihilating infinite abyss, Blackwood in particular draws on environmental setting to curtail these forays with formal and organic limits. Sometimes these are linked to particular spaces, like the island in the Danube of "The Willows," while at other times they are connected to broader categories of economic and social class within the turn-of-the-century English milieu. "The Transfer," included in *Pan's Garden,* tells the story of an ominous bare patch in a suburban garden, "a hideous bit of emptiness yawning to be fed and nourished" that aggressively takes the vitality from a "human vampire" of a London businessman.[44] This "battle" between "the emissaries of the two kingdoms, the human and the vegetable," is in fact no contest at all; the businessman's oversized animation, sponged up by him from countless human victims, is easily seized by the grasping consciousness within the garden's bare patch: "All the vitality and life he had transferred from others to himself for years was now in turn being taken from him and transferred—elsewhere."[45] While the businessman fades away, absenting himself entirely from "public mention," the narrating governess finds that "the after-life of that empty patch of garden, however, was quite otherwise. Nothing, so far as I know, was done to it by gardeners, or in the way of draining it or bringing in new earth, but even before I left in the following summer it had changed. It lay untouched, full of great, luscious, driving weeds and creepers, very strong, full-fed, and bursting thick with life."[46] The implied unreliability of a departed governess blurs our reading of what she calls "a glimpse of death amid life, a centre of disease that cried for healing lest it spread" at the end of the rose garden; as earlier genre fiction has shown, servants and caretakers can most easily be blinded by what the governess calls "the rich luxuriance of the whole amazing garden."[47] Even if the malevolence of this bare patch has not been imagined, though, its containment seems assured; the transfer works with singular specificity of time, place, and victim. The governess shares with Ezra Jennings and Sherlock Holmes, as well as the Time Traveler and countless nonfiction plant-writers, a sense that individual plant specimens prompted a continuity of narrative that recalled and supported the personal history of a singular self. But her class and gender, as well as her possibly unreliable psychology, calls into question the stability of both her specific story as well as the overall project of storytelling as a solely human endeavor. The garden patch is bursting to tell its side of the story.

"The Man Whom the Trees Loved," *Pan's Garden*'s opening story—in its near-one-hundred-page length a novella, though devoid of much in the way of conventional plot incident—goes further to relate the plant's side of the story than any other fiction I have yet considered. The story's titular man, "old David Bittacy, C.B., late of the Woods and Forests," is, significantly, a former ranger in the Indian Forest Service, the same bureaucracy that gave Mowlgi his pension.[48] Bittacy and his wife have returned to England and settled on the edge of the New Forest in Hampshire; there, Bittacy "understood trees, felt a subtle sense of communion with them, born perhaps of those years he had lived in caring for them, guarding, protecting, nursing, years of solitude among their great shadowy presences."[49] David Punter, situating Blackwood within a larger field that Andrew Smith and William Hughes have termed the "ecoGothic," has thoughtfully accounted for the ways that Blackwood's fiction hints at both "an escape from the confines of that inevitable humanness but also the possibility of rapturous, fully engaged experience which is otherwise not available to us."[50] I want to build on Punter's analysis by placing Blackwood's text within the sphere of global plant acculturation that I have been describing throughout this book. The forests of England, as Blackwood shows them, are part vengeful colonizers and part subjugated colonial; Bittacy wonders "whether a tree—er—in any lawful meaning of the term can be—alive. I remember some writing fellow telling me long ago that trees had once been moving things, animal organisms of some sort, that had stood so long feeding, sleeping, dreaming, or something, in the same place, that they had lost the power to get away . . . !"[51] Blackwood's aim throughout what passes for the plot of the story is to revise our understanding of what "getting away" may mean for trees, and to resituate a mobile consciousness and perception through techniques of narration that do not fit with human present-progressive verb forms. Bittacy's work in cultivating forests with the Indian Forest Service, as well as his aesthetic sensibilities, give him an openness to these techniques that his wife, by virtue of her gender and her expectations about narrative, can never possess—for, as we have seen throughout this book, female cultivators may tend flower gardens but never forests.

The story opens with the introduction of the artist Sanderson, whose offer to paint a portrait of a Lebanon cedar that stands at the edge of the Bittacy's woods has allowed dimly held understandings on the part of both the husband and the wife to rise more directly to the surface. For David Bittacy, these are reflections on the "queerness" of his unexamined affinity to the trees as a colonial power that Sanderson's portrait has provoked and amplified: "Awfully queer, that trees should bring me such a sense of dim, vast living! I used to feel it particularly, I remember, in India; in Canadian woods as well; but never in little English woods till here."[52] His wife, on the other hand, understands more thoroughly, if equally nonspecifically, the "power which [trees] wielded over [her husband's] life," even if Bittacy "did not know, or realize at any rate. . . . Her fear, he judged, was simply due to those years in India, when for weeks at a time his calling took him away from her into the jungle forests."[53] This connection to "jungle forests" gives important botanical context to what may be otherwise understood as an allegory for other colonial queerings: "It was long after marriage, during his months of loneliness spent with trees and forests in India, his wife waiting at home in the Bungalow, that his other, deeper side had developed the strange passion that she could not understand. And after one or two serious attempts to let her share it with him, he had given up and learned to hide it from her."[54] From Mrs. Bittacy's side, this passion is understood as a bodily sickness that Bittacy unaccountably conceals: "Mr. Sanderson did not know how easily those attacks of Indian fever came back, but David surely might have told him."[55]

The presence of the artist not only prompts a renegotiation of the couple's Anglo-Indian legacy, but also of the way in which that legacy can be narrated. Mrs. Bittacy's constant displeasure with Sanderson is framed as a disagreement with his indirect discourse: "Her mind retained the disagreeable impression that he meant more than he said. In his tone lay quite another implication. It was not actually 'wind' he spoke of, and it would not remain 'further out' . . . rather, it was coming in. Another impression she got too—still more unwelcome—was that her husband understood his hidden meaning."[56] The intimacy of men, the alliance of colonial returnees and artists who wear "big balloon ties like a Frenchman . . . unnecessarily flowing," and those men's shared secret consciousness of seeing into the life of things as a conspiratorially held secret all fit within a development of queer literary modernism seen in the novels of E. M. Forster, D. H. Lawrence, and others.[57] Thus, while so much of this story is an ecological attack on the domestic pedantry of Mrs. Bittacy, it is also a study in questions of narrative form, neither of which comply with the limits that kept the garden patch of "The Transfer" contained between rosebush and birch tree. More than any other text taken up in this study, Blackwood's finds ways to locate narrating consciousness within a form that is both nonhuman and collective, even as it uses the paranoid surveillance of the singular human to relay that broader realm.

The story returns again and again to the particularities of cultivation and isolation as dangerously limiting constraints. This comes both in Bittacy's own observations of the contrast between "the great encircling mass of gloom that was the forest" and "the prim garden with its formal beds of flowers" that "seemed an impertinence almost."[58] The border between forest gloom and impertinent garden is defended by the single Lebanon cedar, understood to be a harmless, if wrongly cultivated, stray. This is in contrast to other trees, which Sanderson describes in a language that recalls some of *Proserpina*'s—"Trees in a mass are good; alone, you may take it generally, are—well, dangerous. Look at a monkey-puzzler, or better still, a holly. Look at it, watch it, understand it. Did you ever see more plainly an evil thought made visible?"[59] The solitary cedar, he reassures them, is "not evil" but "alien, rather. Cedars grow in forests all together. The poor thing has drifted, that is all. . . . That cedar will protect you here, though, because you both have humanized it by your thinking so lovingly of its presence. The others can't get past it, as it were."[60] Later, as David grows more possessed by the forest, he gains in cedar sympathy: "My dear, I felt the loneliness—suddenly realized it—the alien desolation of that tree, set here upon our little lawn in England when all her Eastern brothers call her in sleep."[61] Sanderson's interpretations, so useful at the start of the story to ease the reader into the setting, show their restrictions; by the story's end, his style of humanized thinking inevitably indicates the inadequate limits of anthropomorphic perception. The idea that a human could think or speak for the trees, evident in Sanderson's conclusion that "some trees obviously seem to prefer the human," rings falser the further we read on.[62]

In the same way, the trees of the town and countryside are held vulnerable and separate from the mass in their cultivation: "The houses threatened them; they knew themselves in danger. . . . They were civilised, cared for—but cared for in order that some day they might be put to death. . . . They knew, moreover, that the Forest with its august deep splendor despised and pitied them. They were a thing of artificial gardens, and belonged to beds of flowers all forced to grow one way."[63] The question of the narratorial location here is paramount. At first it seems that this musing on the terrors of cultivation for trees trapped as immobile prisoners amid the "scream and shriek of clattering traffic" can be identified as the voice of a not-yet-amalgamated David Bittacy's. Yet closer reading of the narrative's distributed consciousness already seems to go far beyond either the "knowing" or the "realizing" that are the twin perceptual and cognitive modes the story proposes, and it is increasingly unclear who, if anyone, is providing the emotional and narrative details of the interior lives of the plants.

We register this confusion at first as an absorption in and then an abandonment of the representational efforts necessary to render tree preferences legible by human minds. Initially, Bittacy's grasp of the lives of the trees finds articulation in a wide range of extratextual citation drawn from aesthetic sources including the artists Dante Rossetti and William Holman Hunt; the poet W. E. Henley; the American and proponent of the New Thought movement Prentice Mulford and his essay "God in the Trees," a piece "with a fine true beauty in it"; articles from the London *Times* claiming that "a big forest may possess a sort of Collective Personality"; and more. Most attended to, however, is Francis (son of Charles) Darwin's 1908 address to the Royal Society, which is read aloud with excitement by Bittacy to his wife within the story:

> "It is impossible to know whether or not plants are conscious; but it is consistent with the doctrine of continuity that in all living things there is something psychic, and if we accept this point of view"
>
> "*If*," she interrupted, scenting danger.
>
> He ignored the interruption as a thing of slight value he was accustomed to.
>
> "If we accept this point of view," he continued, "we must believe that in plants there exists a faint copy *of what we know as consciousness in ourselves*?"
>
> He laid the paper down and steadily stared at her. Their eyes met. He had italicised the last phrase.[64]

Blackwood makes use of the actual text of Francis Darwin's address for both scientific imprimatur and, more important, narratorial validation. The heavily overdetermined scene, which repeats both Bittacy's italicized reading and Mrs. Bittacy's repeated "if" again before the passage is over, ends with Mrs. Bittacy's familiar recourse to the dismissal of the vegetable kingdom's "very right to existence" on biblical and moral grounds. The full text of Francis Darwin's address, however, is more concerned with practical evidence than Christian dictate. Recalling his father's claim in *The Power of Movement in Plants* (1880) that "it is impossible not to be struck with the resemblance between the foregoing movements of plants and many of the actions performed unconsciously by the lower animals," Francis Darwin asserts this is "an example of the way in which science returns to the obvious."[65] He continues: "Here we find revived, in a rational form, the point of view of the child or of the writer of fairy stories. We do not go so far as the child; we know that flowers do not talk or walk; but the fact that plants must be classed with animals as regards their manner of reaction to stimuli has now become almost a commonplace of physiology. And inasmuch as we ourselves are animals, this conception gives us a certain insight into the reactions of plants which we should not otherwise possess."[66] Skirting as he does the "sin" of anthropomorphism, Francis Darwin reaffirms the power of narrative in its most amplified and credulous form to do the necessary work of explaining the organic world to its rational inhabitants. And, like Darwin, Bittacy uses the acknowledgment of the absence of negative evidence only to emphasize the positive possibility—"if we accept this point of view" is a genuinely conditional turn of phrase only for his wife, since he has already made up his mind. This sense of derived consciousness has become fundamental to Michael Marder's plant theories of mind or ecological ethnographies like Eduardo Kohn's *How Forests Think* (2013), but here, in Blackwood's fiction, it is also vital to a reconceptualized narrative subjectivity for the postcolonial forest.[67] The propositional relationship to represented knowledge that rests in Mrs. Bittacy's heavily emphasized "if" is not precluded by the narrative's operations; rather, such conditionality is made necessary in a story with multiple centers of narrative focus—including the Bittacys, Sanderson, and the forest both local and global.

Soon, however, the force of the story's import moves beyond what can be quoted from journals, newspapers, or even poetry. Mrs. Bittacy, more than her husband, perceives the successive attempts by the forest to "amalgamate" her husband: "It's come at last! . . . Beyond the cedar!"[68] The terror for Mrs. Bittacy is not only the loss of her husband but the gain of the trees. "How could she know them too?" she asks herself, staking out the grounds of what Mrs. Bittacy conceives as a clear and jealous "battle between herself and the Forest for his soul."[69] This she describes as a sensation "as clear as though Thompson had come into the room and quietly told her that the cottage was surrounded.

'Please, ma'am, there are trees come up around the house,' she might have suddenly announced."[70] This imagined moment of indirect narration would seem to grant heightened ecological awareness to lower-class minds in ways that have been explored throughout this book, except, of course, for the fact that the information the maid Thompson relays is only Mrs. Bittacy's hypothetical thinking—as her "as though" makes clear. We have come to know that the trees are advancing without being exactly sure how we know it, since neither the Bittacys, their servant, nor even Sanderson has directly narrated their encroachment. Instead, in the negation of the direct assignation of narrating perception and thought, Blackwood makes space for the trees to advance themselves.

The narrative's pull away from focus on Bittacy in the shift from the first half of the story to the second is necessary for the plot to demonstrate his dissolution into the life of the forest, but the refocusing is also necessary to better understand Mrs. Bittacy. Her attempts to reclaim her husband force her to skirt around an acknowledgment of the fragmentary nature of knowledge: "Could this be part of what her husband felt—this sense of thick entanglement with stems, boughs, roots, and foliage?" she asks, in a question she and we both know she cannot answer. The consciousness of being perceived while having limited capacity for reciprocal perception is so horrible that Mrs. Bittacy attempts to physically shut her eyes against its incursions, a blockage that of course has no consequence, given that tree perception disregards visual input.[71] Equally ineffective is Mrs. Bittacy's wish to escape the unsettling forest for the seaside, a possibility thwarted when she realizes that the seaweed offshore from her beach town makes up a forest just as much as the trees that terrify her, its "millions of feelers spreading through the darkened watery depths the power of their ocean foliage."[72] Of course, none of Mrs. Bittacy's attempts to supplant the consciousnesses of the trees can ever be successful, as she partially realizes in the course of a nervous breakdown. The narrative model that Blackwood proposes is one in which there is neither genre nor directive narration, only a kind of wild and windy collective forest consciousness circumnavigating the globe forever. As we learn, the forest is both singular and infinite: "Their number was a host with endless reinforcements, and once it realised its passion was returned the power increased."[73]

The story's inevitable conclusion finds the protecting Lebanon cedar knocked down by a massive storm and Mr. Bittacy amalgamated at last: "For he was out with all that clamoring turmoil. The part of him that she had lost was there. The form that slept so calmly at her side was but the shell, half emptied . . . In the distance she heard the roaring of the Forest further out. Her husband's voice was in it."[74] The vision Mrs. Bittacy has seen of "the figure of her husband moving among the trees—a man, like a tree, walking" uses the comma-delimited clause to attack the pathetic fallacy and what Francis Darwin called the "sin" of anthropomorphism, but also to abandon representational figure more generally. Even in Mrs. Bittacy's heavily humanized perception, the analogy between man and tree is rerouted through the action of movement itself, at least propositionally, so that we don't know if the man is like a tree, or if the man and tree are both alike in their walking.[75] If "the power of movement in plants" is the route which both Darwins (and botanists to this day) propose as the likely indicative force of intelligence and/or consciousness, Blackwood here wants to explore how narrative focalization and its concurrent dissolution into the multitude proposes consciousness differently. Though we know that the simile, along with other forms of "seeming" that we have encountered throughout the story, is inadequate for evoking what is meant by either man or tree, Blackwood is left with no other choice. His ecogothic can give us only that much to understand what has become of Mr. Bittacy.

Thus, for the readers, neither observing Bittacy observing the trees, nor observing Mrs. Bittacy observing Bittacy observing the trees can properly return us to the causal operations of the human narrative, at least not on terms that we understand. Blackwood and weird fiction propose an iteration of the posthuman that is also the more-than-human; this revision fits well in our current moment with recent explanations of nonhuman studies, object-oriented ontologies, and other anthrodecenterings. The goal for Blackwood is neither to hew the forest down to manageable human scale, nor to propose that the union the forest offers Bittacy is an ecstatic one—as Robert Mitchell explains, "literal or metaphorical tree hugging is simply a confused way of embracing the obscurity of plant vitality."[76] Instead, in attending to Blackwood's currently little-read plant horror, I want to connect his writing with that of better-studied genre authors of the end of the century, whether H. Rider Haggard or Arthur Conan Doyle, Robert Louis Stevenson or Bram Stoker, or even modernist forerunners Rudyard Kipling or Joseph Conrad, in order to root fictional investigations of nonhuman vitality in earlier and different genres than have previously been proposed. For all of these authors, and for countless others who also contributed works of antirealist romance, the major problem of fiction was how to perceive and understand the nature of another, particularly when that other may be self-replicating, divided, multiple, obscured, invisible, or otherwise fractured and dispersed. At the edge of modernism, fiction sought new ways to apprehend and explain the operations of an external subjectivity. Thinking about the possible thoughts of plants helped such writers work through difficulties of obscure and fractured consciousness by demonstrating just how obscure and how fractured such external subjectivities could be. Fictions of carnivorous plants depended on a concern (however sensationalized) for discernable traces of subjectivity across the foreign and colonized worlds and beyond the bounds of the human or animal body.

For this reason, I don't think that stories of plant carnivory and plant amalgamation should not be read exclusively in a category with other "monster" stories of vampires and mummies that proliferated at the end of the nineteenth century. They should equally importantly be read as examples of the growing canon of environmental literature, in which plant life gained a history, a coherent range of cause and effect, and a particular scale of engagement. All these served a perpetual investigation of intentionality as a revelatory condition of mind, and depended on a concern (however sensationalized) for that discernable conceptual quality across the foreign and colonized worlds and beyond the bounds of the mobile human/animal body. Though environmental epistemology has become a field embarked upon beyond or outside of a theory of mind, the grasping continuing presence of the killer plant narrative shows that the urge to reground environmental epistemology in individual subjects can never entirely be laid aside. The goals of this redefinition of the purposes of such carnivorous fiction fit within this book's larger attempts to find the space granted for plant thoughts in the form of the popular Victorian novel resistant to realism. In making these attempts, I have been especially able to think about the interplay between the narrative diegesis and the fictional world of the text as negotiated by its setting and characters, or, as might be more accurate when considering plants, the characters of its setting. Acknowledging the submerged but ongoing concurrent lives of plants within that zone of interplay brings attention back to some of the key formal markers distinguishing genre fictions of the late Victorian era and beyond. I've argued that genre fictions, from the detective to the gothic to the adventure, diminished that fiction's ability to depend on novelistic conditions still a priority within realism. These include 1) standardization of temporal progress and its ability to mark beginnings and ends, life and death, when perennial plants are the measuring sticks; 2) distinctions between the kinds of people who matter enough to tell their own stories and the kind who stand silently aside from the telling, distinctions challenged by servants, natives, and happy and unhappy plants themselves; 3) boundaries of selfhood, blurred around the edges once free indirect discourse nudges narrative consciousness from the man regarding the flower to the flower itself; and 4) designations of the beings to which ethical and moral duties are owed, which may or may not include smoke-suffocated plants and ivy-burdened trees. These were problems, I've suggested, that plants brought to genre fiction; implicit in my argument is the question if genre fiction also brought those questions to plants.

In the spring of 2010, the conceptual artist Jonathon Keats staged a viewing of "television for plants," during which a collection of New York City-based rubber plants were treated to a lengthy, ceiling-projected video of an Italian sky shading from day to night. As with his previous project providing pornography—in the form of macro-close-ups of pollinating bees—for zinnias and rhododendrons, Keats's "travel documentary" spurred media responses ranging from bemusement to mockery, as did his proposal that gallery visitors might bring their own houseplants to join in the transportive Italian enjoyment.[77] Hailed by Keats himself as "today's metaphysics," such cooperations of art and science meant to point out plant sentience with provocative wit can be included under the efforts of the field of "human-plant studies" that I have given some hints of within this book. This field, which includes geographers, philosophers, historians, and others engaged in what has been termed "philosophical botany" or "critical plant studies," seeks to investigate human systems of thought and feeling as contingent or cooperative with the decidedly nonhuman thoughts and feelings of plants.[78] As the reaction to Keats's work shows, his is a question that attracts widespread interest. Even without more specialized texts like Michael Marder's *Plant-Thinking* and the field of plant philosophy it is a part of, there remain many more popular investigations into the question of "What would it be like if plants could think?", with recent answers ranging from Michael Pollan's bestselling history *Botany of Desire: A Plant's Eye View of the World* (2001) to M. Night Shylaman's plant-based horror film *The Happening* (2008), a frightful encounter between

Mark Wahlberg and lawns.[79] To imagine the thoughts of trees, however, is not a pleasure reserved solely for twenty-first-century provocateurs. Long before the plant specimen of *WALL-E* (2008) restored humanity from the orgies of late capitalism, nineteenth-century writers and readers found promise (and some peril) in rethinking their world from a plant's perspective.

Adela Pinch has pointed out in her study of the priority of other people's thoughts to readers and writers of the nineteenth-century that "we have grown accustomed to thinking of Victorian Britain as a realm of science, but it was also a realm of metaphysical speculation."[80] When thinking about the thoughts of plants, Victorian writers and readers found a double redirection: in one sense, plants grew narratively more vigorous as they gained agency and direction commensurate with animals and even monstrous or villainous humans, while in another sense, plants grew inaccessible to narrative and rhetorical figure as they became weighted with specific and situated forms of geographical and scientific knowledge. Robert Mitchell writes that "the deictic character of Romantic representations of plants—the attempt to trace cryptogamia in such a way that readers could learn to draw themselves closer to the life of plants—was not, fundamentally, a conservative desire to retain what had come before, but rather a desire to become otherwise than one had been."[81] It has been the work of this book to show that Victorians of many kinds, as well as those who carried forward their fictional forms and genres, were also possessed of this desire, and used the lives of plants to become a part of their expanding world in ways which imagined a kind of liberation even as they, in the scouring exhaustions of their industries, more readily ensured botanical and planetary destruction.

NOTES

Introduction

1. Bewell, "Erasmus Darwin's Cosmopolitan Nature," 22.
2. Loudon, *An Encyclopaedia of Gardening,* 1835, I:351. Or, as Judith Taylor has more recently explained, "A good place to start the examination of plant migration is with England." See her *The Global Migrations of Ornamental Plants: How the World Got into Your Garden* (St. Louis: Missouri Botanical Garden Press, 2009), 13.
3. Thomas, *Man and the Natural World,* 226.
4. On the term "second nature," see William Cronon, *Nature's Metropolis: Chicago and the Great West* (Norton, 1992), and Cronon's caution that such distinctions between tiers of the natural world are "profoundly problematic" (xix). See also Michael Pollan, *Second Nature: A Gardener's Education* (New York: Grove/Atlantic, 2007), and A. J. Lustig, "Cultivating Knowledge in Nineteenth-Century English Gardens," *Science in Context* 13, no. 2 (2000): 155–81.
5. See, on the former, Elizabeth Carolyn Miller, "Dendrography and Ecological Realism," *Victorian Studies* 58, no. 4 (2016): 696–718; and, on the latter, Price, "Vegetable Monsters."
6. Philip Pauly, expanding beyond my synthesis of plants and literature, asserts that "attention to the history of horticulture advances our aspirations to . . . see together the histories of the environment, agriculture, science, art and national development." See his *Fruits and Plains: The Horticultural Transformation of America* (Cambridge: Harvard University Press, 2007), 8. See also his "Mums as the Measure of Men" and "Is Environmental History a Subfield of Garden History?."
7. *Household Words* calls it "not . . . the least of the blessings referable to steam and commerce, that our dinners have pleasanter vegetables, and our desserts richer fruits, than in the days when Queen Elizabeth ruled" (24). "The Growth Of Our Gardens," *Household Words* 18.430 (June 19, 1858): 21–24. On imported vegetables and fruits, see also James Walvin, *Fruits of Empire: Exotic Produce and British Taste, 1660-1800* (New York: New York University Press, 1997).
8. Botanical historians have traced these circulations long prior to the nineteenth century, while also acknowledging the dramatic escalation in scale and significance of botanical exchanges in the Victorian era. See Haripriya Rangan, Judith Carney, and Tim Denham, "Environmental History of Botanical Exchanges in the Indian Ocean World," *Environment and History* 18, no. 3 (August 1, 2012): 311–42; Eric Pawson, "Plants, Mobilities and Landscapes"; Dave Kendal,

Nicholas S. G. Williams, and Kathryn J. H. Williams, "A Cultivated Environment: Exploring the Global Distribution of Plants in Gardens, Parks and Streetscapes," *Urban Ecosystems* 15, no. 3 (2012): 637–52; and James Beattie, Edward D. Melillo, and Emily O'Gorman, eds., *Eco-Cultural Networks and the British Empire: New Views on Environmental History* (London: Bloomsbury Academic, 2016).

9. This argument has been made influentially and also much more broadly by Timothy Morton; for starters, see his landmark *Ecology without Nature: Rethinking Environmental Aesthetics* (Cambridge: Harvard University Press, 2007).

10. Cooke, *Freaks and Marvels of Plant Life*, 19.

11. Curry, "Naturalising the Exotic and Exoticising the Naturalised," 346.

12. This is of course not at all true for British Romanticism. For work focusing especially on aspects of human-aided cultivation of plants in and around Romantic-era literature, see Harriet Ritvo, "At the Edge of the Garden: Nature and Domestication in Eighteenth- and Nineteenth-Century Britain," *Huntington Library Quarterly* 55, no. 3 (July 1, 1992): 363–78; Greg Garrard, "An Absence of Azaleas: Imperialism, Exoticism and Nativity in Romantic Biogeographical Ideology"; Alan Bewell, "Romanticism and Colonial Natural History," *Studies in Romanticism* 43, no. 1 (April 1, 2004): 5–34; Timothy Morton, "Wordsworth Digs the Lawn," *European Romantic Review* 15, no. 2 (June 1, 2004): 317–27; Deidre Shauna Lynch, "'Young Ladies Are Delicate Plants': Jane Austen and Greenhouse Romanticism"; and Theresa M. Kelley, *Clandestine Marriage: Botany and Romantic Culture* (Baltimore: Johns Hopkins University Press, 2012).

13. Hudson, *A Crystal Age*, 164.

14. See John Plotz's discussion of this in "Speculative Naturalism and the Problem of Scale: Richard Jefferies's *After London*, After Darwin," *Modern Language Quarterly* 76, no. 1 (March 1, 2015): 31–56, particularly 39 and 50–51.

15. Woolf, *Mr. Bennett and Mrs. Brown*, 4.

16. Recent works include, on climate, Taylor, *The Sky of Our Manufacture*; on geology, Adelene Buckland, *Novel Science: Fiction and the Invention of Nineteenth-Century Geology* (Chicago: University of Chicago Press, 2013); on energy, Barri J. Gold, *ThermoPoetics: Energy in Victorian Literature and Science* (Cambridge: MIT Press, 2010) and Allen MacDuffie, *Victorian Literature, Energy, and the Ecological Imagination* (Cambridge: Cambridge University Press, 2014); and, on planetary scale as measure of literary reckoning, Benjamin Morgan, "*Fin du Globe*: On Decadent Planets."

17. Work directing the development of the still-nascent field includes Karen Houle, "Animal, Vegetable, Mineral: Ethics as Extension or Becoming? The Case of Becoming Plant," *Journal for Critical Animal Studies* 9, nos. 1–2 (2011): 89–116; Matthew Hall, *Plants as Persons: A Philosophical Botany* (Albany: SUNY Press, 2011); and Michael Marder, *Plant-Thinking: A Philosophy of Vegetal Life*.

18. See Alex Woloch, *The One vs. the Many: Minor Characters and the Space of the Protagonist in the Novel* (Princeton: Princeton University Press, 2003). Other recent nonbotanical reconsiderations of character that make space for the possibility of considering plants as characters include Deidre Shauna Lynch, *The Economy of Character: Novels, Market Culture, and the Business of Inner Meaning* (Chicago: University of Chicago Press, 1998) and Blakey Vermeule, *Why Do We Care about Literary Characters?* (Baltimore: Johns Hopkins University Press, 2010). These queries of character are indebted to the cultural cognitive theories of Lisa Zunshine; see

her *Why We Read Fiction: Theory of Mind and the Novel* (Columbus: Ohio State University Press, 2006).
  19. Bennett, *Vibrant Matter*, 99; Tsing, *The Mushroom at the End of the World*.
  20. Watson, *Flowers and Gardens*, 120.
  21. The development of these questions is indebted to the work of the field of "thing theory"; key texts for the field of Victorian studies include John Plotz, *Portable Property: Victorian Culture on the Move* (Princeton: Princeton University Press, 2008); Elaine Freedgood, *The Ideas in Things: Fugitive Meaning in the Victorian Novel* (Chicago: University of Chicago Press, 2010); and Jonathan Lamb, *The Things Things Say* (Princeton: Princeton University Press, 2016).
  22. Morton, *The Ecological Thought*, 15.
  23. Mitchell, "Cryptogamia."
  24. Wilde, *The Picture of Dorian Gray*, 75.
  25. Brontë, *Villette*, 358, emphasis original. For one study of this memorable pronouncement that takes a nonbotanical focus, see Karen Chase Levenson, "'Happiness Is Not a Potato': The Victorian Cultivation of Happiness," *Nineteenth-Century Contexts* 33, no. 2 (2011): 161–69.
  26. On the social consequences of Victorian cultivations, see David Wayne Thomas, *Cultivating Victorians: Liberal Culture and the Aesthetic* (Philadelphia: University of Pennsylvania Press, 2004).
  27. The language in fact reworked existing nonfiction publications by Butler in New Zealand dating from the 1860s, as Gillian Beer and others have discussed; see Gillian Beer, "Butler, Memory, and the Future" in *Samuel Butler, Victorian Against the Grain: A Critical Overview*, ed. James G. Paradis (Toronto: University of Toronto Press, 2007), 45–57.
  28. Armstrong, "Samuel Butler's Sheep," 452.
  29. Butler, *Erewhon, Or, Over the Range*, 191–92.
  30. On Ruskin's versions of this sympathy, see Katelin Krieg, "Ruskin, Darwin, and Looking Beneath Surfaces," *Victorian Literature and Culture* 45, no. 4 (December 2017): 709–26.
  31. Beinart and Middleton, "Plant Transfers in Historical Perspective," 11. On the potato's history, see Redcliffe N. Salaman, *The History and Social Influence of the Potato* (Cambridge: Cambridge University Press, 1970) as well as, nonbotanically, David Lloyd, "The Political Economy of the Potato," *Nineteenth-Century Contexts* 29, nos. 2–3 (June 1, 2007): 311–35.
  32. Beattie and Stenhouse, "Empire, Environment and Religion," 419.
  33. Blackwood, "The Man Whom the Trees Loved," 24.
  34. Dennis Denisoff has read attention to the lives of the plants as part of an ecopaganist emphasis on human deindividuation, and while I agree with that assessment, I want to alter the emphasis of the equation; here I am as interested in the individuation of the plants as the deindividuation of the humans. See his "The Dissipating Nature of Decadent Paganism from Pater to Yeats" and "Fluid Margins: Natural Environments in Victorian Culture," *Victorian Review* 36, no. 2 (Fall 2010): 7–10, among other recent work.
  35. "Whereas it is possible to conceive of a world without animals ... there could be no life for us and our sister-species in a world without plants," concludes M. M. Mahood bluntly; see *The Poet as Botanist*, 3. This kind of "disanthropic"

conceiving has been explored critically by Greg Garrard; see "Worlds Without Us: Some Types of Disanthropy," *Sub-Stance*, no. 1 (2012): 40-60.

36. I have not in this book given much attention to orchids, largely because they, as perhaps the best-known example of an exotic plant brought to Britain in the nineteenth century, have already been the subject of much excellent scholarship. See Devin Griffiths, "Flattening the World: Natural Theology and the Ecology of Darwin's Orchids," *Nineteenth-Century Contexts* 37, no. 5 (2015): 431-52; Lynn M. Voskuil, "Victorian Orchids and the Forms of Ecological Society," in *Strange Science: Investigating the Limits of Knowledge in the Victorian Age*, ed. Laura Pauline Karpenko and Shalyn R. Claggett, 19-39 (Ann Arbor: University of Michigan Press, 2016); and Jim Endersby's "Deceived by Orchids: Sex, Science, Fiction and Darwin" as well as his *Orchid: A Cultural History* (Chicago: University of Chicago Press, 2016).

37. Grahame, *The Wind in the Willows*, 92.

38. Goody, *The Culture of Flowers*.

39. White, "Environmental History, Ecology, and Meaning," 1113.

40. Seaton, "Considering the Lilies," 256.

41. Secord, *Visions of Science;* Gates, *Kindred Nature;* Shteir, *Cultivating Women, Cultivating Science: Flora's Daughters and Botany in England, 1760-1860;* Secord, "Science in the Pub."

42. A partial list of some recent scholarship around these themes includes Lara Kriegel, "Culture and the Copy: Calico, Capitalism, and Design Copyright in Early Victorian Britain," *Journal of British Studies* 43, no. 2 (April 1, 2004): 233-65; Ann B. Shteir, "Victorian Wax Flower Modelling," *Victorian Literature and Culture* 35, no. 2 (2007): 649-61; Robin Veder, "Flowers in the Slums: Weavers' Floristry in the Age of Spitalfields' Decline," *Journal of Victorian Culture* 14, no. 2 (2009): 261-81; Dominic Janes, "'The Catholic Florist': Flowers and Deviance in the Mid-Nineteenth-Century Church of England," *Visual Culture in Britain* 12, no. 1 (March 2011): 77-95; and Laura Anne Kalba, "Blue Roses and Yellow Violets: Flowers and the Cultivation of Color in Nineteenth-Century France," *Representations* 120, no. 1 (November 2012): 83-114.

43. Moore, "'The Modern World-System' as Environmental History?," 312.

44. See Alfred W. Crosby, *Ecological Imperialism: The Biological Expansion of Europe, 900-1900* (Cambridge: Cambridge University Press, 1986); Richard Grove, *Green Imperialism*; Richard Drayton, *Nature's Government: Science, Imperial Britain, and the "Improvement" of the World* (New Haven: Yale University Press, 2000); and the reference volume *Environment and Empire*, ed. William Beinart and Lotte Hughes, Oxford History of the British Empire Companion Series (Oxford: Oxford University Press, 2007).

Crosby has received most of the rebukes; in a representative critique, Lance van Sittert calls Crosby's concept of "ecological imperialism" a "naive biological Eurocentricism which denied any reciprocal invasion of Europe by plants, animals and pathogens from the colonies in order to preserve the cherished primacy of human agency in the historical narrative." See "'Our Irrepressible Fellow-Colonist': The Biological Invasion of Prickly Pear (Opuntia Ficus-Indica) in the Eastern Cape c. 1890-c. 1910."

45. As Sverker Sörlin and Paul Warde have pointed out, "Environmental

themes of course dovetail neatly, and provide ready analogies, with colonial and postcolonial history. Processes of invasion, acculturation, the confrontation of the 'indigenous' and the 'colonizer,' or the 'indigenous' and the 'exotic,' of 'local' and 'scientific' knowledge, intensive and extensive forms of cultivations, all these find ready resonance in various discourses associated with the 'global south.'" See their "The Problem of the Problem of Environmental History: A Re-Reading of the Field," *Environmental History* 12, no. 1 (January 1, 2007): 107–30, 111.

46. Some of the many histories of these cultural changes include Anne Helmreich, *The English Garden and National Identity: The Competing Styles of Garden Design, 1870-1914* and Sarah Dewis, *The Loudons and the Gardening Press: A Victorian Cultural Industry.*

47. Pawson, "Plants, Mobilities and Landscapes," 1465; Cresswell, *On the Move*, 20.

48. Pfeiffer and Voeks, "Biological Invasions and Biocultural Diversity," 282. On weeds in particular, see the range of treatments from popular to academic between Richard Mabey, *Weeds: How Vagabond Plants Gatecrashed Civilisation and Changed the Way We Think about Nature*, rev. ed. (London: Profile, 2012), and C. A. Kull and H. Rangan, "The Political Ecology of Weeds: A Scalar Approach to Landscape Transformation," in *The International Handbook of Political Ecology*, ed. R. L. Bryant (Cheltenham: Edward Elgar), 487–500.

49. Allen, *Flowers and Their Pedigrees*, 5. The identification of Allen as the "busiest man in England" is one he shares with Joseph Paxton, Victorian gardener. See Peter Morton, *The Busiest Man in England: Grant Allen and the Writing Trade, 1875-1900* (New York: Palgrave Macmillan, 2005) and Kate Colquhoun, *"The Busiest Man in England": A Life of Joseph Paxton, Gardener, Architect, and Victorian Visionary* (Boston: David R. Godine, 2006).

On Grant Allen's nature writing in the context of his contemporaries, see Linda H. Peterson, "Writing Nature at the Fin de Siècle: Grant Allen, Alice Meynell, and the Split Legacy of Gilbert White," *Victorian Review* 36, no. 2 (2010): 80–91. On popular science writing more generally, see Bernard Lightman, *Victorian Popularizers of Science: Designing Nature for New Audiences* (Chicago: University of Chicago Press, 2010) as well as James A. Secord, *Visions of Science Books and Readers at the Dawn of the Victorian Age* (Oxford: Oxford University Press, 2014).

50. Allen, 3–4.

51. Watson, *Cybele Britannica*, 63; Garrard, "An Absence of Azaleas: Imperialism, Exoticism and Nativity in Romantic Biogeographical Ideology," 154.

52. Dümpelmann, "Introduction," 2.

53. Pawson, "Plants, Mobilities and Landscapes," 1474.

54. Braddon, *Lady Audley's Secret*, 1. For more on rhododendron exchange, see Katharina Dehnen-Schmutz and Mark Williamson, "Rhododendron Ponticum in Britain and Ireland: Social, Economic and Ecological Factors in Its Successful Invasion," *Environment & History* 12, no. 3 (August 2006): 325–50.

55. On these circulations in environmental history, see, among many others, Jodi Frawley, "Prickly Pear Land"; Brett M. Bennett, "A Global History of Australian Trees"; and Kate B. Showers, "Prehistory of Southern African Forestry: From Vegetable Garden to Tree Plantation."

56. Pfeiffer and Voeks, "Biological Invasions and Biocultural Diversity," 284.
57. Hibberd, *Brambles and Bay Leaves,* 302.
58. Eliot, *The Mill on the Floss,* 188.
59. Endersby, "Deceived by Orchids," 207.
60. Ryan, "Cultural Botany," 126.
61. Tsing, "Wreckage and Recovery: Four Papers Exploring the Nature of Nature," 7.
62. See Jan Alber's overview of the field, "Unnatural Narratology: The Systematic Study of Anti-Mimeticism," *Literature Compass* 10, no. 5 (May 2013): 449-60, as well as Lars Bernaerts, Marco Caracciolo, Luc Herman, and Bart Vervaeck's "The Storied Lives of Non-Human Narrators," which considers talking objects and talking animals (but not talking plants) to emphasize such narration's "double dialectic of empathy and defamiliarization, human and nonhuman experientiality." *Narrative* 22, no. 1 (2014): 68-93, 69.
63. Murphy, "Dialoguing with Bakhtin over Our Ethical Responsibility to Anothers," 157.
64. Luciano and Chen, "Has the Queer Ever Been Human?," 195.
65. Sandilands, "Fear of a Queer Plant?," 426.
66. Elliott, *Victorian Gardens;* Waters, *The Garden in Victorian Literature*; Cunningham, "The Culture of Gardens"; Dümpelmann, ed., *A Cultural History of Gardens in the Age of Empire.*
67. "Why are gardens so much a part of English identity, why are the English such 'plantaholics'?" asks Eugenia Herbert in *Flora's Empire,* 309, collapsing the two propositions.
68. For recent treatments of gardens in literature, see Shelley Saguaro, *Garden Plots: The Politics and Poetics of Gardens* (Aldershot: Ashgate, 2006); Linda Parshall, "Verbal Representations," in *A Cultural History of Gardens in the Age of Empire,* 135-52.
69. Pauly, "Is Environmental History a Subfield of Garden History?," 71.
70. Cooke, *Freaks and Marvels of Plant Life,* 21.

1. Detecting the Global Plant Specimen

1. Collins, *The Moonstone,* 417.
2. Collins, 417. Studies of *The Moonstone* making plain the complexities of the novel's engagement with the British Empire include Ashish Roy, "The Fabulous Imperialist Semiotic of Wilkie Collin's *The Moonstone,*" *New Literary History* 24, no. 3 (1993): 657-81; Ian Duncan, "The Moonstone, the Victorian Novel, and Imperialist Panic," *Modern Language Quarterly* 55, no. 3 (1994): 297-319; and Melissa Free, "'Dirty Linen': Legacies of Empire in Wilkie Collins's *The Moonstone,*" *Texas Studies in Literature and Language* 48, no. 4 (Winter 2006): 340-71.
3. See, for example, Mark Mossman's "Representations of the Abnormal Body in *The Moonstone,*" *Victorian Literature and Culture* 37, no. 2 (September 2009): 483, which, like Audrey Fisch's "Collins, Race, and Slavery," in *Reality's Dark Light: The Sensational Wilkie Collins,* ed. Maria K. Bachman and Don Richard Cox (Knoxville: University of Tennessee Press, 2003), 313-28, reads Ezra Jennings's mixed racial status as a marker of Collins's efforts at progressive integration of the novel's notion of Englishness. See also the chapter on *The Moonstone* in

Timothy L. Carens's *Outlandish English Subjects in the Victorian Domestic Novel* (Basingstoke: Palgrave Macmillan, 2005), 117–41.

4. Collins, *The Moonstone*, 420.
5. Collins, 420.
6. Collins, 84.
7. "The Moonstone," 106.
8. Eliot, "Introduction," xii.
9. Collins, *The Moonstone*, 254.
10. Collins, 269.
11. Collins, 507.
12. Collins, 491.
13. Collins, 348.
14. Ousby, "Wilkie Collins's *The Moonstone* and the Constance Kent Case," 25.
15. Aylmer, "The Detective in Real Life," 505.
16. Loudon, *Arboretum Et Fruticetum Britannicum, or, The Trees and Shrubs of Britain, Native and Foreign, Hardy and Half-Hardy, Pictorially and Botanically Delineated, and Scientifically and Popularly Described; with Their Propagation, Culture, Management, and Uses in the Arts, In Useful and Ornamental Plantations, and in Landscape-Gardening; Preceded by a Historical and Geographical Outline of the Trees and Shrubs of Temperate Climates Throughout the World*, 780.
17. See Sarah Dewis, *The Loudons and the Gardening Press: A Victorian Cultural Industry*. See also the section on Loudon in A. J. Lustig, "Cultivating Knowledge in Nineteenth-Century English Gardens," *Science in Context* 13, no. 2 (June 2000): 155–81.
18. For a survey of Victorian horticultural periodicals, see Ray Desmond, "Loudon and Nineteenth-Century Horticultural Journalism," in *John Claudius Loudon and the Early Nineteenth Century in Great Britain* (Washington, DC: Dumbarton Oaks, Trustees for Harvard University, 1980), 77–98, as well as his "British Nineteenth Century Gardening Periodicals: A Chronological List" (99–104) in the same volume.
19. Allen, "The Daisy's Pedigree," 170. This essay was later expanded and republished in *Flowers and Their Pedigrees* (London: Longmans, Green, 1883).
20. Beattie, "Recent Themes in the Environmental History of the British Empire," 133.
21. Laird, *The Flowering of the English Landscape Garden*.
22. Cunningham, "The Culture of Gardens," 52.
23. Bewell, "Erasmus Darwin's Cosmopolitan Nature," 27.
24. Grove, *Green Imperialism*.
25. Cushing, *The Exotic Gardener*, 1; Loudon, *The Green-House Companion*, 37.
26. Harrison, "Introduction," 1.
27. Darby, "Un-Natural History," 639.
28. Ward, *On the Growth of Plants in Closely Glazed Cases*, vii.
29. Lynch, "Young Ladies Are Delicate Plants," 693.
30. Tachibana and Watkins, "Botanical Transculturation" 46.
31. Milligan, *Pleasures and Pains*.
32. Reitz, *Detecting the Nation*.
33. In this he is akin to the title character of Harriet Beecher Stowe's *Dred*:

A Tale of the Great Dismal Swamp (1856) as Mary Kuhn has read him. She writes: "Stowe's association of humans with an elastic botanical aesthetic is a clear departure from the way male ethnologists like Louis Agassiz, Comte Joseph A. de Gobineau, Robert Knox, and Samuel George Morton classified race. . . . Dred's alignment with living, dynamic botanical tropes challenges prevalent racial theorists who sought proof of racial difference by projecting nature as immutable" (503); see her "Garden Variety: Botany and Multiplicity in Harriet Beecher Stowe's Abolitionism," *American Literature* 87, no. 3 (2015): 489–516.

34. Goodlad, *The Victorian Geopolitical Aesthetic*, 114.
35. Kelley, *Clandestine Marriage*.
36. Freedgood, "Fictional Settlements," 399.
37. Freedgood, 399, 408.
38. Haggard, *Allan and the Holy Flower*, 24.
39. Clausson, "Degeneration, Fin-de-Siècle Gothic, and the Science of Detection," 78.
40. For accounts of these within detective fiction, see Lawrence Frank, *Victorian Detective Fiction and the Nature of Evidence: The Scientific Investigations of Poe, Dickens, and Doyle* (New York: Palgrave Macmillan, 2003) and Ronald R. Thomas, *Detective Fiction and the Rise of Forensic Science* (Cambridge: Cambridge University Press, 1999).
41. After an initial development in the chapter "Clues" in his *Signs Taken for Wonders: Essays in the Sociology of Literary Forms* (London: Verso, 1988, 130–56), he expands further on the consequences of the clue's introduction for the genre's evolution in "The Slaughterhouse of Literature," *MLQ: Modern Language Quarterly* 61, no. 1 (2000): 207–27.
42. Kermode, "Secrets and Narrative Sequence," 87.
43. Meade and Eustace, "The Talk of The Town," 79, 80.
44. Meade and Eustace, 80.
45. Meade and Eustace, 80.
46. Loudon, *The Green-House Companion*, 1.
47. Doyle, "The Adventure of the Naval Treaty, Cont.," 467.
48. Doyle, "The Adventure of the Naval Treaty," 400.
49. Doyle, *A Study in Scarlet*, 21.
50. Doyle, Arthur Conan, "The Adventure of the Copper Beeches," 618.
51. Braddon, *Lady Audley's Secret*, 93.
52. Jaffe, *The Victorian Novel Dreams of the Real*, 4.
53. Doyle, *The Sign of Four*, 43.
54. Doyle, "The Adventure of the Naval Treaty, Cont.," 464.
55. Doyle gave this explanation in his autobiography *Memories and Adventures*, of the genesis of Sherlock Holmes: "I had been reading some detective stories . . . and it struck me what nonsense they were, to put it mildly, because for getting the solution of the mystery the authors always depended upon some coincidence," which is "not a fair way of playing the game." Quoted in Stephen Knight, *Form and Ideology in Crime Fiction* (London: Macmillan, 1980), 67.
56. Siddiqi, *Anxieties of Empire and the Fiction of Intrigue*, 7.
57. Wells, *The Time Machine: An Invention*, 121.
58. Wells, 151.

59. Wells, 152.
60. Wells, 121.
61. Kingdon-Ward of course did not inaugurate this linkage; a long previous tradition of popular natural history writing, like Philip Gosse's *The Romance of Natural History* (1860), used fantasy techniques to relay the facts of organic life. On Gosse, see Lynn L. Merrill, *The Romance of Victorian Natural History* (Oxford: Oxford University Press, 1989).
62. Ward, *The Romance of Plant Hunting, by Capt. F. Kingdon-Ward*, 267.
63. Ward, 267.
64. Ward, 268.
65. Ward, 268–69.
66. For more on these, see Londa L. Schiebinger, *Plants and Empire: Colonial Bioprospecting in the Atlantic World* (Cambridge: Harvard University Press, 2004). Other studies of plant hunters include Alice M. Coats, *The Plant Hunters: Being a History of the Horticultural Pioneers, Their Quests, and Their Discoveries from the Renaissance to the Twentieth Century* (New York: McGraw-Hill, 1970); Toby Musgrave, *The Plant Hunters: Two Hundred Years of Adventure and Discovery Around the World* (London: Seven Dials, 1999); Mary Gribbin, *Flower Hunters* (Oxford: Oxford University Press, 2008); and Carolyn Fry, *The Plant Hunters: The Adventures of the World's Greatest Botanical Explorers* (London: Andre Deutsch, 2012).

For critical interrogations of the operations of European plant hunters, see Erik Mueggler, *The Paper Road: Archive and Experience in the Botanical Exploration of West China and Tibet* (Berkeley: University of California Press, 2011) and Fa-ti Fan, *British Naturalists in Qing China: Science, Empire, and Cultural Encounter* (Cambridge: Harvard University Press, 2004).

2. STRANGE CITY GARDENS

1. Dickens, *The Mystery of Edwin Drood*, 215.
2. Dickens, 247.
3. Morrison, *A Child of the Jago*, 50–51. See also Margaret Willes, *The Gardens of the British Working Class* (New Haven: Yale University Press, 2014).
4. Doyle, *The Lost World*, 115.
5. As Ross Forman has shown, Doyle's novel makes parodic use of such adventure novel conventions, see R. G. Forman, "Room for Romance: Playing with Adventure in Arthur Conan Doyle's The Lost World."
6. On indoor plants, see Tovah Martin, *Once Upon a Windowsill. A History of Indoor Plants* (Portland: Timber Press, 1988), and Catherine Horwood, *Potted History: The Story of Plants in the Home* (London: Frances Lincoln, 2007). On indoor gardening in a European context, see also Andreas Stynen, "'Une Mode Charmante': Nineteenth Century Indoor Gardening between Nature and Artifice," *Studies in the History of Gardens and Designed Landscapes* 29, no. 3 (September 1, 2009): 217–34.
7. The environmental historians Dave Kendal, Nicholas S. Williams, and Kathryn J. Williams explain: "As the world becomes more urbanised, cultivated vegetation within human settlements in gardens, parks, and streetscapes is becoming increasingly important to many peoples' experience of biological life." See their "A Cultivated Environment: Exploring the Global Distribution of

Plants in Gardens, Parks and Streetscapes," *Urban Ecosystems* 15, no. 3 (September 2012): 637–52, 638.

8. Schmitt, "The Gothic Romance in the Victorian Period," 305.

9. Armstrong, "A Gothic History of the British Novel," 106.

10. Armstrong, 117.

11. Stephanie Ross explores this further in the introduction to her study of eighteenth-century English garden design, demonstrating through a series of negative examples that an adequately accommodating definition of a garden is remarkably difficult to achieve. See her *What Gardens Mean* (Chicago: University of Chicago Press, 1998), 6–10.

12. Hunt and Leslie, "General Editor's Preface," xii–xiii.

13. Loudon, *An Encyclopædia of Gardening*, 1.

14. Loudon, *An Encyclopaedia of Gardening*, 1835, 1, emphasis mine.

15. For a history of earlier city gardens, see Todd Longstaffe-Gowan. *The London Town Garden 1740-1840* (New Haven: Published for the Paul Mellon Centre for Studies in British Art by Yale University Press, 2001).

16. See Taylor, *The Sky of Our Manufacture*.

17. Fairchild, *The City Gardener*, 5.

18. Hibberd, *The Town Garden*, xi.

19. On the mythos of the "black hole," see Partha Chatterjee, *The Black Hole of Empire: History of a Global Practice of Power* (Princeton: Princeton University Press, 2012).

20. Hibberd, *The Town Garden*, xiii. As with most manuals of instruction, each text on city gardening presents itself as the first to have considered the problem; for example, "It has often been a matter of great surprise to me, that amongst all the various books that have been written upon Botany, and the cultivation of Plants, none should ever have been written upon the treatment plants require when placed in a London sitting room," begins *The Bouquet; or, Ladies' Flower Garden: Being a Description of Those Plants Which Will Flower in the Room* by "A Florist," (London: Simpkin, Marshall, 1839). For other examples of guides to city gardening from the Victorian era, see E. A Maling, *A Handbook for Ladies: On In-Door Plants, Flowers for Ornament, and Song Birds* (London: Smith, Elder, 1870) and Mary Eliza Joy Haweis, *Rus in Urbe: Or Flowers That Thrive in London Gardens & Smoky Towns* (London: Field & Tuer, 1886).

21. Isobel Armstrong addresses the culture of larger conservatories in part 2 of her comprehensive *Victorian Glassworlds: Glass Culture and the Imagination 1830-1880* (Oxford: Oxford University Press, 2008); other recent studies of these spaces from interdisciplinary perspectives include Margaret Flanders Darby, "Joseph Paxton's Water Lily," in *Bourgeois and Aristocratic Cultural Encounters in Garden Art, 1550-1850*, ed. Michael Conan (Washington, DC: Dumbarton Oaks Research Library and Collection, 2002), 255–84; William M. Taylor, *The Vital Landscape: Nature and the Built Environment in Nineteenth-Century Britain*; Samantha Burton, "Champagne in the Shrubbery: Sex, Science, and Space in James Tissot's London Conservatory," *Victorian Studies* 57, no. 3 (2015): 476–89; and Dustin Valen, "On the Horticultural Origins of Victorian Glasshouse Culture," *Journal of the Society of Architectural Historians* 75, no. 4 (December 2016): 403–23.

22. Ward, *On the Growth of Plants in Closely Glazed Cases*, 35.

23. Ward, 93-94. This proposal follows Loudon's earlier, even more ill-conceived proposal that "when subsequent improvements in communicating heat, and in ventilation, shall have rendered the artificial climates produced, equal or superior to those which they imitate, then will such an appendage to a family seat be not less useful in a medical point of view, than elegant and luxurious as a lounge for exercise or entertainment in inclement weather. Perhaps the time may arrive when such artificial climates will not only be stocked with appropriate birds, fishes, and harmless animals, but with examples of the human species from the different countries imitated, habited in their particular costumes, and who may serve as gardeners or curators of the different productions." He concludes that "this subject is too new and strange to admit of discussion, without incurring the ridicule of general readers." See John Claudius Loudon, *Remarks on the Construction of Hothouses: Also, a Review of the Various Methods of Building Them in Foreign Countries as Well as in England* (London: J. Taylor, 1817), 49.

24. "Back Street Conservatories," 273.

25. "Back Street Conservatories," 272.

26. Hooker writes that Ward's cases "have been the means, in the last fifteen years, of introducing more new and valuable plants to our gardens than were imported during the preceding century; and in the character of 'Domestic Green-houses' . . . as a means of cultivating plants with success in our parlours, our halls, and our drawing-rooms, they have constituted a new era in horticulture." See *On the Growth of Plants in Closely Glazed Cases*, 132.

27. Loudon, "Domestic Notices: England," 163.

28. Taylor, *The Vital Landscape*, xv.

29. Taylor, *The Sky of Our Manufacture*, 23.

30. Ryan, "Cultural Botany," 129.

31. Darwin, *The Voyage of the Beagle*, 444. See Benjamin Morgan, "Fin du Globe: On Decadent Planets."

32. King, "Reorienting the Scientific Frontier," 196.

33. On Kew, see Ray Desmond, *The History of the Royal Botanic Gardens Kew* (London: Royal Botanic Gardens, Kew, 2007); on royal gardens (in a French context), see Chandra Mukerji, *Territorial Ambitions and the Gardens of Versailles* (Cambridge: Cambridge University Press, 1997); and on private gardens, see Longstaffe-Gowan. On challenges to the unifying natures of public parks, see Joe Crowdy, "Queer Undergrowth: Weeds and Sexuality in the Architecture of the Garden," *Architecture and Culture* 5, no. 3 (2017): 423-33.

34. See Patrick Brantlinger, *Rule of Darkness: British Literature and Imperialism, 1830-1914* (Ithaca: Cornell University Press, 1988).

35. Collins, *Basil*, 146.

36. Ablow, *Victorian Pain*, 119.

37. Dickens, *Our Mutual Friend*, 219.

38. Jacobus, *Women Writing and Writing about Women*, 58.

39. Among the many distinguished feminist critics considering *Villette*, see Sandra M. Gilbert and Susan Gubar, *The Madwoman in the Attic: The Woman Writer and the Nineteenth-Century Literary Imagination* (New Haven: Yale University Press, 1979), 399-440; Nina Auerbach, *Communities of Women: An Idea in Fiction* (Cambridge: Harvard University Press, 1978), 97-114; and Mary Jacobus, "The Buried

Letter: Feminism and Romanticism in Villette," in *The Brontë Sisters: Critical Assessments*, ed. Eleanor McNees, 4 vols. (Mountfield, East Sussex: Helm Information, 1996), 3:673–88.

40. Gibson, "Charlotte Bronte's First Person," 205; Braun, "A Great Break in the Common Course of Confession," 190. See also Emily W. Heady, "Must I Render an Account?': Genre and Self-Narration in Charlotte Brontë's *Villette*," *Journal of Narrative Theory* 36, no. 3 (2006): 341–364; and Elisha Cohn, "Still Life: Suspended Animation in Charlotte Brontë's *Villette*," whose argument I will take up later in the chapter.

41. Schmitt, "The Gothic Romance in the Victorian Period," 209. On the Brontë's interest in the slave trade in particular, see Maja-Lisa von Sneidern, "Wuthering Heights and the Liverpool Slave Trade," *ELH* 62, no. 1 (1995): 171–96; Humphrey Gawthrop, "Slavery: Idée Fixe of Emily and Charlotte Brontë," *Brontë Studies* 28, no. 2 (2003): 113–21; and Mark Celeste, "Metonymic Chains: Shipwreck, Slavery, and Networks in *Villette*," *Victorian Review* 42, no. 2 (2016): 343–60.

42. Brontë, *Villette*, 103.
43. Brontë, 147.
44. Brontë, 147–48.
45. Brontë, 148.
46. Brontë, 150.
47. Brontë, 161.
48. Brontë, 161–62.
49. Brontë, 684.
50. Brontë, 668.
51. Brontë, 595–96.
52. Brontë, 326.
53. Brontë, 653.
54. Brontë, 667, 675.
55. Cohn, "Still Life," 851.
56. Brontë, *Villette*, 669, 663.
57. Brontë, 424.
58. Milbank, "The Victorian Gothic in English Novels and Stories, 1830–1880," 424.
59. On the genre of the ecogothic broadly defined, see Smith and Hughes, *EcoGothic*.
60. Brontë, *Villette*, 714.
61. Collins, *The Woman in White*, 69.
62. On the earlier history of suburban development see Sarah Bilston, "'Your Vile Suburbs Can Offer Nothing but the Deadness of the Grave': The Stereotyping of Early Victorian Suburbia," *Victorian Literature and Culture* 41, no. 4 (December 2013): 621–42.
63. Kuchta, *Semi-Detached Empire*, 5–6, 6.
64. Doyle, *The Sign of Four*, 35; Marsh, *The Beetle*, 258–59.
65. Doyle, *The Sign of Four*, 33.
66. Machen, *The Three Imposters, Or, The Transmutations*, 141–42.
67. Hibberd, *The Town Garden*, xi.
68. Haweis, *Rus in Urbe*, 3.

69. Stevenson, *The Strange Case of Dr. Jekyll and Mr. Hyde,* 50.
70. Stevenson, 35.
71. Stevenson, 50.
72. Jefferies, *After London, Or, Wild England,* 1.
73. Morris, *News from Nowhere,* 119.
74. On anti-urban movements in Britain, see Jan Marsh, *Back to the Land: The Pastoral Impulse in England, from 1880 to 1914* (New York: Quartet, 1982). The urban renewal projects known as the "Garden City" movements led by Ebenezer Howard were contemporary efforts to realize some measure of these future reinhabitations in modern life. See Standish Meacham, *Regaining Paradise: Englishness and the Early Garden City Movement* (New Haven: Yale University Press, 1999); Kermit C. Parsons and David Schuyler, eds., *From Garden City to Green City: The Legacy of Ebenezer Howard,* Center Books on Contemporary Landscape Design (Baltimore: Johns Hopkins University Press, 2002); and, in a colonial context, Liora Bigon and Yossi Katz, eds. *Garden Cities and Colonial Planning: Transnationality and Urban Ideas in Africa and Palestine* (Manchester: Manchester University Press, 2014).
75. Morris, *News from Nowhere,* 100.
76. Wells, *The Time Machine: An Invention,* 90. For more on the constructedness of landscape in Wells and other authors of scientific romance of the late nineteenth century, see Emily Alder, "'Buildings of the New Age': Dwellings and the Natural Environment in the Futuristic Fiction of H. G. Wells and William Hope Hodgson," in *H.G. Wells: Interdisciplinary Essays,* ed. Steven McLean (Newcastle: Cambridge Scholars, 2008).
77. On bioregionalism, see Tom Lynch, Cheryll Glotfelty, Karla Armbruster, and Ezra J. Zeitler, eds., *The Bioregional Imagination: Literature, Ecology, and Place* (Athens: University of Georgia Press, 2012); on reinhabitation in particular as a tool of bioregionalism, see Martin Delveaux, "'O Me! O Me! How I Love the Earth': William Morris's *News from Nowhere* and the Birth of Sustainable Society," *Contemporary Justice Review* 8, no. 2 (June 2005): 131–46.
78. Stoker, *Dracula,* 60.
79. Fabian, *Time and the Other.*
80. Arata, *Fictions of Loss in the Victorian Fin de Siècle.*
81. Machen, *The Three Imposters, Or, The Transmutations,* 143.
82. Darby, "Joseph Paxton's Water Lily," 277.
83. Denisoff, "The Dissipating Nature of Decadent Paganism from Pater to Yeats," 431.
84. Morgan, "Fin du Globe," 612.
85. King, *Bloom,* 219.
86. Esty, "The Colonial Bildungsroman."
87. Wilde, *The Picture of Dorian Gray,* 63.
88. Wilde, 170.
89. Wilde, 43.
90. Webster, *London Trees,* 72. On city trees, see also H. J. Dyos, *Victorian Suburb: A Study of the Growth of Camberwell* (Leicester: University Press, 1966) and Mark Johnston, *Trees in Towns and Cities: A History of British Urban Arboriculture* (Bollington: Windgather Press, 2015).
91. Wilde, *The Picture of Dorian Gray,* 159.

92. Davis, "Decadence and the Organic Metaphor," 145.
93. Wilde, *The Picture of Dorian Gray*, 60.
94. Davis, "'I Seemed to Hold Two Lives,'" 199.
95. See Robyn Warhol, "Neonarrative; or, How to Render the Unnarratable in Realist Fiction and Contemporary Film," in *A Companion to Narrative Theory* (New York: Wiley-Blackwell, 2005), 220-31.
96. Wilde, *The Picture of Dorian Gray*, 46.
97. Wilde, 47.
98. Wilde, 47, 61.
99. Wilde, 61.
100. Wilde, 63.
101. Wilde, 53.
102. Wilde, 187.
103. Wilde, 187.
104. See Richard Ellmann, *Oscar Wilde* (London: Penguin Books 1988), 43, 84, 158; and Ellmann, "The Uses of Decadence," in *a long the riverrun: Selected Essays* (New York: Knopf 1989), 3-4.
105. Wilde, *The Picture of Dorian Gray*, 161.
106. Wilde, 164.
107. Wilde, 165.
108. Wilde, 165.
109. Wilde, 202.
110. Goldstone, "Servants, Aestheticism, and 'The Dominance of Form,'" 616.
111. Wilde, *The Picture of Dorian Gray*, 223-34.
112. Wilde, 232.
113. Watson, *Flowers and Gardens*, 140.
114. Dakers, *The Holland Park Circle*, 1.
115. Barrie, *The Little White Bird*, 182.
116. Barrie, 209.
117. Wells, "The Door in the Wall," 514.
118. Wells, 517.
119. Wells, 519, 518.
120. Wells, 534.
121. Wells, 519.
122. Wells, 533.

3. Strange Country Gardens

1. Carroll, *Through the Looking-Glass*, 26.
2. Carroll, 138.
3. Carroll, 135.
4. Campbell, "Don't Say It with Nightshades," 608; Seaton, "Considering the Lilies"; Shteir, *Cultivating Women, Cultivating Science Flora's Daughters and Botany in England, 1760-1860*; King, *Bloom*.
5. Carroll, *Through the Looking-Glass*, 140, emphasis original.
6. Doyle, *The Hound of the Baskervilles*, 107.
7. Haggard, *The Days of My Life*, 266.
8. Haggard, *Colonel Quaritch*, 1.

9. Haggard, 6.
10. Haggard, 173, 3.
11. Haggard, 7.
12. Miller, "The Environmental Politics and Aesthetics of Rider Haggard's *King Solomon's Mines*: Capital, Mourning, and Desire," 171.
13. Haggard, *Rural England*, viii.
14. Haggard, *Colonel Quaritch*, 14–15.
15. Haggard, 8.
16. Chapter 2, "The Auction Room," explains at great length Allan Quatermain's shock at a man who would pay £2300 for a single orchid.
17. Haggard, *A Gardener's Year*, 93.
18. Haggard, *Colonel Quaritch*, 81.
19. Haggard, 83.
20. It was a chrysanthemum variety possessed of "very fine guard florets of a pinkish white"; see "Anemone-Flowered Chyrsanthemums," 459.
21. Growing interest in Japanese varieties over the older Chinese forms was spurred by increased aesthetic exchange with Japan and a growing number of plant and gardening texts produced by Britons resident in that country, see Josiah Conder, *The Flowers of Japan and the Art of Floral Arrangement* (Tokio: Hakubunsha, 1891) as well as Florence Du Cane, *The Flowers and Gardens of Japan* (London: A. & C. Black, 1908).

An interest in recreations of Japanese gardens within London also drove collectors of Asian cultivars. See Wybe Kuitert, "Japonaiserie in London and the Hague: A History of the Japanese Gardens at Shepherd's Bush (1910) and Clingendael (c. 1915)," *Garden History* 30, no. 2 (December 1, 2002): 221–38; and Setsu Tachibana, Stephen Daniels, and Charles Watkins, "Japanese Gardens in Edwardian Britain: Landscape and Transculturation," *Journal of Historical Geography* 30, no. 2 (April 2004): 364–94.

22. Pauly, "Mums as the Measure of Men: Horticulture and Culture," 18.
23. Haggard, *A Gardener's Year*, 355–56.
24. Engleheart, "Chrysanthemum Reform"; Watson, *Flowers and Gardens*, 188.
25. Haggard, *Colonel Quaritch*, 222.
26. Haggard, 250, emphasis original.
27. For a comprehensive survey of the liberations afforded by the structure and content of women's garden books, see Sarah Bilston, "Queens of the Garden: Victorian Women Gardeners and the Rise of the Gardening Advice Text," *Victorian Literature and Culture* 36, no. 1 (2008): 1–19. See also a more inclusive work that contains an analysis of women's gardening texts: Judith W. Page and Elise L. Smith, *Women, Literature, and the Domesticated Landscape: England's Disciples of Flora, 1780-1870* (Cambridge: Cambridge University Press, 2011). On women's botany, see Ann B. Shteir, *Cultivating Women, Cultivating Science: Flora's Daughters and Botany in England, 1760-1860* (Baltimore: Johns Hopkins University Press, 1996).
28. Loudon, *Instructions in Gardening for Ladies*; Lindley, *Ladies' Botany*.
29. Ansell, *The Happy Garden*, 3. See also Michael Waters, *The Garden in Victorian Literature* (Aldershot: Scolar, 1988, 241–45).
30. Drury, *Home Gardening*, 1; Robinson, *Alpine Flowers for English Gardens*, xv.
31. The range of scope for intervention granted by Ruskin has recently

been debated by critics, amid the legacy of Kate Millet's dismissal of the work. See Linda H. Peterson, "The Feminist Origins of 'Of Queens' Gardens'," in *Ruskin and Gender,* ed. Dinah Birch and Francis O'Gorman (Houndsmills: Palgrave Macmillan, 2002, 86–106) and Sharon Aronofsky Weltman, "Be No More Housewives, But Queens: Queen Victoria and Ruskin's Domestic Mythology," in *Remaking Queen Victoria,* ed. Margaret Homans and Adrienne Munich (Cambridge: Cambridge University Press, 1997, 105–122).

32. Ruskin, *Sesame and Lilies,* 92.
33. Millett, "The Debate Over Women," 64.
34. Mill writes: "When people are brought up, like many women of the higher classes (though less so in our own country than in any other) as a kind of hothouse plants, shielded from the wholesome vicissitudes of air and temperature, and untrained in any of the occupations and exercises which give stimulus and development to the circulatory and muscular system, while their nervous system, especially in its emotional department, is kept in unnaturally active play; it is no wonder if those of them who do not die of consumption, grow up with constitutions liable to derangement from slight causes, both internal and external, and without stamina to support any task, physical or mental, requiring continuity of effort." *The Subjection of Women* (London: Longmans, 1869), 112.
35. Pierce, "From Garden to Gardener," 757.
36. Pierce, 759. For another perspective on the "Of Queens's Gardens"/*Through the Looking Glass* comparison, see Laura Mooneyham White, "Domestic Queen, Queenly Domestic: Queenly Contradictions in Carroll's Through the Looking-Glass," *Children's Literature Association Quarterly* 32, no. 2 (Summer 2007): 110–28.
37. Other horticultural approaches to *Proserpina* include Beverly Seaton, "Considering the Lilies: Ruskin's 'Proserpina' and Other Victorian Flower Books," and John Illingworth, "Ruskin and Gardening," *Garden History* 22, no. 2 (1994): 218–33.
38. Ruskin, *Love's Meine and Proserpina,* 207.
39. Ruskin, 207, emphasis original.
40. Ruskin, 532.
41. Birch, "Ruskin and the Science of Proserpina," 144.
42. On this, see Mahood, *The Poet as Botanist,* 147–82.
43. Ruskin, *Love's Meine and Proserpina,* 369.
44. Ruskin, 283.
45. Ruskin, 283, emphasis original.
46. Ruskin, 285.
47. Ruskin, 451.
48. Ruskin, 345.
49. Ruskin, 286.
50. Robinson, *The Wild Garden,* xix, emphasis original.
51. Robinson, *The English Flower Garden,* iv.
52. Helmreich, *The English Garden and National Identity.*
53. Cartwright, "The Portfolio," 218.
54. Jekyll, *Wood and Garden,* 5.
55. Robinson, *The Wild Garden,* xiv.

56. Kehler, "Gertrude Jekyll and the Late-Victorian Garden Book: Representing Nature-Culture Relations," 620, 618.
57. Jekyll, *Wood and Garden*, 1.
58. Jekyll, *Home and Garden*, 55.
59. Kehler, "Gertrude Jekyll and the Late-Victorian Garden Book: Representing Nature-Culture Relations," 628.
60. Burnett, *A Little Princess*, 149.
61. Burnett, *The Secret Garden*, 3.
62. Burnett, 3.
63. Burnett, 4.
64. Burnett, 3.
65. Richardson, *Flowers and Flower-Gardens,* 1. On the broader culture of Anglo-Indian gardening, see Eugenia W. Herbert, *Flora's Empire: British Gardens in India* (Philadelphia: University of Pennsylvania Press, 2012).
66. Duncan, *The Simple Adventures of a Memsahib*, 166.
67. Burnett, *The Secret Garden*, 7.
68. Burnett, 64.
69. Burnett, 64.
70. Burnett, 53.
71. Burnett, 137.
72. See Anne Stiles, "Christian Science versus the Rest Cure in Frances Hodgson Burnett's *The Secret Garden*," MFS: Modern Fiction Studies 61, no. 2 (June 25, 2015): 295-319.
73. See especially Danielle E. Price, "Cultivating Mary: The Victorian Secret Garden," *Children's Literature Association Quarterly* 26, no. 1 (2001): 4-14, whose claim that "Mary's cultivation follows the steps of nineteenth-century garden theorists in their plans for the perfect garden: namely, enclosure, imprisonment, instruction, and beautification. Although Mary does not easily relinquish her wildness, she becomes a girl who, like the ideal garden, can provide both beauty and comfort, and who can cultivate her male cousin, the young patriarch-in-training" (4) is one I follow here.

Other studies include Jerry Phillips's on the novel's colonialism, "The Mem Sahib, the Worthy, the Rajah and His Minions: Some Reflections on the Class Politics of The Secret Garden," *The Lion and the Unicorn* 17, no. 2 (1993): 168-94. More recent work has considered *The Secret Garden* through theoretical lenses of global space and place; see Katharine Slater, "Putting Down Routes: Translocal Place in *The Secret Garden*," *Children's Literature Association Quarterly* 40, no. 1 (March 3, 2015): 3-23, and Sandra Dinter, "Spatial Inscriptions of Childhood: Transformations of the Victorian Garden in *The Secret Garden*, *Tom's Midnight Garden*, and *The Poison Garden*," *Children's Literature Association Quarterly* 40, no. 3 (August 10, 2015): 217-37.

On links between *The Secret Garden* and the mythological figure that inspires Ruskin's *Proserpina*, see Holly Blackford, *The Myth of Persephone in Girls' Fantasy Literature* (London: Routledge, 2012).

74. Burnett, *The Secret Garden*, 79.
75. Burnett, 51.
76. Burnett, 118.

77. Bewell, "John Clare and the Ghosts of Natures Past," 573.
78. Burnett, 70.
79. Johns-Putra, "Environmental Care Ethics."
80. Burnett, *The Secret Garden*, 165.
81. Burnett, 165.
82. Burnett, 172.
83. Burnett, 173.
84. Hogle, "Introduction," 11. On twentieth-century gothic romance, see Janice A. Radway, *Reading the Romance: Women, Patriarchy, and Popular Literature* (Chapel Hill: University of North Carolina Press, 1991).
85. See Daphne du Maurier, *Vanishing Cornwall* (Garden City: Doubleday, 1967).
86. Helmreich, *The English Garden and National Identity*, 171.
87. Helmreich, 188. On Hooker's rhododendron collections, see Felix Driver and Luciana Martins, *Tropical Visions in an Age of Empire* (Chicago: University of Chicago Press, 2005).
88. Pauly, "Mums as the Measure of Men: Horticulture and Culture," 12.
89. Radovíc, "Outside Within," 150.
90. I have not gone into great detail on the distinction between the showy, likely Asian cultivars that are planted close to the house at Manderley and the widespread growth of the *rhododendron ponticum* present on an estate of this size and class. *R. ponticum*, a hardy and easily self-sowing variety initially planted to grant cover in hunting grounds, has now come to be considered an invasive alien in Britain. See Katharina Dehnen-Schmutz and Mark Williamson, "Rhododendron Ponticum in Britain and Ireland: Social, Economic, and Ecological Factors in Its Successful Invasion," *Environment and History* 12, no. 3 (August 2006): 325–50, and Harriet Ritvo, "Invasion/Invasive."
91. Ritvo, "Invasion/Invasive," 173.
92. Du Maurier, *Rebecca*, 1–2.
93. Du Maurier, 2–3.
94. Du Maurier, 36.
95. Du Maurier, 36. Making plain that du Maurier is following the ideas of Gertrude Jekyll quite closely here, Maxim and Jekyll share similar thoughts on the possibilities of primroses as exceptions to this rule. Jekyll writes that "I think the delicious wild Primrose must have some special quality of kindly sympathy with humanity, and particularly with children, and that it really likes to be gathered and brought into our houses; for not only does it live well after being picked and carried home, but even bunches, long held tight in hot little hands, will flourish when released and put in water" (*Home and Garden* 134). Meanwhile, Maxim tells the narrator, "The primrose was more vulgar, a homely pleasant creature who appeared in every cranny like a weed." Unlike the bluebells, which wilted upon being picked and presented "ravaged stalks straggling naked and unclean" on the handlebars of foraging bicyclists, "the primrose did not mind it quite so much, although a creature of the wilds it had a leaning towards civilisation, and preened and smiled in a jam-jar in some cottage window without resentment, living quite a week if given water" (36).
96. Du Maurier, *Rebecca*, 34–35.

97. Du Maurier, 33.
98. Du Maurier, 77.
99. Du Maurier, 99.
100. Du Maurier, 100.
101. Du Maurier, 159.
102. Du Maurier, 286.
103. Du Maurier, 3.

4. ACCLIMATIZATION ABROAD

1. Allen, "Hilda Wade.," August 1899, 192.
2. Allen, "Hilda Wade.," September 1899, 321.
3. Allen, 209–10.
4. Showers, "Prehistory of Southern African Forestry," 296.
5. Forman, "Room for Romance."
6. Kestner, *Masculinities in British Adventure Fiction, 1880–1915*; Deane, *Masculinity and the New Imperialism*.
7. Murray, "Catastrophe and Development in the Adventure Romance."
8. Rivière, *The Ideal Reader: Selected Essays*, 116.
9. Esty, "The Colonial Bildungsroman," 407.
10. Brantlinger, *Rule of Darkness*; Veracini, "'Settler Colonialism.'"
11. Esty, *Unseasonable Youth*.
12. Haggard, *King Solomon's Mines*, 43.
13. Kipling, "'In the Rukh': Mowgli's Introduction to White Men," 23.
14. Allen, "Prickly-Pears," 223.
15. Allen, 227.
16. Van Sittert, "'Our Irrepressible Fellow-Colonist,'" 398.
17. Van Sittert, 412; Frawley, "Prickly Pear Land," 328. See also Christina Alt, "Prickly Pears and Martian Weeds: Ecological Invasion Narratives in History and Fiction."
18. Frawley, "Prickly Pear Land," 326, emphasis original.
19. Lidström et al., "Invasive Narratives and the Inverse of Slow Violence."
20. Cohen, "The Right to Mobility in Adventure Fiction," 294.
21. McClintock, *Imperial Leather*. See also Wendy R. Katz, *Rider Haggard and the Fiction of Empire: A Critical Study of British Imperial Fiction* (Cambridge: Cambridge University Press, 1987); Laura Chrisman, *Rereading the Imperial Romance*; and Lindy Stiebel, *Imagining Africa: Landscape in H. Rider Haggard's African Romances*.
22. Pratt, *Imperial Eyes*.
23. Belich, *Replenishing the Earth*; Steer, "Gold and Greater Britain."
24. Moretti, *Atlas of the European Novel, 1800–1900*, 62.
25. Steer, "Romances of Uneven Development," 344.
26. Chrisman, *Rereading the Imperial Romance*.
27. Conrad, *Heart of Darkness*, 100.
28. Jeffrey Mathes McCarthy, "A Choice of Nightmares," 623.
29. "The Story of an African Farm," 424.
30. Some recent assessments include McClintock, *Imperial Leather*; Carolyn Burdett, *Olive Schreiner and the Progress of Feminism: Evolution, Gender, Empire* (New

York: Palgrave Macmillan, 2001); and John Kucich, "Olive Schreiner, Masochism, and Omnipotence: Strategies of a Preoedipal Politics," *Novel* 36.1 (Fall 2002): 79–109.

31. Esty, "The Colonial Bildungsroman," 418, 419.

32. Freeman, "Dissolution and Landscape in Olive Schreiner's Story of an African Farm," 30.

33. Schreiner, *The Story of an African Farm*, 47.

34. The significance of the plant has been discussed as allegory (albeit from very different perspectives) in Gerald Cornelius Monsman, *Olive Schreiner's Fiction: Landscape and Power* (New Brunswick: Rutgers University Press, 1991) and Jade Munslow Ong, *Olive Schreiner and African Modernism: Allegory, Empire and Postcolonial Writing* (New York: Routledge, 2017).

35. Bryden, *Kloof and Karroo*, 88.

36. Hobson, *The Farm in the Karoo*, 269.

37. Schreiner, *The Story of an African Farm*, 53.

38. Schreiner, 54.

39. Schreiner, 54.

40. Schreiner, 237.

41. Schreiner, 250.

42. Haggard, "About Fiction.," 180.

43. Lang, "A Dip in Criticism.," 498.

44. H. Rider Haggard, *The Days of My Life*, 265. "About the Transvaal and Majuba it is not agreeable to me to read," Lang explains in "A Dip in Criticism" (498).

45. Haggard, *The Days of My Life*, 265.

46. Hultgren, *Melodramatic Imperial Writing*,71.

47. Hultgren, 73.

48. Haggard, *Jess*, 336.

49. Haggard, 5.

50. Lang, "Realism and Romance.," 691.

51. Miller, "The Environmental Politics and Aesthetics of Rider Haggard's King Solomon's Mines: Capital, Mourning, and Desire."

52. Haggard, *Jess*, 44.

53. Haggard, 46, 44.

54. Anonymous [John Watson], "The Fall of Fiction.," 333–34.

55. Haggard, *Jess*, 175, 174.

56. Mill, *On Liberty*, 68n.

57. Haggard, *Jess*, 199.

58. Haggard, 86–87.

59. Haggard, 191.

60. Haggard, 248, 261.

61. Bryce, *Impressions of South Africa*, 34.

62. Bennett, "A Global History of Australian Trees."

63. Showers, "Prehistory of Southern African Forestry"; Grove, "Scottish Missionaries, Evangelical Discourses and the Origins of Conservation Thinking in Southern Africa 1820-1900."

64. Comaroff and Comaroff, *Of Revelation and Revolution.*
65. Flikke, "South African Eucalypts," 20.
66. Haggard, *Jess,* 104, 108.
67. Haggard, 109–10.
68. Haggard, 110.
69. Haggard, 116, 112.
70. Haggard, 120.
71. Haggard, 120–21.
72. Haggard, 335.
73. On the vexed place of Australian Acacia in the South African landscape, see Jane Carruthers and Libby Robin, "Taxonomic Imperialism in the Battles for Acacia: Identity and Science in South Africa and Australia," *Transactions of the Royal Society of South Africa* 65, no. 1 (February 2010): 48–64. See also Jane Carruthers, Libby Robin, Johan P. Hattingh, Christian A. Kull, Haripriya Rangan, and Brian W. van Wilgen, "A Native at Home and Abroad: The History, Politics, Ethics and Aesthetics of Acacias," *Diversity and Distributions* 17, no. 5 (September 2011): 810–21, and Christian A. Kull and Haripriya Rangan, "Acacia Exchanges: Wattles, Thorn Trees, and the Study of Plant Movements," *Geoforum,* 39, no. 3 (May 2008): 1258–72. More generally see Brett M. Bennett and Frederick J. Kruger, "Ecology, Forestry, and the Debate over Exotic Trees in South Africa," *Journal of Historical Geography* 42 (October 2013): 100–109.
74. Haggard, *The Days of My Life,* 116.
75. Haggard, *A Gardener's Year,* 267.
76. Mitchell, "Cryptogamia," 636.
77. Chang, "Hollow Earth Fiction and Environmental Form in the Late Nineteenth Century."
78. Haggard, *Allan Quatermain,* 155; Poon, *Enacting Englishness in the Victorian Period.*
79. Deane, "Imperial Barbarians: Primitive Masculinity in Lost World Fiction," 217.
80. Haggard, *Allan Quatermain,* 3.
81. Haggard, 7.
82. Haggard, 32.
83. Haggard, 33.
84. Haggard, 44.
85. Stiebel, *Imagining Africa,* 70.
86. Haggard, *Allan Quatermain,* 53.
87. Haggard, 60.
88. Haggard, 71.
89. Haggard, 72, 73.
90. Quoted in Ferrall and Jackson, *Juvenile Literature and British Society, 1850-1950,* 162.
91. Haggard, *Allan Quatermain,* 54.
92. Flint, *The Woman Reader, 1837-1914,* 202–3.
93. Haggard, *Allan Quatermain,* 102.
94. Haggard, 108.

95. Reid, *The Plant Hunters*, 1–2.

96. Goodyear, *The Rhetoric of English India*.

97. Given that Kipling included "In the Rukh" with other *Jungle Book* stories in the American *Outward Bound* edition of his works, but kept it with *Many Inventions* for his collected works published in Britain, critical consensus on the proper place of the story has not yet been achieved.

98. "Rukh" itself is a term difficult to define in modern context. The OED identifies it as "Indian English, now rare. . . . In South Asia, esp. the Punjab: wasteland, wilderness; (also) a forest; a forest reserve," citing Kipling's story as one of its usage examples. See "rukh, n." OED Online, Oxford University Press, accessed July 17, 2017, http://www.oed.com/view/Entry/168715?redirectedFrom=rukh&.

99. Kipling, "'In the Rukh': Mowgli's Introduction to White Men," 23.

100. Kipling, *The Jungle Book*, 131.

101. Guha, "The Prehistory of Community Forestry in India," 234; Barton and Bennett, "'There Is a Pleasure in the Pathless Woods,'" 220.

102. Barton and Bennett, 225.

103. Though Gregory Barton has claimed that "empire forestry" in general, and the formation of the IFS in particular, mark the start of modern environmentalism, this claim has not been widely accepted. See Gregory Allen Barton, *Empire Forestry and the Origins of Environmentalism* (Cambridge: Cambridge University Press, 2002).

104. Kipling, "In the Rukh," 222.

105. Kipling, 222–23.

106. Bennett, "A Global History of Australian Trees," 135.

107. Kipling, "In the Rukh," 223–24.

108. Kipling, 224–25.

109. Kipling, 246.

110. Arnold, "Globalization and Contingent Colonialism."

111. Kipling, "In the Rukh," 247.

112. Brandis, "Indian Forestry: The Extended Employment of Natives," 253; Kipling, "In the Rukh," 247.

113. Kipling, "In the Rukh," 232.

114. Kipling, 251.

115. Kipling, 254.

116. Kipling, 237.

117. Kipling, 229.

118. Kipling, 233.

119. Kipling, 236.

120. Kipling, 236.

121. Kipling, 239.

122. Kipling, 226.

123. Kipling, 240.

124. Kipling, 253.

125. Kipling, 253–54.

126. Kipling, 244.

127. Kipling, 249.
128. Kipling, 255.
129. Kipling, 234.
130. Kipling, 264.
131. Milne, "'Fully Motile and AWAITING FURTHER INSTRUCTIONS': Thinking the Feral into Bioregionalism," 332.
132. Milne, 332. On feral citizens, see N. Garside, *Democratic Ideals and the Politicization of Nature: The Roving Life of a Feral Citizen* (New York: Palgrave Macmillan, 2013).
133. Sandilands, "Some 'F' Words for the Environmental Humanities: Feralities, Feminisms, Futurities," 445.
134. Sandilands, 445.
135. Hotchkiss, "The Jungle of Eden," 441.
136. McBratney, *Imperial Subjects, Imperial Space*, 101.
137. Randall, *Kipling's Imperial Boy*, 67; Bivona, *British Imperial Literature, 1870-1940*, 85.
138. Straley, *Evolution and Imagination in Victorian Children's Literature*, 128; Sergeant, *Kipling's Art of Fiction 1884-1901*, 129.

5. THE SENTIENT SPECIMEN RETURNS

1. Ruskin, *Love's Meine and Proserpina*, 507.
2. Recent surveys and studies of man-eating plant fictions include Price, "Vegetable Monsters"; Miller, "Lives of the Monster Plants"; Arment, *Flora Curiosa*; and Arment, *Botanica Delira*.
3. Doyle, "The American's Tale"; Robinson, "The Man-Eating Tree"; Aubrey, *The Devil-Tree of El Dorado*; White, "The Purple Terror."
4. Taylor, *The Sagacity and Morality of Plants*, 2.
5. Marder, *Plant-Thinking*, 35; Taylor, v.
6. Taylor, *The Sagacity and Morality of Plants*, 2.
7. Hamilton, "Bad Flowers," 192; Darwin, *The Power of Movement in Plants*.
8. Vieira, "Phytographia," 208.
9. Sandilands, "Fear of a Queer Plant?," 421.
10. Montgomery, *The Annotated Anne of Green Gables*, 81. See also Shelley Boyd, "The Geranium in the Window: One Plant's Literary Hardiness in the Canadian Imagination," in *Material Cultures in Canada*, ed. Thomas Allen, and Jennifer Blair (Waterloo: Wilfrid Laurier University Press, 2015), 83-106.
11. Brontë, *Jane Eyre*, 181.
12. Haggard, *A Gardener's Year*, 183-84, emphasis original.
13. Haggard, 184.
14. Haggard, 243.
15. Kelley, *Clandestine Marriage*, 86-87.
16. Chase et al., "Murderous Plants."
17. Allen, "Queer Flowers," 404.
18. Allen, 403, 404.
19. Allen, 404.
20. Allen, 404.

21. Robinson, "The Man-Eating Tree," 299.
22. Hurley, *The Gothic Body*, 62.
23. Robinson, "The Man-Eating Tree," 297.
24. Doyle, "The American's Tale," 31.
25. Aubrey, *The Devil-Tree of El Dorado*, 273.
26. White, "The Purple Terror," 243.
27. Price, "Vegetable Monsters," 327.
28. White, "The Purple Terror," 245.
29. Rieder, *Colonialism and the Emergence of Science Fiction*, 56.
30. Wells, *The War of the Worlds*, 147.
31. Wells, 161.
32. Wells, 145.
33. Wells, 145, 144.
34. Arata, "The Occidental Tourist," 623.
35. Chew, "The Monstering of Tamarisk," 235; Alt, "Prickly Pears and Martian Weeds: Ecological Invasion Narratives in History and Fiction."
36. Wells, *The War of the Worlds*, 180.
37. Hodgson, "A Voice in the Night," 178.
38. Hodgson, 182, 184.
39. On one female botanist and social reformer's debates with Darwin over such fungi, see Tina Gianquitto, "Botanical Smuts and Hermaphrodites: Lydia Becker, Darwin's Botany, and Education Reform," *Isis* 104, no. 2 (2013): 250–77.
40. Blackwood, "The Willows," 160.
41. Blackwood, 147, emphasis original.
42. Blackwood, 145.
43. Joshi, *The Weird Tale*.
44. Blackwood, "The Transfer," 351, 350.
45. Blackwood, 353, 356.
46. Blackwood, 357.
47. Blackwood, 346.
48. Blackwood, "The Man Whom the Trees Loved," 4.
49. Blackwood, 4.
50. Smith and Hughes, *EcoGothic*; Punter, "Algernon Blackwood: Nature and Spirit," 55.
51. Blackwood, "The Man Whom the Trees Loved," 9.
52. Blackwood, 9.
53. Blackwood, 4.
54. Blackwood, 12.
55. Blackwood, 18.
56. Blackwood, 38.
57. On Lawrence in particular, whose undergraduate training in botany returned throughout his fiction, see M. M. Mahood, *The Poet as Botanist*.
58. Blackwood, "The Man Whom the Trees Loved," 8.
59. Blackwood, 26.
60. Blackwood, 27.
61. Blackwood, 65.
62. Blackwood, 24.

63. Blackwood, 10–11.

64. Blackwood, 14, emphasis original.

65. Darwin, *The Power of Movement in Plants,* 571; Darwin, "The Address of the President of the British Association for the Advancement of Science," 354.

66. Darwin, "The Address of the President of the British Association for the Advancement of Science," 354–55.

67. Marder, *Plant-Thinking*; Kohn, *How Forests Think*.

68. Blackwood, "The Man Whom the Trees Loved," 34.

69. Blackwood, 68.

70. Blackwood, 69.

71. Blackwood, 75–76.

72. Blackwood, 94.

73. Blackwood, 70.

74. Blackwood, 98–99.

75. Blackwood, 79.

76. Mitchell, "Cryptogamia," 646.

77. Coverage included Adam Gopnik, "Plant TV," *New Yorker,* March 15, 2010, 23.

78. These methodologies are both explored by John Ryan in his survey of the field, in which he proposes a "renewed conceptualization of plants as autonomous, agentic beings, rather than as mute materials or mere messages." See John Charles Ryan, "Passive Flora? Reconsidering Nature's Agency through Human-Plant Studies (HPS)," *Societies* 2, no. 3 (August 14, 2012): 101–21, 103. See also Matthew Hall, *Plants as Persons: A Philosophical Botany* (New York: SUNY Press, 2011), and the special issue of *PAN: Philosophy Action Nature,* no. 9 (2012).

79. See Marder and Michael Pollan, *The Botany of Desire: A Plant's-Eye View of the World* (New York: Random House, 2001).

80. Pinch, *Thinking About Other People in Nineteenth-Century British Writing,* 6–7.

81. Mitchell, "Cryptogamia," 643.

WORKS CITED

Ablow, Rachel. *Victorian Pain.* Princeton: Princeton University Press, 2017.
Allen, Grant. "The Daisy's Pedigree." *Cornhill Magazine* 44 (1881): 168–81.
———. *Flowers and Their Pedigrees.* London: Longmans, Green, 1883.
———. "Hilda Wade." *Strand Magazine* 18, no. 104 (August 1899): 184–95.
———. "Hilda Wade." *Strand Magazine* 18, no. 105 (September 1899): 321–32.
———. *Hilda Wade: A Woman with Tenacity of Purpose.* New York: G. P. Putnam's Sons, 1900.
———. "Queer Flowers." *Cornhill Magazine* 3, no. 16 (1884): 397–409.
———. "Prickly-Pears." *North American Review* 151, no. 405 (1890): 223–27.
Alt, Christina. "Prickly Pears and Martian Weeds: Ecological Invasion Narratives in History and Fiction." In *Rethinking Invasion Ecologies from the Environmental Humanities,* edited by Jodi Frawley and Iain McCalman, 137–48. New York: Routledge, 2014.
"Anemone-Flowered Chrysanthemums." *Gardening Illustrated* 18 (October 17, 1897): 459.
Anonymous [John Watson]. "The Fall of Fiction." *Fortnightly Review* 44, no. 261 (September 1888): 324–36.
Ansell, Mary. *The Happy Garden.* London: Cassell & Co., 1912.
Arata, Stephen. *Fictions of Loss in the Victorian Fin de Siècle.* Cambridge: Cambridge University Press, 2009.
———. "The Occidental Tourist: 'Dracula' and the Anxiety of Reverse Colonization." *Victorian Studies* 33, no. 4 (Summer 1990): 621–45.
Arment, Chad. *Botanica Delira: More Stories of Strange, Undiscovered, and Murderous Vegetation.* Landisville, Pa.: Coachwhip Publications, 2010.
———. *Flora Curiosa: Cryptobotany, Mysterious Fungi, Sentient Trees, and Deadly Plants in Classic Science Fiction and Fantasy.* Landisville, Pa.: Coachwhip Publications, 2008.
Armstrong, Nancy. "A Gothic History of the British Novel." In *New Directions in the History of the Novel,* edited by Patrick Parrinder, Andrew Nash, and Nicola Wilson, 103–120. New York: St. Martin's Press, 2014.
Armstrong, Philip. "Samuel Butler's Sheep." *Journal of Victorian Culture* 17, no. 4 (December 2012): 442–53.
Arnold, David. "Globalization and Contingent Colonialism: Towards a Transnational History of 'British' India." *Journal of Colonialism and Colonial History* 16, no. 2 (2015): Project MUSE.
Aubrey, Frank. *The Devil-Tree of El Dorado.* New York: New Amsterdam, 1897.

Aylmer, Arthur. "The Detective in Real Life." *Windsor Magazine* 1 (1895): 499-510.
"Back Street Conservatories." *Household Words* 2, no. 38 (December 14, 1850): 271-75.
Barrie, James Matthew. *The Little White Bird*. Leipzig: B. Tauchnitz, 1903.
Barton, Gregory A., and Brett M. Bennett. "'There Is a Pleasure in the Pathless Woods': The Culture of Forestry in British India." *British Scholar* 3, no. 2 (2010): 219-34.
Beattie, James. "Recent Themes in the Environmental History of the British Empire." *History Compass* 10, no. 2 (February 1, 2012): 129-39.
Beattie, James, and John Stenhouse. "Empire, Environment, and Religion: God and the Natural World in Nineteenth-Century New Zealand." *Environment and History* 13, no. 4 (2007): 413-46.
Beinart, William, and Karen Middleton. "Plant Transfers in Historical Perspective: A Review Article." *Environment and History* 10, no. 1 (2004): 3-29.
Belich, James. *Replenishing the Earth: The Settler Revolution and the Rise of the Anglo-World, 1783-1939*. Oxford: Oxford University Press, 2011.
Bennett, Brett M. "A Global History of Australian Trees." *Journal of the History of Biology* 44, no. 1 (2011): 125-45.
Bennett, Jane. *Vibrant Matter: A Political Ecology of Things*. Durham: Duke University Press, 2010.
Bewell, Alan. "Erasmus Darwin's Cosmopolitan Nature." *ELH* 76, no. 1 (2009): 19-48.
———. "John Clare and the Ghosts of Natures Past." *Nineteenth-Century Literature* 65, no. 4 (2011): 548-78.
Birch, Dinah. "Ruskin and the Science of Proserpina." In *New Approaches to Ruskin*, edited by Robert Hewison, 142-56. London: Routledge & Kegan Paul, 1981.
Bivona, Daniel. *British Imperial Literature, 1870-1940: Writing and the Administration of Empire*. Cambridge: Cambridge University Press, 1998.
Blackwood, Algernon. "The Man Whom the Trees Loved." In *Pan's Garden: A Volume of Nature Stories*, 3-104. London: Macmillan, 1919.
———. "The Transfer." In *Pan's Garden: A Volume of Nature Stories*, 343-62. London: Macmillan, 1919.
———. "The Willows." In *The Listener and Other Stories*, 127-204. London: Eveleigh Nash, 1907.
Braddon, Mary Elizabeth. *Lady Audley's Secret*. Toronto: Broadview, 2003.
Brandis, Dietrich. "Indian Forestry: The Extended Employment of Natives." *Imperial and Asiatic Quarterly Review and Oriental and Colonial Record*, third series, 3, no. 6 (April 1897): 245-57.
Brantlinger, Patrick. *Rule of Darkness: British Literature and Imperialism, 1830-1914*. Ithaca: Cornell University Press, 1988.
Braun, Gretchen. "'A Great Break in the Common Course of Confession': Narrating Loss in Charlotte Brontë's Villette." *ELH* 78, no. 1 (2011): 189-212.
Brontë, Charlotte. *Jane Eyre*. New York: A. L. Burt, 1864.

———. *Villette*. Edited by Herbert Rosengarten and Margaret Smith. Clarendon Edition of the Novels of the Brontës. Oxford: Oxford University Press, 1984.
Bryce, James. *Impressions of South Africa*. London: Macmillan, 1897.
Bryden, Henry Anderson. *Kloof and Karroo: Sport, Legend and Natural History in Cape Colony, with a Notice of the Game Birds, and of the Present Distribution of Antelopes and Larger Game*. London: Longmans, Green, 1889.
Burnett, Frances Hodgson. *A Little Princess*. New York: Penguin, 2002.
———. *The Secret Garden*. New York: W. W. Norton, 2006.
Butler, Samuel. *Erewhon, Or, Over the Range*. London: David Bogue, 1880.
Campbell, Elizabeth A. "Don't Say It with Nightshades: Sentimental Botany and the Natural History of Atropa Belladonna." *Victorian Literature and Culture* 35, no. 2 (2007): 607–15.
Carroll, Lewis. *Alice's Adventures in Wonderland and Through the Looking-Glass and What Alice Found There*. New York: Penguin, 1998.
Cartwright, Julia. "Gardens." *Portfolio: An Artistic Periodical* 23 (1892): 211–18.
Chang, Elizabeth Hope. "Hollow Earth Fiction and Environmental Form in the Late Nineteenth Century." *Nineteenth-Century Contexts* 38, no. 5 (2016): 387–97.
Chase, Mark W., J. M. Maarten, Dawn Sanders Christenhusz, and Michael F. Fay. "Murderous Plants: Victorian Gothic, Darwin, and Modern Insights into Vegetable Carnivory." *Botanical Journal of the Linnean Society* 161, no. 4 (2009): 329–56.
Chew, Matthew K. "The Monstering of Tamarisk: How Scientists Made a Plant into a Problem." *Journal of the History of Biology* 42, no. 2 (2009): 231–66.
Chrisman, Laura. *Rereading the Imperial Romance: British Imperialism and South African Resistance in Haggard, Schreiner, and Plaatje*. Oxford: Oxford University Press, 2000.
Clausson, Nils. "Degeneration, Fin-de-Siècle Gothic, and the Science of Detection: Arthur Conan Doyle's The Hound of the Baskervilles and the Emergence of the Modern Detective Story." *Journal of Narrative Theory* 35, no. 1 (2005): 60–87.
Cohen, Margaret. "The Right to Mobility in Adventure Fiction." *Novel* 42, no. 2 (2009): 290–96.
Cohn, Elisha. "Still Life: Suspended Animation in Charlotte Brontë's *Villette*." *SEL: Studies in English Literature, 1500–1900* 52, no. 4 (Autumn 2012): 843–60.
Collins, Wilkie. *Basil*. London: Richard Bentley, 1852.
———. *The Moonstone*. New York: Penguin, 1986.
———. *The Woman in White*. Toronto: Broadview, 2006.
Comaroff, Jean, and John L. Comaroff. *Of Revelation and Revolution*. Vol. 2. Chicago: University of Chicago Press, 1991.
Conrad, Joseph. *Heart of Darkness*. Toronto: Broadview, 1999.
Cooke, Mordecai Cubitt. *Freaks and Marvels of Plant Life*. London: Society for Promoting Christian Knowledge, 1881.
Cresswell, Tim. *On the Move: Mobility in the Modern Western World*. New York: Routledge, 2006.
Cunningham, Andrew. "The Culture of Gardens." In *Cultures of Natural History,*

rev. ed., edited by N. Jardine, J. A. Secord, and E. C. Spary, 38–56. Cambridge: Cambridge University Press, 1997.
Curry, Helen Anne. "Naturalising the Exotic and Exoticising the Naturalised: Horticulture, Natural History, and the Rosy Periwinkle." *Environment and History* 18, no. 3 (August 1, 2012): 343–65.
Cushing, John. *The Exotic Gardener: In Which the Management of the Hot-House, Green-House, and Conservatory, Is Fully and Clearly Delineated According to Modern Practice: With an Appendix Containing Observation on the Soils Suitable to Tender Exotics*. 2nd ed. London: G. & W. Nicoll, 1814.
Dakers, Caroline. *The Holland Park Circle: Artists and Victorian Society*. New Haven: Yale University Press, 1999.
Darby, Margaret Flanders. "Joseph Paxton's Water Lily." In *Bourgeois and Aristocratic Cultural Encounters in Garden Art, 1550–1850*, edited by Michael Conan, 255–84. Washington, DC: Dumbarton Oaks Research Library and Collection, 2002.
———. "Un-Natural History: Ward's Glass Cases." *Victorian Literature and Culture* 35, no. 2 (2007): 635–47.
Darwin, Charles. *The Power of Movement in Plants*. New York: D. Appleton, 1888.
———. *The Voyage of the Beagle: Journal of Researches into the Natural History and Geology of the Countries Visited During the Voyage of the H.M.S. Beagle Round the World*. New York: Modern Library, 2001.
Darwin, Francis. "The Address of the President of the British Association for the Advancement of Science." *Science* 28 (September 18, 1908): 353–62.
Davis, Helen H. "'I Seemed to Hold Two Lives': Disclosing Circumnarration in *Villette* and *The Picture of Dorian Gray*." *Narrative* 21, no. 2 (2013): 198–220.
Davis, Whitney. "Decadence and the Organic Metaphor." *Representations* 89, no. 1 (2005): 131–49.
Deane, Bradley. "Imperial Barbarians: Primitive Masculinity in Lost World Fiction." *Victorian Literature and Culture* 36, no. 1 (2008): 205–25.
———. *Masculinity and the New Imperialism: Rewriting Manhood in British Popular Literature, 1870–1914*. Cambridge: Cambridge University Press, 2014.
Denisoff, Dennis. "The Dissipating Nature of Decadent Paganism from Pater to Yeats." *Modernism/Modernity* 15, no. 3 (December 3, 2008): 431–46.
Dewis, Sarah. *The Loudons and the Gardening Press: A Victorian Cultural Industry*. Farnham, England: Ashgate, 2014.
Dickens, Charles. *The Mystery of Edwin Drood*. New York: Penguin, 2002.
———. *Our Mutual Friend*. New York: Penguin, 1997.
Doyle, Arthur Conan. "The Adventure of the Copper Beeches." *Strand Magazine* 3 (1892): 613–48.
———. "The Adventure of the Naval Treaty." *Strand Magazine* 6 (1893): 392–403.
———. "The Adventure of the Naval Treaty, Cont." *Strand Magazine* 6 (1893): 459–68.
———. "The American's Tale." In *My Friend the Murderer: And Other Mysteries and Adventures*. London: Lovell, Coryell, 1893.
———. *The Hound of the Baskervilles*. Toronto: Broadview, 2006.

———. *The Lost World*. New York: Penguin, 2007.
———. *The Sign of Four*. Toronto: Broadview, 2001.
Drury, William D. *Home Gardening: A Manual for the Amateur*. London: L. Upcott Gill, 1898.
Du Maurier, Daphne. *Rebecca*. New York: Modern Library, 1943.
Dümpelmann, Sonja. "Introduction." *A Cultural History of Gardens in the Age of Empire*, 1–36. Vol. 5 of A Cultural History of Gardens, edited by Michael Leslie and John Dixon Hunt. London: Bloomsbury, 2013.
Dümpelmann, Sonja, ed. *A Cultural History of Gardens in the Age of Empire*. Vol. 5 of A Cultural History of Gardens, edited by Michael Leslie and John Dixon Hunt. London: Bloomsbury, 2013.
Duncan, Sara Jeannette. *The Simple Adventures of a Memsahib*. New York: D. Appleton, 1893.
Eliot, George. *The Mill on the Floss*. Toronto: Broadview, 2007.
Eliot, T. S. "Introduction" to *The Moonstone* by Wilkie Collins. Oxford: Oxford University Press, 1928.
Elliott, Brent. *Victorian Gardens*. Portland, OR: Timber Press, 1986.
Endersby, Jim. "Deceived by Orchids: Sex, Science, Fiction, and Darwin." *British Journal for the History of Science* 49, no. 2 (June 2016): 205–29.
Engleheart, G. H. "Chrysanthemum Reform." *Garden* 24, no. December 1 (1883): 475.
Esty, Jed. "The Colonial Bildungsroman: *The Story of an African Farm* and the Ghost of Goethe." *Victorian Studies*, no. 3 (2007): 407–30.
———. *Unseasonable Youth: Modernism, Colonialism, and the Fiction of Development*. Modernist Literature and Culture. New York: Oxford University Press, 2012.
Fabian, Johannes. *Time and the Other: How Anthropology Makes Its Object*. New York: Columbia University Press, 1983.
Fairchild, Thomas. *The City Gardener. Containing the Most Experienced Method of Cultivating and Ordering Such Ever-Greens, Fruit-Trees, Flowering Shrubs, Flowers, Exotick Plants, &c. as Will Be Ornamental, and Thrive Best in the London Gardens*. London: Printed for T. Woodward, and J. Peele, 1722.
Ferrall, Charles, and Anna Jackson. *Juvenile Literature and British Society, 1850-1950: The Age of Adolescence*. New York: Routledge, 2010.
Flikke, Rune. "South African Eucalypts: Health, Trees, and Atmospheres in the Colonial Contact Zone." *Geoforum* 76 (November 1, 2016): 20–27.
Flint, Kate. *The Woman Reader, 1837-1914*. Oxford: Oxford University Press, 1993.
Forman, R. G. "Room for Romance: Playing with Adventure in Arthur Conan Doyle's *The Lost World*." *Genre* 43, nos. 1–2 (January 1, 2010): 27–59.
Frawley, Jodi. "Prickly Pear Land." *Australian Historical Studies* 38, no. 130 (October 2007): 323–38.
Freedgood, Elaine. "Fictional Settlements: Footnotes, Metalepsis, the Colonial Effect." *New Literary History* 41, no. 2 (2010): 393–411.
Freeman, Hannah. "Dissolution and Landscape in Olive Schreiner's *The Story of an African Farm*." *English Studies in Africa* 52, no. 2 (2009): 18–34.

Garrard, Greg. "An Absence of Azaleas: Imperialism, Exoticism, and Nativity in Romantic Biogeographical Ideology." *Wordsworth Circle* 28, no. 3 (1997): 148–55.
Gates, Barbara T. *Kindred Nature: Victorian and Edwardian Women Embrace the Living World*. Chicago: University of Chicago Press, 1998.
Gibson, Anna. "Charlotte Bronte's First Person." *Narrative* 25, no. 2 (May 2017): 203–26.
Goldstone, Andrew. "Servants, Aestheticism, and 'The Dominance of Form.'" *ELH* 77, no. 3 (Fall 2010): 615–43.
Goodlad, Lauren M. E. *The Victorian Geopolitical Aesthetic: Realism, Sovereignty, and Transnational Experience*. Oxford: Oxford University Press, 2015.
Goody, Jack. *The Culture of Flowers*. Cambridge: Cambridge University Press, 1993.
Goodyear, Sara Suleri. *The Rhetoric of English India*. Chicago: University of Chicago Press, 1992.
Grahame, Kenneth. *The Wind in the Willows*. New York: Charles Scribner's Sons, 1915.
Grove, Richard. *Green Imperialism: Colonial Expansion, Tropical Island Edens, and the Origins of Environmentalism, 1600–1860*. Studies in Environment and History. Cambridge: Cambridge University Press, 1995.
———. "Scottish Missionaries, Evangelical Discourses, and the Origins of Conservation Thinking in Southern Africa, 1820–1900." *Journal of Southern African Studies* 15, no. 2 (1989): 163–87.
Guha, Ramachandra. "The Prehistory of Community Forestry in India." *Environmental History* 6, no. 2 (2001): 213–38.
Haggard, H. Rider. "About Fiction." *Contemporary Review* 51 (February 1887): 172–80.
———. *Allan Quatermain: Being an Account of His Further Adventures and Discoveries in Company with Sir Henry Curtis, Bart., Commander John Good, R. N., and One Umslopogaas*. London: Longmans, Green, 1913.
———. *Allan and the Holy Flower*. London: Longmans, Green, 1915.
———. *Colonel Quaritch, V.C.: A Tale of Country Life*. London: Longmans, Green, 1911.
———. *The Days of My Life: An Autobiography*. London: Longmans, Green, 1926.
———. *A Gardener's Year*. London: Longmans, Green, 1905.
———. *Jess: A Novel*. London: Longmans, Green, 1908.
———. *King Solomon's Mines*. Toronto: Broadview, 2002.
———. *Rural England; Being an Account of Agricultural and Social Researches Carried out in the Years 1901 & 1902*. London: Longmans, Green, 1906.
Hamilton, Jennifer. "Bad Flowers: The Implications of a Phytocentric Deconstruction of the Western Philosophical Tradition for the Environmental Humanities." *Environmental Humanities* 7, no. 1 (January 1, 2015): 191–202.
Harrison, Joseph. "Introduction." *Floricultural Cabinet, and Florists' Magazine* 1 (1833): 1–3.

Haweis, Mary Eliza Joy. *Rus in Urbe: Or Flowers That Thrive in London Gardens & Smoky Towns*. London: Field & Tuer, 1886.
Helmreich, Anne. *The English Garden and National Identity: The Competing Styles of Garden Design, 1870-1914*. New York: Cambridge University Press, 2002.
Hibberd, James Shirley. *Brambles and Bay Leaves: Essays on the Homely and the Beautiful*. London: Groombridge & Sons, 1862.
———. *The Town Garden: A Manual for the Management of City and Suburban Gardens*. London: Groombridge & Sons, 1859.
Hobson, Mary Ann Carey. *The Farm in the Karoo: Or, What Charley Vyvyan and His Friends Saw in South Africa*. London: Juta, Heelis, 1883.
Hodgson, William Hope. "A Voice in the Night." In *Men of Deep Waters*. London: Holden & Hardingham, 1921.
Hogle, Jerrold E., "Introduction." *The Cambridge Companion to Gothic Fiction*, 1–20. Cambridge: Cambridge University Press, 2002.
Hotchkiss, Jane. "The Jungle of Eden: Kipling, Wolf Boys, and the Colonial Imagination." *Victorian Literature and Culture* 29, no. 2 (September 2001): 435–49.
Hudson, William Henry. *A Crystal Age*. London: T. Fisher Unwin, 1906.
Hultgren, Neil. *Melodramatic Imperial Writing: From the Sepoy Rebellion to Cecil Rhodes*. Columbus: Ohio University Press, 2014.
Hunt, John Dixon and Michael Leslie. "General Editor's Preface." *A Cultural History of the Gardens in the Age of Empire*, xi–xiii, edited by Sonja Dümpelmann. Vol. 5 of A Cultural History of Gardens, edited by Michael Leslie and John Dixon Hunt. London: Bloomsbury, 2013.
Hurley, Kelly. *The Gothic Body: Sexuality, Materialism, and Degeneration at the Fin de Siècle*. Cambridge: Cambridge University Press, 1996.
Jacobus, Mary. *Women Writing and Writing about Women*. London: Routledge, 2012.
Jaffe, Audrey. *The Victorian Novel Dreams of the Real: Conventions and Ideology*. Oxford: Oxford University Press, 2016.
Jefferies, Richard. *After London, Or, Wild England*. London: Cassell, 1886.
Jekyll, Gertrude. *Home and Garden: Notes and Thoughts, Practical and Critical, of a Worker in Both*. London: Longmans, Green, 1900.
———. *Wood and Garden: Notes and Thoughts, Practical and Critical, of a Working Amateur*. London: Longmans, Green, 1899.
Johns-Putra, Adeline. "Environmental Care Ethics: Notes Toward a New Materialist Critique." *Symploke* 21, no. 1 (December 22, 2013): 125–35.
Joshi, S. T. *The Weird Tale: Arthur Machen, Lord Dunsany, Algernon Blackwood, M. R. James, Ambrose Bierce, H. P. Lovecraft*. Austin: University of Texas Press, 1990.
Kehler, Grace. "Gertrude Jekyll and the Late-Victorian Garden Book: Representing Nature-Culture Relations." *Victorian Literature and Culture* 35, no. 2 (2007): 617–33.
Kelley, Theresa M. *Clandestine Marriage: Botany and Romantic Culture*. Baltimore: Johns Hopkins University Press, 2012.

Kermode, Frank. "Secrets and Narrative Sequence." *Critical Inquiry* 7, no. 1 (October 1, 1980): 83–101.
Kestner, Joseph A. *Masculinities in British Adventure Fiction, 1880–1915*. Farnham, England: Ashgate, 2010.
King, Amy M. *Bloom: The Botanical Vernacular in the English Novel*. Oxford: Oxford University Press, 2003.
———. "Reorienting the Scientific Frontier: Victorian Tide Pools and Literary Realism." *Victorian Studies* 47, no. 2 (2005): 153–63.
Kipling, Rudyard. "In the Rukh." In *Many Inventions*, 222–64. New York: Appleton, 1893.
———. "'In the Rukh': Mowgli's Introduction to White Men." *McClure's* 7, no. 1 (June 1896): 23–38.
———. *The Jungle Book*. New York: Century, 1920.
Kohn, Eduardo. *How Forests Think*. Berkeley: University of California Press, 2013.
Kuchta, Todd. *Semi-Detached Empire: Suburbia and the Colonization of Britain, 1880 to the Present*. Charlottesville: University of Virginia Press, 2010.
Laird, Mark. *The Flowering of the Landscape Garden: English Pleasure Grounds, 1720–1800*. Penn Studies in Landscape Architecture. Philadelphia: University of Pennsylvania Press, 1999.
Lang, Andrew. "A Dip in Criticism." *Contemporary Review* 54 (October 1888): 495–503.
———. "Realism and Romance." *Contemporary Review* 52 (November 1887): 683–93.
Leslie, Michael, and John Dixon Hunt, eds. *A Cultural History of Gardens*. London: Bloomsbury, 2013.
Lidström, Susanna, Simon West, Tania Katzschner, M. Isabel Pérez-Ramos, and Hedley Twidle. "Invasive Narratives and the Inverse of Slow Violence: Alien Species in Science and Society." *Environmental Humanities* 7, no. 1 (May 1, 2016): 1–40.
Lindley, John. *Ladies' Botany, or, A Familiar Introduction to the Study of the Natural System of Botany, Illustrated with Numerous Wood-Cuts*. London: Henry G. Bohn, 1841.
Loudon, Jane. *Instructions in Gardening for Ladies*. London: John Murray, 1840.
Loudon, John. *Arboretum Et Fruticetum Britannicum, or, The Trees and Shrubs of Britain, Native and Foreign, Hardy and Half-Hardy, Pictorially and Botanically Delineated, and Scientifically and Popularly Described; with Their Propagation, Culture, Management, and Uses in the Arts, In useful and Ornamental Plantations, and in Landscape-Gardening; Preceded by a Historical and Geographical Outline of the Trees and Shrubs of Temperate Climates Throughout the World*. 2nd ed. London: Longman, Brown, Green, & Longman, 1844.
———. *An Encyclopædia of Gardening: Comprising the Theory and Practice of Horticulture, Floriculture, Arboriculture and Landscape-Gardening Including All the Latest Improvements*. London: Longman, 1822.
———. *An Encyclopaedia of Gardening: Comprising the Theory and Practice of Horticulture, Floriculture, Arboriculture, And landscape-Gardening, Including All the Latest*

Improvements; a General History of Gardening in All Countries; and a Statistical View of Its Present State; with Suggestions for Its Future Progress in the British Isles. A new ed. London: Longman, Rees, Orme, Brown, Green & Longman, 1835.

———. "Domestic Notices: England." *Gardener's Magazine, and Register of Rural and Domestic Improvement for Gardening and Gardeners* 10 (1834): 160–68.

———. *The Green-House Companion: Comprising a General Course of Green-House and Conservatory Practice Throughout the Year; a Natural Arrangement of All the Green-House Plants in Cultivation.* London: Printed for Harding, Triphook & Lepard, & J. Harding, 1824.

Luciano, D., and M. Y. Chen. "Has the Queer Ever Been Human?" *GLQ* 21, nos. 2–3 (January 2015): 183–207.

Lynch, Deidre Shauna. "'Young Ladies Are Delicate Plants': Jane Austen and Greenhouse Romanticism." *ELH* 77, no. 3 (2010): 689–729.

Machen, Arthur. *The Three Imposters, Or, The Transmutations.* London: John Lane, 1895.

Mahood, M. M. *The Poet as Botanist.* Cambridge: Cambridge University Press, 2008.

Marder, Michael. *Plant-Thinking: A Philosophy of Vegetal Life.* New York: Columbia University Press, 2013.

Marsh, Richard. *The Beetle.* Toronto: Broadview, 2004.

McBratney, John. *Imperial Subjects, Imperial Space: Rudyard Kipling's Fiction of the Native-Born.* Columbus: Ohio State University Press, 2002.

McCarthy, Jeffrey Mathes. "'A Choice of Nightmares': The Ecology of *Heart of Darkness.*" *MFS Modern Fiction Studies* 55, no. 3 (2009): 620–48.

McClintock, Anne. *Imperial Leather: Race, Gender, and Sexuality in the Colonial Conquest.* New York: Routledge, 1995.

Meade, L. T., and Robert Eustace. "The Talk of The Town." *Strand Magazine* 25, no. 145 (January 1903): 67–80.

Milbank, Alison. "The Victorian Gothic in English Novels and Stories, 1830–1880." In *The Cambridge Companion to Gothic Fiction,* edited by Jerrold E. Hogle, 145–66. Cambridge: Cambridge University Press, 2002.

Mill, John Stuart. *On Liberty.* New York: Penguin, 2006.

Miller, John. "The Environmental Politics and Aesthetics of Rider Haggard's *King Solomon's Mines*: Capital, Mourning, and Desire." In *Victorian Writers and the Environment: Ecocritical Perspectives,* edited by Laurence W. Mazzeno and Ronald D. Morrison, 157–73. New York: Routledge, 2017.

Miller, T. S. "Lives of the Monster Plants: The Revenge of the Vegetable in the Age of Animal Studies." *Journal of the Fantastic in the Arts* 23, no. 3 (2012): 460–79.

Millett, Kate. "The Debate Over Women: Ruskin Versus Mill." *Victorian Studies* 14, no. 1 (Summer 1970): 63–82.

Milligan, Barry. *Pleasures and Pains: Opium and the Orient in Nineteenth-Century British Culture.* Charlottesville: University Press of Virginia, 1995.

Milne, Anne. "'Fully Motile and AWAITING FURTHER INSTRUCTIONS: Thinking the Feral into Bioregionalism." In *The Bioregional Imagination: Literature, Ecology, and Place,* edited by Tom Lynch, Cheryll Glotfelty, and Karla Armbruster, 329-44. Athens: University of Georgia Press, 2012.

Mitchell, Robert. "Cryptogamia." *European Romantic Review* 21, no. 5 (2010): 631-51.

Montgomery, L. M. *The Annotated Anne of Green Gables.* Edited by Wendy E. Barry, Margaret Anne Doody, and Mary E. Doody Jones. Oxford: Oxford University Press, 1997.

Moore, Jason W. "'The Modern World-System' as Environmental History? Ecology and the Rise of Capitalism." *Theory and Society* 32, no. 3 (June 1, 2003): 307-77.

Moretti, Franco. *Atlas of the European Novel, 1800-1900.* London: New York: Verso, 1998.

Morgan, Benjamin. "Fin du Globe: On Decadent Planets." *Victorian Studies,* no. 4 (2016): 609-35.

Morris, William. *News from Nowhere; or an Epoch of Rest, Being Some Chapters from a Utopian Romance.* Toronto: Broadview, 2003.

Morrison, Arthur. *A Child of the Jago.* London: Duffield, 1906.

———. "The Ivy Cottage Mystery." In *Chronicles of Martin Hewitt,* 1-41. New York: D. Appleton, 1896.

Morton, Timothy. *The Ecological Thought.* Cambridge: Harvard University Press, 2010.

———. *Hyperobjects.* Minneapolis: University of Minnesota Press, 2013.

Murphy, Patrick D. "Dialoguing with Bakhtin over Our Ethical Responsibility to Anothers." In *Ecocritical Theory: New European Approaches,* edited by Axel Goodbody and Kate Rigby, 155-67. Charlottesville: University of Virginia Press, 2011.

Murray, Cara. "Catastrophe and Development in the Adventure Romance." *English Literature in Transition, 1880-1920* 53, no. 2 (April 2010): 150-69.

Ousby, Ian. "Wilkie Collins's *The Moonstone* and the Constance Kent Case." *Notes and Queries* 21, no. 1 (1974): 25.

Pauly, Philip J. "Is Environmental History a Subfield of Garden History?" *Environmental History* 10, no. 1 (January 1, 2005): 70-71.

———. "Mums as the Measure of Men: Horticulture and Culture." *Raritan* 27, no. 3 (2008): 1-25.

Pawson, Eric. "Plants, Mobilities, and Landscapes: Environmental Histories of Botanical Exchange." *Geography Compass* 2, no. 5 (September 1, 2008): 1464-77.

Pfeiffer, Jeanine M., and Robert A. Voeks. "Biological Invasions and Biocultural Diversity: Linking Ecological and Cultural Systems." *Environmental Conservation* 35, no. 4 (2008): 281-93.

Pierce, Joanna Tapp. "From Garden to Gardener: The Cultivation of Little Girls in Carroll's Alice Books and Ruskin's 'Of Queens' Gardens.'" *Women's Studies* 29, no. 6 (October 2000): 741-61.

Poon, Angelia. *Enacting Englishness in the Victorian Period: Colonialism and the Politics of Performance*. New York: Routledge, 2017.
Pratt, Mary Louise. *Imperial Eyes: Travel Writing and Transculturation*. New York: Routledge, 2007.
Price, Cheryl Blake. "Vegetable Monsters: Man-Eating Trees in Fin-de-Siècle Fiction." *Victorian Literature and Culture* 41, no. 2 (2013): 311–27.
Punter, David. "Algernon Blackwood: Nature and Spirit." In *EcoGothic*, edited by Andrew Smith and William Hughes, 44–57. Manchester: Manchester University Press, 2013.
Radović, Stanka. "Outside Within: Natural Environment and Social Place in Daphne du Maurier's *Rebecca*." In *Ecocriticism and Geocriticism: Overlapping Territories in Environmental and Spatial Literary Studies*, edited by Robert T. Tally Jr. and Christine M. Battista, 137–53. Houndmills, England: Palgrave Macmillan, 2016.
Randall, Don. *Kipling's Imperial Boy: Adolescence and Cultural Hybridity*. New York: Palgrave Macmillan, 2000.
Reid, Mayne. *The Plant Hunters: Or, Adventures among the Himalaya Mountains*. London: Ticknor & Fields, 1858.
Reitz, Caroline. *Detecting the Nation: Fictions of Detection and the Imperial Venture*. Columbus: Ohio State University Press, 2004.
Richardson, David Lester. *Flowers and Flower-Gardens*. Calcutta: D'Rozario, 1855.
Rieder, John. *Colonialism and the Emergence of Science Fiction*. Wesleyan Early Classics of Science Fiction Series. Middletown: Wesleyan University Press, 2008.
Ritvo, Harriet. "Invasion/Invasive." *Environmental Humanities* 9, no. 1 (May 1, 2017): 171–74.
Rivière, Jacques. *The Ideal Reader: Selected Essays*. New York: Meridian, 1960.
Robinson, Phil. "The Man-Eating Tree." In *Under the Sun*. Boston: Roberts Brothers, 1882.
Robinson, William. *Alpine Flowers for English Gardens*. London: John Murray, 1870.
———. *The English Flower Garden*. London: John Murray, 1889.
———. *The Wild Garden, or, The Naturalization and Natural Grouping of Hardy Exotic Plants, with a Chapter on the Garden of British Wild Flowers*. 4th ed. London: John Murray, 1894.
Ruskin, John. *Love's Meine and Proserpina*. London: G. Allen, 1906.
———. *Sesame and Lilies*. New Haven: Yale University Press, 2002.
Ryan, John C. "Cultural Botany: Toward a Model of Transdisciplinary, Embodied, and Poetic Research into Plants." *Nature and Culture* 6, no. 2 (June 2011): 123–48.
Sandilands, Catriona. "Fear of a Queer Plant?" *GLQ: A Journal of Lesbian and Gay Studies* 23, no. 3 (May 25, 2017): 419–29.
———. "Some 'F' Words for the Environmental Humanities: Feralities, Feminisms, Futurities." In *The Routledge Companion to the Environmental Humanities*, edited by Ursula K. Heise, Jon Christensen, and Michelle Niemann, 443–51. New York: Routledge, 2016.

Schmitt, Cannon. "The Gothic Romance in the Victorian Period." In *A Companion to the Victorian Novel*, edited by Patrick Brantlinger and William B. Thesing, 302-17. Oxford: Blackwell, 2005.
Schreiner, Olive. *The Story of an African Farm*. Toronto: Broadview, 2003.
Seaton, Beverly. "Considering the Lilies: Ruskin's 'Proserpina' and Other Victorian Flower Books." *Victorian Studies* 28, no. 2 (January 1, 1985): 255-82.
Secord, Anne. "Science in the Pub: Artisan Botanists in Early Nineteenth-Century Lancashire." *History of Science* 32, no. 3 (September 1, 1994): 269-316.
Secord, James A. *Visions of Science: Books and Readers at the Dawn of the Victorian Age*. Chicago: University of Chicago Press, 2014.
Sergeant, David. *Kipling's Art of Fiction, 1884-1901*. Oxford: Oxford University Press, 2013.
Showers, Kate B. "Prehistory of Southern African Forestry: From Vegetable Garden to Tree Plantation." *Environment and History* 16, no. 3 (August 2010): 295-322.
Shteir, Ann B. *Cultivating Women, Cultivating Science: Flora's Daughters and Botany in England, 1760-1860*. Baltimore: Johns Hopkins University Press, 1996.
Siddiqi, Yumna. *Anxieties of Empire and the Fiction of Intrigue*. New York: Columbia University Press, 2012.
Sittert, Lance van. "'Our Irrepressible Fellow-Colonist': The Biological Invasion of Prickly Pear (Opuntia Ficus-Indica) in the Eastern Cape c. 1890-c. 1910." *Journal of Historical Geography* 28, no. 3 (July 1, 2002): 397-419.
Smith, Andrew, and William Hughes, eds. *EcoGothic*. Manchester: Manchester University Press, 2013.
Steer, Philip. "Gold and Greater Britain: Jevons, Trollope, and Settler Colonialism." *Victorian Studies* 58, no. 3 (2016): 436-63.
———. "Romances of Uneven Development: Spatiality, Trade, and Form in Robert Louis Stevenson's Pacific Novels." *Victorian Literature and Culture* 43, no. 2 (2015): 343-56.
Stevenson, Robert Louis. *The Strange Case of Dr. Jekyll and Mr. Hyde*. Toronto: Broadview, 2005.
Stiebel, Lindy. *Imagining Africa: Landscape in H. Rider Haggard's African Romances*. Westport: Greenwood, 2001.
Stoker, Bram. *Dracula*. Boston: Bedford/St. Martins, 2002.
Straley, Jessica. *Evolution and Imagination in Victorian Children's Literature*. Cambridge: Cambridge University Press, 2016.
Tachibana, Setsu, and Charles Watkins. "Botanical Transculturation: Japanese and British Knowledge and Understanding of *Aucuba Japonica* and *Larix Leptolepis*, 1700-1920." *Environment & History* 16, no. 1 (February 2010): 43-71.
Taylor, Jesse Oak. *The Sky of Our Manufacture: The London Fog and British Fiction from Dickens to Woolf*. Under the Sign of Nature: Explorations in Ecocriticism. Charlottesville: University of Virginia Press, 2016.
Taylor, John Ellor. *The Sagacity and Morality of Plants: A Sketch of the Life and Conduct of the Vegetable Kingdom*. London: Chatto & Windus, 1884.

Taylor, William M. *The Vital Landscape: Nature and the Built Environment in Nineteenth-Century Britain.* Aldershot, England: Ashgate, 2004.
"The Moonstone: A Romance." *Athenaeum,* no. 2126 (July 25, 1868): 106.
"The Story of an African Farm." *Dublin Review, 1836–1910; London* 17, no. 2 (April 1887): 423–24.
Thomas, Keith. *Man and the Natural World: Changing Attitudes in England, 1500–1800.* London: Allen Lane, 1983.
Tsing, Anna. *The Mushroom at the End of the World: On the Possibility of Life in Capitalist Ruins.* Princeton: Princeton University Press, 2015.
———. "Wreckage and Recovery: Four Papers Exploring the Nature of Nature." In *Wreckage and Recovery: Exploring the Nature of Nature,* 2:2–15. More than Human: AURA Working Papers. Aarhus University Research on the Anthropocene, 2013. http://anthropocene.au.dk/fileadmin/Anthropocene/Workingpapers/AURA_workingpaperVol2.pdf.
Veracini, Lorenzo. "'Settler Colonialism': Career of a Concept." *Journal of Imperial and Commonwealth History* 41, no. 2 (June 1, 2013): 313–33.
Vieira, Patrícia. "Phytographia: Literature as Plant Writing." *Environmental Philosophy* 12, no. 2 (Fall 2015): 205–20.
Ward, Francis Kingdon. *The Romance of Plant Hunting, by Capt. F. Kingdon-Ward.* London: E. Arnold, 1924.
Ward, Nathaniel B. *On the Growth of Plants in Closely Glazed Cases.* London: J. Van Voorst, 1842.
Waters, Michael. *The Garden in Victorian Literature.* Aldershot, England: Scolar, 1988.
Watson, Forbes. *Flowers and Gardens: Notes on Plant Beauty.* London: Strahan, 1872.
Watson, Hewett Cottrell. *Cybele Britannica: Or British Plants and Their Geographical Relations.* London: Longman, 1847.
Webster, Angus Duncan. *London Trees: Being an Account of the Trees That Succeed in London, with a Descriptive Account of Each Species and Notes on Their Comparative Value and Cultivation. With Guide to Where the Finest London Trees May Be Seen.* London: Swarthmore, 1920.
Wells, H. G. "The Door in the Wall." In *The Country of the Blind, and Other Stories,* 513–37. London: T. Nelson, 1913.
———. *The Time Machine: An Invention.* Toronto: Broadview, 2001.
———. *The War of the Worlds.* Toronto: Broadview, 2003.
White, Fred. "The Purple Terror." *Strand Magazine* 18, no. 105 (1899): 243–51.
White, Richard. "Environmental History, Ecology, and Meaning." *Journal of American History* 76, no. 4 (1990): 1111–16.
Wilde, Oscar. *The Picture of Dorian Gray.* Toronto: Broadview, 2005.
Woolf, Virginia. *Mr. Bennett and Mrs. Brown.* London: Hogarth, 1924.

INDEX

acclimatization: of characters, 122, 144; of plants, 14, 19, 124, 142, 168–69
"Adventure of the Naval Treaty, The" (Doyle), 38–43
After London (Jeffries), 70
Allan and the Holy Flower (Haggard), 32, 90
Allan Quatermain (Haggard), 141–46
Allen, Grant, 30, 44, 160; "The Daisy's Pedigree," 29; *The Flowers and their Pedigrees*, 12; *Hilda Wade,* 121–22; "In Nature's Workshop," 124–25; "Queer Flowers," 163
"American's Tale, An" (Doyle), 159, 165
Anne of Green Gables (Montgomery), 161
anthrodecentrism, 17, 101
Anthropocene, 56
anthropocentrism, 13, 17, 160
anthropomorphism, 4, 85, 101, 115, 160, 164, 176
Arata, Stephen, 168
Arboretum et Fruticetum Britannicum (Loudon), 28
A rebours (Huysmans), 74, 78
Aubrey, Frank, *The Devil Tree of El Dorado,* 2, 159, 165, 170

Barrie, J. M., *The Little White Bird,* 81–82
Basil (Collins), 58
Beast and Man in India (Kipling), 151
Beattie, James, 30
Beetle, The (Marsh), 68–69, 71
Belich, James, 127
Bewell, Alan, 30, 109
bildungsroman, 123, 128–29, 156
Blackwood, Algernon, 20; "The Man Whom the Trees Loved," 8–9, 156, 172–78; "The Transfer," 171; "The Willows," 170
Bleak House (Dickens), 16

Bloomfield, Reginald, *Formal Gardens in England,* 99
bonsai, 162
botanical gardens: Calcutta, 153; Cape Town, 124; colonial, 30, 126; Royal Botanical Gardens (Kew), 29, 57–58
botany, 11, 161–62; botanical geographies, 12–13; botanical transculturation, 31, 86; Sherlock Holmes and, 39; philosophical, 180; *Proserpina* and, 97–99; women and, 86, 95–96
Braddon, Mary Elizabeth, *Lady Audley's Secret,* 14, 39
Brandis, Dietrich, 151, 155. *See also* Indian Forest Service
Brontë, Charlotte, 59–60; *Jane Eyre,* 59, 104, 112, 161–62; *Villette,* 6–8, 52, 59–67, 75
Brotherhood of Seven Kings, The (Meade), 43
Burnett, Frances Hodgson: *A Little Princess,* 101–2; *The Secret Garden,* vii, 19, 83, 85, 87, 101–12
Butler, Samuel, 185n27; *Erewhon,* 7–8, 158

Cape Colony, 14, 137
Cape Town, 124, 137
Carroll, Lewis, *Through the Looking Glass,* 84–85, 97
Cartwright, Julia, 99–100
Chen, Mel, 17
Child of the Jago, A (Morrison), 49
Chrisman, Laura, 127
chrysanthemum (plant), 92–93
circumnarration, 75
clues, 36, 119, 123; in "The Adventure of the Naval Treaty," 38; in *The Moonstone,* 25, 34; Moretti on, 34–35, 190n41; plants as, 26, 30, 35, 42, 47–48; in "The Talk of the Town," 36–37

Cohen, Margaret, 126
Colonel Quaritch V.C. (Haggard), 88–95
colonialism. *See* Empire, British; settler colonies
colonial metalepsis, 32–33, 164
Collins, Wilkie, 32; *Basil*, 58; *The Moonstone*, 23–25, 26–29, 31–32; *The Woman in White*, 67–68
Conrad, Joseph, *Heart of Darkness*, 127–28
Crosby, Alfred, 11, 186n44
Crystal Age, A (Hudson), 3
cultivation: colonial setting for, 122–24, 140, 147, 148–50; dangers of, 174; detective novels and, 25; exotic plants and, 1–7, 15, 26, 30, 37–38, 56, 74, 79, 92–93, 162–63; fictional characters and, 134–35; fictional plants and, 6, 33, 37, 50, 70, 73, 108, 114–16, 118–19, 143–45; forests and, 148–50, 153, 155, 172; gardens and, 50–51, 59, 87–88, 106, 112, 115–18, 142; history of, 52, 142; humans and, 14, 111, 156; landscape and, 90, 122; lost race narrative and, 141; naming and, 47, 161–62; potatoes and, 6–9; readers and, 21; Romantic-era, 184n12; selfhood and, 7, 67; single specimens and, 47, 147–48; time-frame of, 6–7; women and, 94–97, 119, 172, 199n73
Curry, Helen, 2
Cybele (Watson), 13

"Daisy's Pedigree, The" (Allen), 29
Darby, Margaret, 31, 71
Darwin, Charles, 74, 160; *On the Power of Movement in Plants*, 97, 160; *Voyage of the Beagle*, 56–57
Darwin, Erasmus, 163
Darwin, Francis, 175–76, 178
Davis, Helen, 73
Davis, Whitney, 74
Days of My Life, The (Haggard), 140
Denisoff, Dennis, 72, 185n34
detective fiction, 17, 18, 26, 167; clues in, 25, 34, 35–36; as global genre, 31, 43; inductive method in, 29; plants in, 26, 28–29, 33, 87–88; windows in, 40. *See also* "Adventure of the Naval Treaty, The"; *Moonstone, The*; "Talk of the Town, The"

Devil Tree of El Dorado, The (Aubrey), 2, 159, 165, 170
Dewis, Sarah, 28
Dickens, Charles, 128; *Bleak House*, 16; *The Mystery of Edwin Drood*, 49; *Our Mutual Friend*, 58
"Door in the Wall, The" (Wells), 82–83
Doyle, Arthur Conan, 122, 178; "The Adventure of the Naval Treaty," 38–43; "An American's Tale," 159, 165; *The Hound of the Baskervilles*, 87–88; *The Lost World*, 49, 122; *The Sign of Four*, 40, 68; *A Study in Scarlet*, 39
Du Maurier, Daphne, 113; *Rebecca*, 19, 85, 112–19, 200n95
Dümpelmann, Sonja, 13–14
Duncan, Sara, *Simple Adventures of a Memsahib*, 103–4

ecogothic, 71–72, 156, 172, 178
Empire, British: adventure fiction and, 123, 146; botanical collectors and, 46; crime and, 87–88, 121–22; environment and, 11–12, 30, 165–66, 187–88n45; exotic plants and, 16, 30; expansion of, 11–13; forestry and, 137, 147–49; gardens and, 13–14; genre novels and, 3, 16, 21, 43, 68–69, 124, 126–27, 166; gothic and, 51, 58; in "In the Rukh," 146–51, 153–56; in *The Jungle Books*, 156; landscape and, 126–27; London suburbs and, 68; melodrama and, 132; metalepsis and, 32–33; in *The Moonstone*, 32; objects and, 68, 101–2; plant circulation within, 30, 32–33, 44, 55–56, 123–24; potatoes and, 8; revenge plots and, 40, 69, 71; soldiers and, 89; in *The War of the Worlds*, 168–69
empire forestry, 143, 204n103. *See also* Indian Forest Service
Encyclopedia of Gardening, An (Loudon), 52–53
Endersby, Jim, 15–16
environmental history, 11–12, 18, 26, 125–26, 186–87n45
Erewhon (Butler), 7–8, 158
Esty, Jed, 73, 123, 128–29
eucalyptus (plant), 19, 124, 136–40, 149

INDEX   225

"Fall of Fiction, The" (Watson), 131–32, 134
Farmer's Year, A (Haggard), 89
Flikke, Rune, 137–38
"Flowering of the Strange Orchid, The" (Wells), 72
flowers: in *Allan Quatermain,* 143–45; bedding out, 80–81; culture of, 10; as childhood friends, 15; exotic varieties, 30–31; Sherlock Holmes and, 38–43; in hothouses, 71–72; Ezra Jennings and, 23–25; in *Jess,* 133–34; language of, 10–11, 86; in *The Moonstone,* 27–28; naturalized, 12–13; in *The Picture of Dorian Gray,* 73–74, 76–79; in pots, 38, 49; in *Rebecca,* 115–18; in *The Secret Garden,* 103–5, 106, 110–11; in *Through the Looking Glass,* 84–85; in *The Time Machine,* 44–45; in *Villette,* 64–66; women and, 95–99. *See also specific plant names*
Flowers and Gardens, Notes on Plant Beauty (Watson), 80
Flowers and Their Pedigrees, The (Allen), 12
Floricultural Cabinet (periodical), 30
Formal Gardens in England (Bloomfield), 99
Forman, Ross, 122, 191n5
Frawley, Jodi, 125–26
Freedgood, Elaine, 32, 164

Garden (serial), 99
gardeners, 30, 46, 53, 59, 80; female, 87, 95; in *The Moonstone,* 28; in *The Picture of Dorian Gray,* 79–80; in *Rebecca,* 118; in *The Secret Garden,* 107, 112; in *Villette,* 62–64. *See also* Loudon, Jane; Loudon, John
Gardener's Year, A (Haggard), 133, 140, 163
gardens, 18, 51; in *Allan Quatermain,* 142–43; Anglo-Indian, 103–4; in *Basil,* 58; in *The Beetle,* 68; botanical, in *Colonel Quaritch, V.C.,* 90–95; colonial, 43–44, 124, 126; conservatory, 71–72; country, 86–87; crimes in, 87–88; Decadent, 72; in "The Door in the Wall," 82–83; empire and, 13–14, 87; exotic plants and, 30, 45–46, 86; history of, 183n6; in *The Little White Bird,* 81–82; in "The Man Whom the Trees Loved," 174; in *News from Nowhere,* 70; nonfiction writing on, 99–101; in "Of Queen's Gardens," 96–97; in *The Picture of Dorian Gray,* 74–77, 79–80; plantfulness of, 30, 87; plant-hunting and, 45–47, 146; polluted, 53–54; in *Rebecca,* 114–19; scientific, 57, 58; in *The Secret Garden,* 103–12; in *The Strange Case of Dr. Jekyll and Mr. Hyde,* 69–70; in *The Three Imposters,* 69; in *Through the Looking Glass,* 84–85; in *The Time Machine,* 70–71; in "The Transfer," 171; in *Villette,* 60–66; Victorian, 1, 57; urban, 50–59, 67–71; wild, 86–87, 99; in *The Woman in White,* 67–68; women and, 95–97, 119–20, 145, 172. *See also* botanical gardens; gardeners
Garrard, Greg, 13
geranium (plant), 161
Goodlad, Lauren, 32
gothic, 4; architectural, 55; in *Colonel Quaritch, V.C.,* 90; in country house setting, 85–87, 119; imperial, 58, 67–69; and monsters, 164; in *The Picture of Dorian Gray,* 72, 75, 77–78; in *Rebecca,* 113–15, 118; in *The Secret Garden,* 106; in urban setting, 18, 50–52, 58; in *Villette,* 59, 61, 64–66. *See also* ecogothic
Grove, Richard, 11, 30

Haggard, H. Rider, 88, 89, 126–27, 131–32, 134; *Allan and the Holy Flower,* 32, 90; *Allan Quatermain,* 141–46; *Colonel Quaritch, V.C.,* 88–95; *The Days of My Life,* 140; *A Farmer's Year,* 89; *A Gardener's Year,* 133, 140, 163; *Jess,* 131–41; *Rural England,* 89
Heart of Darkness (Conrad), 127–28
Helmreich, Anne, 99
Hibberd, Shirley, 53; *The Town Garden,* 53–54, 69
Hilda Wade (Allen), 121–22
Home and Garden (Jekyll), 100, 200n95
Hooker, W. H., 55, 193n26
horticulture, 10, 183n6; in *A Rebours,* 74; global, 50, 67, 133; H. Rider Haggard and, 89, 92, 93, 162–63; history of, 52–53; importation and, 31, 114; in *The Moonstone,* 28; transculturation and, 31; Wardian cases and, 55–56; writings on, 12, 189n18. *See also* Loudon, John
Hound of the Baskervilles, The (Doyle), 87–88
Hudson, William Henry, *A Crystal Age,* 3

226 INDEX

Hultgren, Neil, 132
Humboldt, Alexander, 97–98
Hurley, Kelly, 164
Huysmans, Joris-Karl, 72; *A rebours,* 74, 78

Indian Forest Service (IFS), 146–47, 149, 151, 172. See also Brandis, Dietrich
"In Nature's Workshop" (Allen), 124–25
Instructions on Gardening for Ladies (Loudon), 95
"In the Rukh" (Kipling), 19, 124, 146–55
invasive species, 12, 19, 114, 126, 166, 200n90

Jane Eyre (Brontë), 59, 104, 112, 161–62
Jeffries, Richard, *After London,* 70
Jekyll, Gertrude, 87, 99–100, 113; *Home and Garden,* 100, 200n95; *Wood and Garden,* 100
Jess (Haggard), 131–41
Jungle Book, The (Kipling), 146–47, 155–56, 204n97

Keats, Jonathon, 180
Kehler, Grace, 100
Kelly, Theresa, 163
Kim (Kipling), 146
King, Amy, 57, 72, 85
Kingdon-Ward, Frank, 45; *The Romance of Plant-Hunting,* 45–47
Kipling, John Lockwood, *Beast and Man in India,* 151
Kipling, Rudyard: "In the Rukh" 19, 124, 146–55; *The Jungle Book,* 146–47, 155–56, 204n97; *Kim,* 146; *Many Inventions,* 146, 204n97
Kuchta, Todd, 68

Lady Audley's Secret (Braddon), 14, 39
Lady's Country Companion, The (Loudon), 95
Laird, Mark, 30
Lang, Andrew, 132, 134, 202n44
Little Princess, A (Burnett), 101–2
Little White Bird, The (Barrie), 81–82
Lost World, The (Doyle), 49, 122
Loudon, Jane, 26; *Instructions on Gardening for Ladies,* 95; *The Lady's Country Companion,* 95

Loudon, John, 1, 28, 30, 37–38, 54–55; *Arboretum et Fruticetum Britannicum,* 28; *An Encyclopedia of Gardening,* 52–53
Luciano, Dana, 17
Lynch, Deirdre, 31

Machen, Arthur, *The Three Imposters,* 69, 71
"Man-eating Tree, The" (Robinson), 159, 164
"Man Whom the Trees Loved, The" (Blackwood), 8–9, 156, 172–78
Many Inventions (Kipling), 146, 204n97
Marder, Michael, *Plant Thinking,* 160, 176, 180
Marsh, Richard, *The Beetle,* 68–69, 71
McClintock, Anne, 126
Meade, L. T.: *The Brotherhood of Seven Kings,* 43; "The Talk of the Town," 36–37; *The Sorceress of the Strand,* 36
Milbank, Alison, 65
Mill, John Stuart, *The Subjection of Women,* 96, 198n34; *On Liberty,* 135
Miller, John, 89, 134
Millet, Kate, 96
Mill on the Floss, The (Eliot), 15
Milne, Anne, 155
Mitchell, Robert, 5, 141, 178, 181
Montgomery, L. M., *Anne of Green Gables,* 161
Moonstone, The (Collins), 23–25, 26–29, 31–32
Moore, Jason, 11
Moretti, Franco, 34–36
Morris, William, *News from Nowhere,* 70
Morrison, Arthur, *A Child of the Jago,* 49
Murphy, Patrick, 17
Mystery of Edwin Drood, The (Dickens), 49

News from Nowhere (Morris), 70
nonhuman turn, 17
novel, British, 21; adventure, 122–23, 126–27, 146; characters and, 158; circumnarration, and, 75; colonial, 104, 123–24; detective, 18, 25, 26, 29, 34–35, 87–88, 119; gardens in, 50–51, 58–59, 86, 87; genre, 1–3, 21, 34, 59, 67, 100, 123, 179–80; gothic, 51–52, 58, 68–70, 71; plants in, 5–6, 16, 25–26, 32, 33, 87, 98, 126, 127–28, 179–80; plots

of, 15, 33, 86; modernist, 3–4, 173; realist, 3–4, 40, 57; sensation, 39, 67, 87–88; setting, 5, 9, 36, 86, 119, 123; utopian, 70; Victorian, 1, 4, 32, 160, 179–80; windows in, 40. *See also* bildungsroman; *specific titles*

"Of Queen's Gardens" (Ruskin), 96–97
On Liberty (Mill), 135
On the Growth of Plants in Closely Glazed Cases (Ward), 31, 54
On the Power of Movement in Plants (Darwin), 97, 160
orchid (plant), 15, 32, 72, 74, 79, 90–91, 186n36
Our Mutual Friend (Dickens), 58

Pauly, Philip, 21, 92, 113, 183n6
Pawson, Eric, 12, 14
Picture of Dorian Gray, The (Wilde), 6, 18, 52, 72–81
Pierce, Joanna Tapp, 96–97
Pinch, Adela, 181
Plant Hunters, The (Reid), 146
plant-hunting, 27, 45–46, 146
plants: acclimatization of, 14, 19, 124, 142, 168–69; agency of, 4, 20, 115, 139–40, 159–60; anthropomorphism and, 4, 17, 84–85; carnivorous, 72, 159, 164–71; circulation of, 10, 12–13, 30, 32–33, 44, 55–56, 123–24, 132; as clues, 26, 30, 35, 42, 47–48; collection of, 27, 45–46, 146; colonial, 123–24, 127–28, 142–44; consciousness in, 160–61, 172–78; cultivation in fiction of, 2, 6, 33, 37, 50, 70, 73, 108, 114–16, 118–19, 143–45; encyclopedias of, 28; epistemology of, 15–16, 34, 42, 124, 179–81; exotic, 1, 11–12, 16, 30, 26, 30, 32, 50, 59, 71, 90–94, 99–100, 113–14; as friends, 5, 15, 47; happiness of, 100; history of, 8–9; human-plant studies and, 4, 160; invasive, 12, 114, 118, 126, 166–68, 186–87n45, 200n90; metalepsis and, 32–33; naming of, 98, 109, 161–62; narrative and, 1, 3, 4, 6, 9, 15, 20, 26, 29, 37, 42, 61–67, 74–77, 81, 87–88, 106, 114–19, 138–39, 178–80; native, 15, 119; novels and, 3, 4, 5, 10, 16, 21, 33, 42, 50, 52, 158–59, 178–80; pain of, 53–54, 58; parasitic, 98–99; potted, 37–38; power of movement of, 120, 160, 176, 178; sentience of, 9–10, 20, 42, 158, 164; Wardian cases and, 31, 54–57; women and, 95–97. *See also* flowers; gardens; *and specific plant names*
Plant Thinking (Marder), 160, 176, 180
potato (plant), 6–9, 158
Pratt, Mary-Louise, 126
Price, Cheryl Blake, 165
Prickly pear (plant), 14, 19, 121, 124–26
Proserpina (Ruskin), 87, 97–99
"Purple Terror, The" (White), 159, 165

"Queer Flowers" (Allen), 163

Rebecca (Du Maurier), 19, 85, 112–19, 200n95
Reid, Mayne, *The Plant Hunters,* 146
Reitz, Caroline, 31
rhododendron (plant), 14, 98, 113–18, 200n90
Rieder, John, 166
Ritvo, Harriet, 114
Robinson, Phil, "The Man-eating Tree," 159, 164
Robinson, William, 95, 100, 113; *Garden,* 99; *The Wild Garden,* 86, 98, 99
Romance of Plant-Hunting, The (Kingdon-Ward), 45–47
Rural England (Haggard), 89
Ruskin, John, 8; "Of Queen's Gardens," 96–97; *Proserpina,* 87, 97–99
Ryan, John, 15, 56, 207n78

Sagacity and Morality of Plants, The (Taylor), 159–60
Sandilands, Catriona, 17, 155, 161
Schreiner, Olive, 127; *The Story of an African Farm,* 14, 123, 128–32
Seaton, Beverly, 10, 85
second nature, 9, 16, 90, 183n4
Secret Garden, The (Burnett), vii, 19, 83, 85, 87, 101–12
settler colonies: in fiction, 19, 126–27; in *Hilda Wade,* 121; landscape of, 123; in *Story of an African Farm,* 128–31

Showers, Kate, 122
Sign of Four, The (Doyle), 40, 68
Simple Adventures of a Memsahib (Duncan), 103–4
Sorceress of the Strand, The (Meade), 36
Steer, Philip, 127
Stevenson, Robert Louis, 127, 178; *The Strange Case of Dr. Jekyll and Mr. Hyde,* 69–70
Story of an African Farm, The (Schreiner), 14, 123, 128–32
Straley, Jessica, 156
Strange Case of Dr. Jekyll and Mr. Hyde, The (Stevenson), 69–70
Study in Scarlet, A (Doyle), 39
Subjection of Women, The (Mill), 96, 198n34
sundew (plant), 163–64

"Talk of the Town, The" (Meade), 36–37
Taylor, Jesse Oak, 53, 56
Taylor, John Ellor, 159; *The Sagacity and Morality of Plants,* 159–60
Taylor, William M., 56
Thomas, Keith, 1
Three Imposters, The (Machen), 69, 71
Through the Looking Glass (Carroll), 84–85, 97
Time Machine, The (Wells), 44, 70–71
Town Garden, The (Hibberd), 53–54, 69
"Transfer, The" (Blackwood), 171
Tsing, Anna, 4, 16

Van Sittert, Lance, 125, 186n44
Villette (Brontë), 6–8, 52, 59–67, 75
"Voice in the Night, A" (Hodgson), 169
Voyage of the Beagle (Darwin), 56–57

War of the Worlds, The (Wells), 166–69
Ward, Nathaniel, 26, 31, 54–56; *On the Growth of Plants in Closely Glazed Cases,* 31, 54
Wardian case, 12, 31, 52, 54–55, 65, 71
Warhol, Robin, 75
Watson, Forbes, *Flowers and Gardens, Notes on Plant Beauty,* 80
Watson, Hewett Cottrell, *Cybele,* 13
Watson, John William, "The Fall of Fiction," 131–32, 134
weeds, 12, 13, 98–99, 125, 168, 187n48. *See also* invasive species; plants
Wells, H. G.: "The Door in the Wall," 82–83; "The Flowering of the Strange Orchid," 72; *The Time Machine,* 44, 70–71; *The War of the Worlds,* 166–69
White, Fred, "The Purple Terror," 159, 165
Wilde, Oscar, *The Picture of Dorian Gray,* 6, 18, 52, 72–81
"Willows, The" (Blackwood), 170
Wind in the Willows, The (Grahame), 9
Woman in White, The (Collins), 67–68
Wood and Garden (Jekyll), 100
Woolf, Virginia, 3–4
Wordsworth, William, 6, 141

Recent Books in the Series
Under the Sign of Nature: Explorations in Ecocriticism

Scott Hess
William Wordsworth and the Ecology of Authorship: The Roots of Environmentalism in Nineteenth-Century Culture

Dan Brayton
Shakespeare's Ocean: An Ecocritical Exploration

Jennifer K. Ladino
Reclaiming Nostalgia: Longing for Nature in American Literature

Byron Caminero-Santangelo
Different Shades of Green: African Literature, Environmental Justice, and Political Ecology

Kate Rigby
Dancing with Disaster: Environmental Histories, Narratives, and Ethics for Perilous Times

Adam Trexler
Anthropocene Fictions: The Novel in a Time of Climate Change

Eric Gidal
Ossianic Unconformities: Bardic Poetry in the Industrial Age

Jesse Oak Taylor
The Sky of Our Manufacture: The London Fog in British Fiction from Dickens to Woolf

Michael P. Branch and Clinton Mohs, editors
"The Best Read Naturalist": Nature Writings of Ralph Waldo Emerson

Lynn Keller
Recomposing Ecopoetics: North American Poetry of the Self-Conscious Anthropocene

Serenella Iovino, Enrico Cesaretti, and Elena Past, editors
Italy and the Environmental Humanities: Landscapes, Natures, Ecologies

Christopher Abram
Evergreen Ash: Ecology and Catastrophe in Old Norse Myth and Literature

Elizabeth Hope Chang
Novel Cultivations: Plants and British Literature in the Global Nineteenth Century

www.ingramcontent.com/pod-product-compliance
Lightning Source LLC
Chambersburg PA
CBHW030825230426
43667CB00008B/1374